GETTING WISE ABOUT GETTING OLD

GETTING WISE ABOUT GETTING OLD

DEBUNKING MYTHS ABOUT AGING

Edited by
Véronique Billette,
Patrik Marier,
and Anne-Marie Séguin

26 25 24 23 22 21 20 19 20   5 4 3 2 1

Printed in Canada on FSC-certified ancient-forest-free paper (100% post-consumer recycled) that is processed chlorine- and acid-free.

Library and Archives Canada Cataloguing in Publication

Title: Getting wise about getting old: debunking myths about aging / edited by
    Véronique Billette, Patrik Marier, and Anne-Marie Séguin.
Other titles: Vieillissements sous la loupe. English
Names: Billette, Véronique, editor. | Marier, Patrik, editor. | Séguin, Anne-Marie,
    editor.
Description: Translation of: Les vieillissements sous la loupe : entre mythes et
    réalités. | Includes bibliographical references and index.
Identifiers: Canadiana (print) 20200296256 | Canadiana (ebook) 20200296531 |
    ISBN 9780774880626 (softcover) | ISBN 9780774880633 (PDF) |
    ISBN 9780774880640 (EPUB) | ISBN 9780774880657 (Kindle)
Subjects: LCSH: Aging – Social aspects. | LCSH: Older people – Social conditions.
Classification: LCC HQ1061 .V6413 2020 | DDC 305.26 – dc23

Canadä

UBC Press gratefully acknowledges the financial support for our publishing program of the Government of Canada (through the Canada Book Fund), the Canada Council for the Arts, and the British Columbia Arts Council.

The publication of this book received financial support from the Fonds de recherche du Québec – Société et culture (FRQSC).

Printed and bound in Canada by Friesens
Set in Macklin and Warnock by Artegraphica Design Co. Ltd.
Translators: Evelyn Lindhorst, Neil Macmillan (Meristem), Kathleen McHugh, Joanne Deller, Ken Larose, Jennifer Strachan, Nick Todd, and John March
Copy editor: Käthe Roth
Proofreader: Kristy Lynn Hankewitz
Indexer: Cheryl Lemmens

Purich Books, an imprint of UBC Press
2029 West Mall
Vancouver, BC, V6T 1Z2
www.purichbooks.ca

To our mothers, fathers, grandparents, great aunts ...
and everyone else who has inspired us with their lives,
their wisdom, and their resilience

Contents

Foreword to the English Edition

Laura Tamblyn Watts, LLB | CEO CanAge, Canada's
National Seniors' Advocacy Organization

The paradox about aging is always the same: Aging is the natural process of successful living, although few wish for death and no one wants to get old. But, as a culture, we wrestle with profound ageism, often referred to as the last acceptable form of discrimination.

I see this in my work in advocacy. But, perhaps most profoundly, I see this in the graduate level classes I teach on aging. Each year, I start the class the same way, asking students to write down in one minute as many words as possible about the word "old." Year after year, the results are stunningly consistent. There are always a few responses that are positive, including "wise," "grandparent," or "knowledge." The others range from heart-breaking to horrid. The words chosen overwhelmingly include such terms as "useless," "fear," "alone," "incapable," "demented," "nursing home," and "frail."

Making it more poignant, these telling responses are from university students who have *chosen* to take courses in the field of aging. By definition, they are students who believe that aging is an important topic to study. They would also identify as anti-ageist – and probably are. It is my belief that the broader socially constructed view of aging is simply worse. Where does this narrative of aging as pain and exclusion originate?

Aging, as a concept, is a story of "other." As individuals and as a society we reject our own aging. We criticize the natural process in others. No one has ever taken the comment "they look really old" as a compliment. No one buys cosmetics to look older. In fact, multibillion-dollar industries exist to try to reverse the aging process. Globally, we also express self-loathing for the very social and biological *successes*, which have resulted in a doubling of life expectancy in the past hundred years.

However, it is my belief that this contradiction about aging cannot continue. Discrimination against our future selves is the ultimate social self-harm not only to ourselves but to others.

At CanAge, Canada's national seniors' advocacy organization (www.CanAge.ca), we are challenging the basis of discriminatory beliefs rooted in ageism. In order to better understand the barriers to positive social aging in this country, we are engaged in an extensive consultation process that combines evidence-based research and the most up-to-date knowledge from experts.

During this process, we have consulted from coast to coast to coast. We have conferred with seniors, care providers, professionals, policy makers, faith leaders, newcomers to Canada, and members of a diverse range of cultural and self-identified perspectives. We have also engaged with Indigenous leaders, housing advocates, veterans, business leaders, community organizations, and members of all five generations.

But mostly we listen. We listen to stories of discrimination. We also listen to those who fear becoming purposeless or hopelessly out of date, and to others anxious about job loss because of mandatory retirement or being pushed out of a workplace. We listen to others talk about the joys of later-life freedom but who worry about outliving their retirement savings. Then there are those who express concerns about living smaller, more isolated lives, or about becoming frail and unable to stay at home. For them there is always a pervasive dread of dementia and of a future where one might experience physical or mental incapability.

In many cases, their worries do not match their current vibrant lives, health, or economic security. But their fears paint a picture of a society at war with itself and reveal the extent of social angst and lack of social planning for our aging society.

At CanAge, we are focused on finding a way forward, to ensure that older adults and our aging society in general have a better path to follow. This attitude is fundamental to our work. We do not just represent seniors; we work tirelessly towards overcoming obstacles associated with aging. We work to lift up, to problem solve, to advocate, and to collaboratively make things better.

From our extensive consultation and research, we have created a platform for the future, entitled the "VOICES of Canada's Seniors: A Roadmap Towards an Age-Inclusive Canada." This roadmap lays out six compass points as areas that we, as a society, must address to move forward and overcome age-based inequalities. These compass points include violence and abuse prevention; optimal health and well-being; infection prevention and disaster management; caregiving, long-term care, and housing supports; economic security; and social inclusion (www.CanAge.ca).

This "Roadmap to an Age-Inclusive Canada" is not just for policy makers or business leaders. Rather it is a call to action for everyone to reimagine a new society. A society where aging is celebrated and normalized. Where no one lives in fear or trauma because they are subject to elder abuse and neglect (which currently one out of every six seniors experience). Where an aging population is viewed as the celebrated accomplishment of a nation, not a health emergency requiring fiscal handwringing. Where the best evidence is made available to consider the impact of infection on older people, especially in light of failures of care during the COVID-19 pandemic, where loss of life in long-term care was both numerically horrifying yet often seen as occurring outside the "general population."

Care for people must be reimagined, with social policy adapting to support tireless essential caregivers. Long-term care must be transformed into "Care at Home" – a new model that allows our most frail to live dignified lives of quality and purpose. Housing must be rethought, redesigned, and redeveloped to make sure that there are enough affordable homes suitable for aging in our new era. People should be given greater supports and flexibility in work, pensions, savings, and in how to fund the new "last third" of their lives. Above all, the underlying barriers to social inclusion must be dragged into the light and systematically overcome. There must be increases to intergenerational programming; supports to reconnect isolated seniors with community; and adoption of age-friendly policies in urban planning and rural infrastructure.

We have known for decades that a demographic age-wave was coming and that social infrastructure and planning would have to change. But we have mostly buried our heads and refused to see what was really happening. Worse still, some of us have deepened our ageist beliefs, predicting that the rising age-wave would engulf us and lead to the demographic apocalypse of society. This is an expression of our own refusal to face our own aging. Our own mortality. Our own fears of exclusion, frailty, and loss of capacity.

The reality is much different. Older adults contribute enormously to society. They work longer, and more capably, than many younger generations. They volunteer tirelessly. They provide enormous unpaid caregiving roles. And their tax dollars fund the very systems that they also use.

A book like *Getting Wise about Getting Old* is critical to understanding why, in the face of the greatest achievement of health and longevity in the history of humankind, we are full of fear, denial, and inaction.

We can make our society age-inclusive. We have a roadmap towards this change. We invite you to join us in making this possible. Together.

Foreword to the French Edition

Danis Prud'homme, Caroline Bouchard, Marco Guerrera, and Sophie Gagnon | Réseau FADOQ (the Federation for Aging in Dignity and Overall Quality in Quebec)

Why does aging, a natural, inevitable, and intrinsic part of life, seem to be regarded with such fear? Yet that is how it is perceived in Quebec – and in many other Western societies. The representation of aging as negative – a view that has changed over time – affects the choices that societies make and, ultimately, the quality of life of the elderly. It is precisely to provide a counterweight to such misleading perceptions of aging that we have gathered this collection of articles.

Aging of the Quebec population as a whole is accelerating, and older people now outnumber younger people in the province. Quebec could position itself as a pioneer in adapting to the trend of population aging and lead the way to innovation and a new kind of intergenerational compact. For decades, however, Quebec has failed to seize this opportunity – the first of its kind in history – because its political class lacks the vision to do so. Not only does this prevent Quebec society from meeting this adaptation challenge, but it also adds fuel to many myths about aging. Collective aging – like individual aging – is thus seen as a threat.

The age pyramid of the Canadian population has undergone a radical shift: in 2015, for the first time, Statistics Canada counted more people 65 and older in the country than children 14 and under. A negative attitude toward aging comes into play when younger generations, and society in general, begin to view the increased longevity and higher demographic weight of older people as a social and economic burden. And yet, the higher life expectancy of the Quebec population is due to remarkable advances and shows that living conditions and health standards have been continually improving.

The persistent myth in Western societies that older people are a heavy burden is compounded by a series of ageist perceptions specific to consumer society. Consider, for example, the perception that older people become useless as soon as they leave the labour market, whereas, in reality, retirees continue to make significant contributions to society as consumers, taxpayers, volunteers, and informal caregivers, as well as in other roles.

The prevailing discourse places a high value on the performance and productivity inherent to working life. As a result, retirees are essentially written off because they seem to give little back to society in comparison with the costs entailed by their aging. This view and the myths that it spawns have become extremely widespread and have acquired considerable legitimacy; they are even reflected in public policy.

Taking Steps to Improve the Living Conditions of Older People

Réseau FADOQ, the largest association of older people in Canada, with more than 535,000 members (https://www.fadoq.ca/reseau/a-propos/qui -sommes-nous), has defended the interests of the most vulnerable older people in Quebec for the past 50 years or so. The organization advocates for respect and an adequate quality of life for seniors, and it condemns the concrete effects of misconceptions about older people that lead to daily and repeated assaults on their dignity. It has to continually adapt to the needs of extremely diverse generations of seniors (mostly baby boomers but also their "Greatest Generation" parents and "Generation X" children).

Despite its solid credibility and recognized expertise, when Réseau FADOQ protests against injustices against older people, it all too often faces a wall of denial from political and economic decision makers or counter-arguments that downplay or belittle their experiences. Many of the senior-related issues raised by Réseau FADOQ – such as poverty, mistreatment, lack of affordable housing, and not enough available places in CHSLDs (centres d'hébergement de soins de longue durée, or residential long-term care centres) – have also been analyzed and critiqued by independent organizations such as the Quebec Ombudsman, the Auditor General of Quebec, and several research groups.

Even when presenting factual evidence, Réseau FADOQ sometimes has difficulty making media outlets and decision makers aware of certain issues.

Myths and false beliefs about older people are deeply entrenched and dehumanizing, and they feed into a negative perception of aging. Their effects are real and harmful, especially for vulnerable people who are dependent on either the state or their relatives and friends. Older people face increased poverty and a lower quality of life. Some consider this inevitable, but it is not. These conditions are very much the pernicious repercussions of prevailing myths about aging.

The Myths in Daily Life

We will examine two situations in which we at Réseau FADOQ intervene: healthcare and experienced older workers. We have absolutely no doubt that the demographic weight of older people is perceived by society as exerting undue budgetary pressure on healthcare costs. This perception also tends to feed into blatant ageism, which is manifested, for instance, in the placement of older people in CHSLDs (residential long-term care centres), about which we receive many heart-wrenching stories from our members. The hygienic conditions and nutritional practices in these establishments speak volumes. Indeed, if confinement to bed, infrequent diaper changes, and rushed meals were standard practice for children – or for anybody other than vulnerable seniors – they would be roundly condemned and changes would be made in short order. However, despite the public outrage provoked by every new case publicized in the media, unfit living conditions persist. In other words, we are facing a situation of institutional ageism (or mistreatment).

The fate of experienced older workers has been one of Réseau FADOQ's main causes for many years, largely as a result of the numerous calls it receives from workers who have difficulty re-entering the job market. Because of rampant ageism, experienced older workers are often put at a disadvantage when they try to pursue their careers or training, change jobs, or rejoin the labour force. Prejudices often curtail the career prospects of these workers, forcing them to accept lower-paid employment, with barely acceptable working conditions. They may even be pressured to retire.

The many problems encountered by experienced older workers are increasingly apparent among our members – especially during economic downturns, which trigger a range of legislative measures designed to redefine the parameters of retirement and pension plans. It is important to recognize that rates of poverty and indebtedness are rising in the 65-and-older age group. This is a new phenomenon, diverging from the trend in recent decades, and it forces many in this group to return to the job market. The problem is so acute and widespread that Réseau FADOQ has launched a provincial web platform to help workers 50 and older maintain, access, or return to employment.

Although the media could theoretically be relied on to deconstruct these myths, in the current context of instantaneous news, media competition, and multiple information sources, research and analysis by media outlets have become rarer or are drowned out in the 24-hour news cycle. There is a tendency to broadcast sensationalist and provocative news, much of which is designed to boost ratings or readership. Unfortunately, many media outlets fuel myths that reinforce negative perceptions about aging by constantly promoting incomplete or contradictory messages that sow confusion and prevent a full and accurate picture of aging from emerging. Coverage of cases of actual mistreatment also accentuates the fear of growing old by leading people to believe that these exceptional cases are the rule.

Myths about aging can also lead to indifference or condescension toward older people, who rarely speak out; it is as if there were an age limit for expressing a valid opinion. This was exemplified when former Quebec minister of health and social services Gaétan Barrette told Claude Castonguay, the "father of public health insurance in Quebec," to retire when the latter called for the resignation of Yves Bolduc, who was the minister of health and social services at the time. This type of attitude tends to marginalize the representation of older people, especially in spaces for democratic participation such as the media and the legislature. Such ageism, often not recognized as such, is tolerated, particularly when few people identify with older people who speak out or the opinions that they express. Yet again, older people are "the others."

Before we deconstruct the many persistent myths about aging and highlight a number of little-known realities, we need to ask who profits from these myths and, concomitantly, who benefits from maintaining them. Fear of aging bolsters the myths that many official bodies subscribe to. In the name of sensationalism or "hard news," the media often showcase stories that are not totally accurate or that give a platform to the expression of negative opinions about the elderly. Politicians exploit these incomplete representations of reality to justify budget cutbacks and discriminatory measures. Furthermore, the fashion industry; manufacturers of anti-aging products, pharmaceuticals, and special products for older people; and firms in other sectors see the fear of aging as a gold mine.

Deconstructing prevailing myths, which is the purpose of this book, is crucial if we are ultimately to obtain an accurate view of aging and define current challenges. When portrayals of aging that do not correspond to reality are debunked and detailed information is available, we will be able to work together to make society more inclusive and more sensitive to older people's needs. We may even be able to transcend the sterile intergenerational quarrels that, unfortunately, continue today and that legitimize discourses asking us to choose between services for young people and for seniors and to tighten our budgetary belts because the aging population is bound to be a burden.

At Réseau FADOQ, we feel that it is essential to maintain and enhance mechanisms of intergenerational solidarity, based on the recognition that growing old is an important, enjoyable, positive, and valid part of life. Recognizing older people's contributions, which may be different from those of other generations but are just as socially meaningful, is also necessary in an inclusive society. If an enlightened message about the natural and essentially human phenomenon of growing old were adopted by every generation, it would have a positive impact on everyone.

So how can we implement this social agenda of offering an adequate quality of life for both present and future seniors – in other words, for all of us? Raising awareness must be a priority across the board, from political and economic decision makers at all levels to people working with older adults, students, families, neighbours, and friends. All of us should therefore take time to reflect on and become familiar with the work of researchers and seniors' advocacy organizations. Extensive collective discussion and consultation are indispensable if we are to lay the foundations of an inclusive, fair, and all-embracing national aging policy, free of measures dictated by erroneous and pejorative perceptions of aging. Policy-making is the business of politicians, but it is likewise the concern of ordinary citizens.

GETTING WISE ABOUT GETTING OLD

Introduction

Multiple Perspectives on Diverse Aging Experiences

Anne-Marie Séguin, Véronique Billette, and Patrik Marier

Aging is sometimes depicted as a demographic disaster or as a heavy social and financial burden on younger generations. In a society that places a high value on image and speed, slowness and other effects of the passage of time on the human body may be considered pathological or undesirable, while attachment to the past is viewed as old-fashioned. Population aging and old age are often subject to negative portrayals and persistent stereotypes – so much so that denying or fighting against aging is commonplace and even a regular part of everyday conversation.[1] The anti-aging industry has exploited this situation (and probably contributes to it as well) with a gamut of natural products, anti-aging creams, hair dyes, aesthetic treatments, medications, injections, surgical procedures, and other "remedies." This global market, now worth an estimated US$140.3 billion, is clearly booming![2]

Are these negative portrayals of aging well founded? This book examines numerous commonly accepted myths, or false beliefs, about aging. To obtain an accurate portrait of seniors, experts from many different fields and disciplines were asked to describe a specific myth and then analyze all of its facets. Without compromising scientific integrity, the short and accessible articles in this book are designed to enable readers to explore many of the social issues that lie behind the common myths. The aim of this exercise is to contribute to a better understanding of the challenges – and advantages – of an aging society.

This book was written prior to the COVID-19 pandemic, which has had unprecedented and widespread impacts around the world. Unfortunately, older adults have been particularly affected by the spread of the virus and by the governmental measures enacted in concert with public health officials. The majority of COVID-19 deaths have been in residential long-term care centres, and confinement measures have been the most restrictive for seniors. Consequently, the myths illustrated in this book have been under a far more intense spotlight. It is our hope that this book will contribute positively to enhance societal discussions in the aftermath of the pandemic.

What Is Meant by "Population Aging"?

More and more Quebecers are joining the highly diversified sociodemographic category called "seniors," which generally includes people 65 years of age and older, as well as, in some cases, adults over the age of 50 in particularly difficult circumstances (for example, people who are homeless, in prison, or living with HIV). Like all of Canada and many other countries, Quebec can be described as an aging society. A few statistics clearly substantiate this phenomenon. In 1970, 6.7 percent of the total population of Quebec consisted of people 65 and older, as opposed to 40.6 percent younger than 20. By 2016, the older age group had grown to 18.1 percent of the total Quebec population, and the younger group stood at 20.6 percent.[3] According to the Institut de la statistique du Québec, the proportion of seniors in Quebec will continue to climb, reaching 25.9 percent by 2036. The aging of Quebec's population will thus continue to accelerate over the next 20 years. This trend, which began several decades ago, is caused by many factors, including a lower birth rate that can be partly attributed to women's increased participation in the labour force and access to more reliable contraception. Population aging also results from longer life expectancy thanks to better overall living conditions, medical and technological advances, and improved understanding of health determinants.

The Social Issues of Aging

Old age is a diverse and complex stage of life that takes many forms and multiple paths. Numerous factors in the past and present lives of individuals affect their experience of growing old. Collective or social factors also affect older adults' experiences and living conditions. These varied social parameters of aging are central to the field of social gerontology, which takes a multidisciplinary approach to the phenomenon – one that stresses the complex and varied dimensions of human aging and the social factors that influence both how older people are portrayed in society and their living conditions. Many social gerontologists around the world, including in Quebec, other Canadian provinces, and the UK, have analyzed aging from the standpoint of social exclusion.[4]

Growing Old and Social Exclusion

In many societies, old age is perceived as the antithesis of beauty, efficiency, productivity, autonomy, and social utility, and seniors are often described in terms of vulnerability, dependency, apathy, and frailty. Such social representations can easily lead to the infantilization or social exclusion of seniors (for "convenience's sake" or "for their own protection"). In Quebec's public consultations on seniors' living conditions, held in 2007, many seniors stated that they were ignored, treated as children, or subjected to long-standing prejudices – in short, they were victims of ageism.[5]

Although seniors do not make up a homogeneous, excluded population subjected to generalized ageism, many older individuals experience exclusion and discrimination in various aspects of their lives. Examples include recognition of their place in society and their social roles; social participation and the exercise of citizenship; access to necessary care and services; mobility in their daily environments; the ability to make choices and act on them until the end of their lives; having sufficient income and other resources to meet their needs; and growing older without rejection or mistreatment.[6]

Recognition: A Key Ingredient in the Social Inclusion of Seniors

How can society be made more inclusive for its seniors? Inclusion requires respect and recognition, for a start. This requirement is highly relevant when we consider the insidious nature of the myths that tend to portray seniors in negative or reductionist terms. According to German philosopher Axel Honneth, lack of recognition of certain social groups can undermine societal values such as respect, integrity, justice, and ethics.[7] Recognition allows for every member of a society to be treated as a full-fledged partner in the life of that society, regardless of individual differences.[8] This concept can also be used to explore and better understand issues such as each person's need to feel acknowledged, respected, and fairly treated. Recognition also requires taking individuals' needs into account by offering them access to society's resources: financial means; appropriate, adequate, and timely care and other services, such as accessible spaces; affordable and adequate housing; and equal rights.[9] Indeed, talking about the recognition of seniors without pro-vision of resources and capabilities needed for their health, well-being, and social participation would be an empty and misleading discussion.

Structure of the Book

This book has six parts, each of which addresses a major theme. In Part 1, social representations of aging are compared with its realities. This section begins with an exploration of the various terms used – seniors, older adults, elders, and so on – in various societies. The authors also challenge the use of the term *aîné* in Quebec society to designate seniors, given the low consider-ation and lack of respect shown to seniors in general in that society (Olazabal and Simard). The myth that seniors are wealthy is then examined; the find-ing is that although poverty among seniors has dropped significantly, most of them are not financially well-off (Marier et al.). The blanket labelling of seniors as conservative is challenged in the following chapter by an analysis that reveals a wide variety of political leanings (Simard and Olazabal). The view that growing old is bound to be associated with loss of interest in the technologies that are increasingly predominant in society is then examined in depth (Sawchuk et al.). In the last chapter in this section, the latest re-search about age-related loss of memory and other cognitive functions is discussed, and the idea that all seniors suffer rapid linear cognitive decline is challenged (Lussier et al.).

In Part 2, seniors' living environments are explored. Many myths about living environments and specific senior populations are dispelled or de-bunked. For a start, the myth that most seniors live in residential long-term care facilities does not stand up to analysis (Séguin et al.). Maintaining seniors in their own homes, an approach advocated by seniors and public authorities alike, raises the question of the related adaptive measures that need to be taken in cities, towns, and villages. Although Municipalité amie des aînés, the Quebec government's age-friendly municipalities program, is often presented as favouring these adaptive measures, its effectiveness is open to scrutiny (Joy et al.). Given that many seniors still drive and try to keep their licences for as long as possible in order to maintain their in-dependence, it might be assumed that they are somewhat obsessed with their vehicles; the accuracy of this view is explored (Negron-Poblete and Séguin). The last two chapters shed light on two groups of seniors who are largely invisible or subject to severe stigmatization: homeless seniors and older prison inmates. The first describes how, contrary to popular opinion, homeless seniors, whose numbers are growing, present a wide variety of profiles and life histories (Burns). In the second, the view that prisons provide older inmates with living conditions that compare favourably with long-term care facilities is countered by an accurate portrait of the little-known world of older prison inmates (Gagnon and Dunn).

Part 3 focuses on the diversity of aging experiences. Seniors constitute a highly diversified population group: there is a huge difference between being 65 years old and being 100. Each senior has a life history with all its accompanying baggage. We age as we have lived throughout our lives – with our individuality, relationships, and community involvement; in other words, the diversity of our individual pasts is coupled with that of our individual futures as a result of the various events that continue to occur in our lives. Growing old with a diagnosis of mental illness or living with recent mental health problems at an advanced age triggers a host of prejudices, as explained by Aubin and Dallaire. The myth of the eternal child attached to individuals with an intellectual disability or a pervasive developmental disorder is explored, as is how older individuals in this group are perceived now that they have a much longer life expectancy (Dickson). The sexual life of seniors is the target of many myths and prejudices. For example, it might be assumed that HIV/AIDS poses no issues for older people, whereas the syndrome has serious repercussions for the lives and health of those living with it (Wallach). Another myth – that of the sexuality of the older women known as "cougars" – is also explored (Alarie). Since the life experience of some seniors involves difficult situations of violence, two chapters are devoted to violence, which is perpetrated mostly against women and persists with age. These chapters examine, respectively, false beliefs about sexual assault (Couture et al.) and spousal violence (Israel et al.).

Part 4 deals with myths related to social roles. The term *seniors* often evokes stereotypical images – of retirees, low-performance workers, and people who engage in a wide range of recreational activities. This section begins with an analysis of recent changes in the labour market, revealing that the dependency ratio of retirees to the working population is far from being as catastrophic as has been portrayed in the media (Carrière et al.). Although the labels applied to workers aged 50, 55, or older are often negative, these workers possess knowledge and experience that can largely offset the effects of growing old. The question of whether they should be retained in their jobs and given appropriate working conditions is examined (Lord and Therriault). Although old age and free time are often associated, the daily reality of many seniors involves severe time constraints due to factors such as numerous medical appointments, schedules imposed by medication, and a slower pace in performing domestic chores or getting around (Wiebe et al.). The last two chapters, which cover volunteering (Castonguay et al.) and social participation (Raymond et al.), describe the pressures on seniors to participate in volunteering or other social activities in order to "age well." These two chapters also explore whether it is possible to live a "full life" in old age without succumbing to these pressures and whether steps are being taken to help seniors participate in society in appropriate and satisfying ways.

Part 5 of the book explores death and bereavement. The first chapter explores the successive bereavements of friends, acquaintances, and family members experienced by seniors and challenges the mistaken belief that, because death is such an integral part of seniors' lives, it has less impact on them (Bourgeois-Guérin et al.). The topic of end of life is then covered in an attempt to understand why so few seniors have access to palliative care, and the question of whether seniors' deaths are more peaceful and freer of suffering because of their age is also analyzed (Van Pevenage et al.). Lastly, the idea that all seniors want – and are able – to die at home is challenged. The current conditions available to them at the end of their lives are evaluated, as is whether they are really given comfort and respect at this stage of their lives (Van Pevenage et al.).

The last part of the book addresses issues relating to caregivers and the support provided to seniors and their family and friends. The first chapter debunks the myth that seniors are regularly abandoned by their families (Van Pevenage et al.). The next chapter addresses various concepts of independent living and highlights the role of evaluation tools used by professionals in decisions regarding the provision of services (Gilbert et al.). The last two chapters cover sources of support and care for lesbian, gay, bisexual, and transgender seniors (Beauchamp et al.) and for immigrant seniors and their families (Ferrer and Brotman).

Conclusion

In the current social context, with its floods of simplified and contradictory information, it is sometimes difficult to differentiate between myths and false beliefs, on the one hand, and the many nuanced realities of aging, on the other hand. This is why it is necessary to take stock of and carefully analyze the social issues of aging. The purpose of this book is to stimulate thought about various approaches to these issues based on the varied expertise and knowledge of its authors in their respective fields. This book can thus serve as a tool not only for seniors but also for students, professionals, researchers, and all those who strive every day to ensure that society is more welcoming, inclusive, and kind toward all of its citizens, regardless of their age or identity.

Notes

1 Amanda Grenier and Ilyan Ferrer (2010), "Âge, vieillesse et vieillissement. Définition controversée de l'âge," in Michèle Charpentier, Nancy Gubennan, Véronique Billette, Jean-Pierre Lavoie, Amanda Grenier and Ignace Olazabal (eds.), *Vieillir au pluriel. Perspectives sociales* (Quebec City: Presses de l'Université du Québec), 35–54.

2 Zion Market Research (2016), *Anti-Aging (Baby Boomer, Generation X and Generation Y) Market, by Product (Botox, Anti-Wrinkle Products, Anti-Stretch Mark Products, and Others), by Services (Anti-Pigmentation Therapy, Anti-Adult Acne Therapy, Breast Augmentation, Liposuction, Chemical Peel, Hair Restoration Treatment, and Others), by Device (Microdermabrasion, Laser Aesthetics, Anti-Cellulite Treatment and Anti-Aging Radio Frequency Devices): Global Industry Perspective, Comprehensive Analysis, Size, Share, Growth, Segment, Trends and Forecast, 2015–2021*, <https://www.zionmarketresearch.com/sample/anti-aging-market>, accessed July 5, 2017.

3 Institut de la statistique du Québec (2014), *Tableau statistique, Effectif et poids démographique des grands groupes d'âge, scénario A – Référence, Québec, régions administratives et régions métropolitaines (RMR), 2011 et 2036*, <http://www.stat.gouv.qc.ca/docs-hmi/statistiques/population-demographie/perspectives/population/age_reg_14.htm>, accessed March 22, 2017; Institut de la statistique du Québec (2016), *Tableau statistique, Population par groupe d'âge, Canada et régions, 1er juillet 2016*, <http://www.stat.gouv.qc.ca/statistiques/population-demographie/structure/104.htm>, accessed July 12, 2017.

4 Véronique Billette and Jean-Pierre Lavoie (2010), "Vieillissements, exclusions sociales et solidarités," in Michèle Charpentier, Nancy Guberman, Véronique Billette, Jean-Pierre Lavoie, Amanda Grenier, and Ignace Olazabal (eds.), *Vieillir au pluriel. Perspectives sociales* (Quebec City: Presses de l'Université du Québec), 1–22; Thomas Scharf and Norah Keating (eds.) (2012), *From Exclusion to Inclusion in Old Age: A Global Challenge* (Bristol: The Policy Press).

5 Lucie Gagnon and Annie Savoie (2008), *Préparons l'avenir avec nos aînés, Rapport de la consultation publique sur les conditions de vie des aînés* (Quebec City: Gouvernement du Québec – Secrétariat aux aînés), 26.

6 Billette and Lavoie (2010), op. cit.; Chris Phillipson (2012), "Globalization, Economic Recession and Social Exclusion: Policy Challenges and Responses," in Scharf and Keating (eds.) (2012), op. cit., 17–32; Jane Jensen (2004), *Canada's New Social Risks: Directions for a New Social Architecture*, Research Report F 43 (Ottawa: Canadian Policy Research Networks [CPRN]).

7   Axel Honneth (2006), "Les conflits sociaux sont des luttes pour la reconnaissance," interview with philosopher Axel Honneth, *Sciences Humaines*, electronic edition, No. 172, June, <https://www.scienceshumaines.com/articleprint2.php?lg=fr&id_article =14475>, accessed August 30, 2017.
8   Nancy Fraser (2005), *Qu'est-ce que la justice sociale? Reconnaissance et redistribution* (Paris: La Découverte).
9   Ibid.

Part 1
PORTRAYALS AND REALITIES OF AGING

1

Myths and Realities about Seniors

Ignace Olazabal and Julien Simard

The French term *aîné*, which can be read as the translation of the English term *elder*, has now been enshrined in both Quebec media and Quebec government publications as the synonym for all the less consensual terms that designate old age (such as "old," "elderly," and "golden ager") and is associated with the concept of old people in general. Semantically, *aîné* in French refers to the oldest sibling in a family. Being the oldest child often comes with the rights of the firstborn (especially with regard to the family estate) and certain responsibilities with regard to the younger siblings. Despite the fact that *aîné* is also employed in Canada to define a specific age group (people aged 65 and older), the use of the term to refer to a segment of the overall population is rarely questioned. For instance, the Dictionnaire Robert defines *aîné* in terms of the hierarchy among siblings, simply adding that the word is used by extension in literature to refer to ancestors or forebears.

Social anthropologists study the position of the older generation in traditional societies and the foundational myths that sustain the social phenomenon of the elderly. Various legends glorify old age as the culmination of a long, well-lived life. Some societies have venerated old age by attributing powers and often supernatural qualities to it that younger generations lack the necessary experience to possess. This idealized image of old age is perfectly encapsulated in the foundational myth of Judeo-Christian culture, as described in Genesis, the first book of the Bible. In that account, three elderly patriarchs – Abraham, Isaac, and Moses – led the Israelites through many trials and tribulations and were the only ones with the authority and status to converse with God.

In the sixteenth century, Michelangelo provided a superb material representation of the archetypal elder governing his community in his statue of Moses. In this Renaissance masterpiece, Moses is a very old man, but he is also wise, physically strong, and exudes a reassuring presence. He is the leader who sets the course for his people to follow.

The figure of the heroic elder is also found in cultural output of Antiquity, such as the *Iliad* and the *Odyssey*, written by Greek poet Homer in the eighth century BCE. In such epics, heroic elders not only become wise with advancing years but conserve all of their mental and physical vigour despite their old age. During the same period, the militarily renowned Kingdom of Sparta revered its older men as heroes for having survived successive wars. Although two elderly kings ruled Sparta, ultimate authority was vested in a Council of Elders – "the *gerousia*, consisting of 30 old men chosen by acclamation among citizens aged over 60."[1]

In many traditional preliterate societies, as in mythology, elders were highly valued because they were considered the repositories of knowledge and collective memory. Because writing did not exist, older people's knowledge and experience were considered indispensable.

Older People in Preliterate Societies

Various societies throughout history, albeit culturally very different in other respects, held their elders in high social esteem – for example, precolonial West African societies and all traditional societies that lived off hunting, fishing, and gathering (the situation of most precolonial Indigenous societies). In those societies, the oldest members actively participated in the transmission of both practical knowledge, such as plant-based healthcare, the art of hunting, and the ability to differentiate between edible and poisonous foodstuffs, and symbolic knowledge, such as religion and genealogy. Preliterate societies were perpetuated from generation to generation via oral tradition, with the individual memories of men and women who had considerable experiential and practical knowledge constituting the society's collective archives. This reality was aptly expressed by Malian writer Amadou Hampâté Bâ: "When an old person dies, it is as if a library goes up in flames."[2] We should also bear in mind that longevity and life expectancy were much shorter in those societies than in contemporary Western societies.

Because people generally died young, older people were a somewhat excep-tional social category.

In most early hunter-fisher-gatherer societies (by definition nomadic, or-ganized into bands, and generally without a single leader), there were two opposing categories: between men and women, and between children and adults.[3] Quebec anthropologist Bernard Arcand notes that the elderly among the Cuiva Indians of Colombia were treated on the same footing as all adults. However, social status was based on social utility and respect for the group's rules of conduct, and these two qualities tended to develop with age. The oldest adults thus enjoyed special social standing thanks to their longer lives and greater accumulated knowledge. This knowledge, transmit-ted through collective memory, constituted the intergenerational driving force of the group, guaranteeing that the practical knowledge essential for survival would be transmitted. Knowledge could be jealously guarded by the elders until the end of their lives, implicitly ensuring that the demand for its transmission – and thus the elders' social value – was maintained despite their old age.[4] The elders were also recognized for their ability to interact with the realm of the sacred as mediators between the living and the dead in these societies, in which dead ancestors or forebears were al-ways an integral part of the world of the living (through ancestor worship).

Still in preliterate times, a typical model of social respect for elders existed in many precolonial West African societies – sedentary societies in which it was easier for older adults to establish their power and authority and that contained, unlike the societies described above, highly differenti-ated social categories whereby men were totally dominant vis-à-vis women, as were elders vis-à-vis the young. Everyone belonged to a tribe, ethnic group, specific lineage, and predetermined caste, but, above all, men and women belonged to a given age-based class. The oldest men were considered *elders* in the true sense of the term: they enjoyed the highest social status and, simply by belonging to the oldest age group, they were generally rich and powerful.[5] But the elders were also the narrators of the traditional stor-ies and transmitted cultural-identity values by conversing with the younger generation. This process has been described by Boucar Diouf, a Senegalese-born humourist, scientist, and broadcaster, in his stories about his grand-father.[6] Although the gerontocratic power of West African elders was not officially challenged prior to colonization, it was nonetheless coveted by the younger members of society. At the same time, the latter generally accepted the prevailing hierarchical order and waited their turn. In such societies, people moved from one age group to the next when the last representative of the immediate older group died. All members of a single age group progressed simultaneously because they were class siblings throughout their lives, with this subjective variable being a particular feature of African societies of bygone days.

In the past half-century, all traditional societies have undergone major social transformations. Not only do they now use writing and documentary records, but many of their members pursue higher education and have fully adopted information and communications technologies. Oral traditions are gradually becoming less important, and the knowledge that was previously held secret or sparingly transmitted by the elders is now recorded in books and accessible via Google. As a consequence, knowledge transmitted by collective memory is no longer considered sacred or indispensable, which has resulted in a considerable decline in older adults' power in those societies as Western technical and legal knowledge, invariably transmitted in written form, is integrated. Older people's privileges have also been diminished as monotheistic religions and capitalist values have taken hold. Older adults are thus gradually losing their prestige and social utility and are now more likely to be considered, simply, old. This social change can also be observed in Quebec and in the West in general, where literacy, the importance of academic education, and access to technologies have contributed to devaluation of the traditional knowledge transmitted by the oldest practitioners of certain trades.

In the 1970s, anthropologists who compared the social status of older people in modern societies with that in ancestral societies observed that this status has declined with modernization.[7] Social change, especially in technological terms, has accelerated in advanced modern societies; this can be a handicap for many older people as societies focus on the future without regard for the past. The social utility of the elderly and the need for younger people to receive knowledge from them have therefore declined accordingly.

The Elderly and the *Aînés:* The Quebec Reality

A Quebec government publication states that "in Quebec, old people are generally designated by the term *aînés*. In other parts of the Francophone world, the terms *'seniors,' 'personnes de l'âge d'or'* [golden-agers], *'personnes du troisième âge'* [senior citizens], *'personnes du quatrième âge'* [elderly], and *'adultes vieillissants'* [aging adults] are also used."[8]

The concept of *aînés* to designate everyone aged 65 or older came into effect in Quebec without much fanfare in the early 1990s. It became the official term in public policy and was also adopted for this segment of the population by civil society, the media, and scientific literature. Does the concept of *aîné* have an explicit meaning, other than simply being 65 or older? And why was a concept with ancestral connotations chosen as a term of reference? It is, in fact, relevant to question the terminology used to describe old age, because the meaning of words is not value-neutral.[9] Could it be that the term *aîné* is being used to valorize elders on the basis of the sacred and mythical character of elders in the past – whereas, in reality, many older people these days are either abandoned or, at best, excluded? Moreover, their knowledge is seldom considered to be worthy of transmission.

In Quebec, there are greater numbers of *aînés* – or the people designated as such when they reach "pension age" – than ever before, and they will become even more numerous over the next 30 years, as the baby-boomer generation gets older. This reality is accentuated by another variable, that of greater longevity. There are actually several categories of old age now due to higher life expectancy, which is currently 81 years for men and over 84 years for women. Increasing numbers of people have exceeded these ages and are said to have reached "old-old age." Between the beginning of old age, in the early 60s, and end of life, two or three stages of old age may occur, with the parents of the current 65-to-70-year-old age group now constituting the oldest of the *aînés*. Moreover, given the increased variability in quality of aging, the 65-and-older age group has become totally heterogeneous.[10]

Some people considered *elders*, in the anthropological sense of the term, do exist, but they are the exception rather than the rule. These people represent a benchmark outside the sphere of their own family because their experience and expertise are valued and they are socially involved, primarily through the quality of what they say and the respect that their words evoke. Many of them are intellectuals, scientists, artists, entrepreneurs, administrators, politicians, media personalities, and other notables – for example, poet and singer-songwriter Gilles Vigneault and former Quebec politician Françoise David. Another example is Janette Bertrand, whose autobiography describes what life is like for her as an elder (although she says she is simply old rather than an elder), because her life experience is also of interest to younger people.[11]

At the same time, we must not forget that it is largely the media that determine which older people deserve to be heard and seen – and it is the media that reflect prevailing ageist prejudices.[12] Society often derides old age by infantilizing older people even though, in reality, many older people are actively involved in their families and communities, and thus in society. Their voices receive scant media coverage: old age, it seems, is a "hard sell."

Conclusion

In social anthropology, the term *aîné* in French, like the term *elder* in English, refers to an old person who, simply by virtue of being old, enjoys high social standing and respect within his or her family and community. The term also evokes knowledge transmission and social utility in general. In some ancestral societies, elders possessed experiential knowledge and enjoyed rights that their younger counterparts did not; they were positioned at the top of the parental and social hierarchy (the right of seniority). However, those called *aînés* in Quebec are generally deprived of such attributes. The concept therefore seems to be out of sync with the observable reality of ageism prevalent in hypermodern societies: those whom we call our elders are simply considered old.

However, we should not view the choice of this concept, which applies more accurately to bygone societies, as a deliberate strategy of paying lip service by its proponents (especially the Quebec government). In practice, the discourses of governments and civil society promote appreciation for people aged 65 and older, especially the oldest among them. Many political initiatives have been envisaged, such as the World Health Organization's strategy for maintaining the vitality and social participation of older people. But social recognition is also largely measured in words and how people are labelled, and there doesn't seem to be an easy answer to what to call such a diversified population category, while also avoiding the discomfort that can arise with terms such as "old," "elderly," "senior," and "golden-ager." However, as Cameroonian anthropologist Manga Bekombo points out, "Speaking about old age consists not solely of pronouncing words from a glossary, but, even more, of attempting to access an entire system of thought and behaviour all at once."[13] Nevertheless, the problem is that the true meaning of this now-official term, which is associated with respect and social recognition, is generally overlooked.

We are living in a society that favours youth and perpetual social change and that tends to view everything that is "dated" with contempt. The value placed on collective memory (emblems, historical figures, historical dates, and other "sites of memory") is directly proportional to the value accorded to the knowledge accumulated by the oldest among us, bearing in mind that anyone who has lived a long life has the potential to transmit his or her varied experience and knowledge, which could be very useful socially. A society that looks only to the future and never to the past is one that, by definition, places little value on the knowledge of its oldest members. It is therefore legitimate to question whether our consciences should be clear when we use the term *aîné* in a society that is not overly enamoured of old age.

Notes

1 Georges Minois (1989), *History of Old Age: From Antiquity to the Renaissance* (Chicago: University of Chicago Press), 64.

2 Amadou Hampâthé Bâ (1991), *Amkoullel l'enfant peul* (Mémoires 1) (Paris: J'ai lu éditions) (our translation).

3 Bernard Arcand (1982), "La construction culturelle de la vieillesse," *Anthropologie et sociétés*, Vol. 6, No. 3, 7–23.

4 Jared Diamond (2012), *The World until Yesterday: What Can We Learn from Traditional Societies?* (New York: Viking).

5 Marc Abélès and Chantal Collard (eds.) (1985), *Âge, pouvoir et société en Afrique noire* (Paris, Montreal, and Khartala: Presses de L'Université de Montréal); Denise Paulme (ed.) (1971), *Classes et associations d'âge en Afrique de l'Ouest* (Paris: Plon).

6 Boucar Diouf (2007), *Sous l'arbre à palabres, mon grand-père disait* (Montreal: Les Intouchables).

7 Donald Cowgill and Lowell D. Holmes (eds.) (1972), *Aging and Modernization* (New York: Appleton-Century-Crofts).

8 Gouvernement du Québec (2002), *L'activité physique, déterminant de la qualité de vie des personnes âgées de 65 ans et plus* (Quebec City: Kino-Québec), 7 (our translation).

9 Alain Montandon (ed.) (2004), *Les mots du vieillir* (Clermont-Ferrand: Centre de recherches sur les littératures modernes et contemporaines); Jacqueline Trincaz, Bernadette Puijalon, and Cédric Humbert (2011), "Dire la vieillesse et les vieux," *Gérontologie et société*, No. 138, September, 113–26.

10 We define "quality of aging" as the level of health and autonomy and the quality of social circles and meaning in life, especially the feeling of social utility, a feeling that gradually declines in society after retirement.

11 Janette Bertrand (2016), *La vieillesse par une vraie vieille* (Montreal: Québec Loisirs).

12 Martine Lagacé, Joëlle Laplante, and André Davignon (2011), "Construction sociale du vieillir dans les médias écrits canadiens: de la lourdeur de la vulnérabilité à l'insoutenable légèreté de l'être," *Communication et organisation*, Vol. 40, 87–101.

13 Manga Bekombo (2004), "Percevoir et dire le vieillir chez les Dwala," in Alain Montandon (ed.), *Les mots du vieillir* (Clermont-Ferrand: CRLMC, Presses universitaires Blaise Pascal), 49 (our translation).

2

Living on Easy Street?

The Myth of the Affluent Senior

Patrik Marier, Yves Carrière, and Jonathan Purenne

Popular beliefs about pensioners and their incomes have been bolstered by numerous magazine articles, including the provocatively titled article "Boomers: riches comme Crésus?" (Baby boomers: Rich as Croesus?) in the finance magazine *Conseiller*.[1] The first line of the article states unequivocally that the financial prosperity that baby boomers are reputed to enjoy is no myth.[2] This message is also conveyed quite clearly in an article on the cottage and country home show in Montreal, which the writer observes is "aimed at a clientele composed largely of baby boomers dreaming about the easy life they'll enjoy in retirement. It's no longer about a modest home on a lake but about prestige."[3] The image of the affluent baby boomer is common elsewhere in the West. In France, a headline in the newspaper *Libération* proclaimed baby boomers to be "the spoiled children of retirement."[4]

But are retirees actually rich? For many years, retirement was synonymous with poverty, but it is now associated with prosperity. Seniors are undeniably in a better position now than in the 1970s, when almost one in three was living under the low income cut-off.[5] Today's seniors are faring better, irrespective of the poverty indicator used. In fact, less than 5 percent of older adults have an after-tax income that places them below the low income cut-off, and just over one in 10 (12.5 percent) falls beneath the low income measure.[6] In light of these statistics, it might be believed that today's seniors have no financial worries and that the problem of poverty among those 65 and over has been solved. In this chapter, we look at seniors' incomes and endeavour to demystify some of the conventional wisdom around this topic. For a better understanding of the myth of the affluent senior, we first take a brief look at Canada's pension system and its objectives. We then explore the following questions: Do seniors have as much money as we think? Which groups of older adults are most likely to be affected by poverty? What does the future hold for pension incomes?

What Is Behind the Widespread Perception of the Recently Retired as Rich?

To learn more about the origin of the myth of the affluent senior, we first need to remember that for many decades, retirement was synonymous with poverty. In 1951, before the introduction of the various income-security programs for seniors, two thirds of Canadian seniors had an annual income of less than $1,000 ($9,500 in 2016 dollars).[7] To mitigate the prevalence of poverty among older adults, in the early 1950s the Government of Canada introduced Old Age Security (OAS). This tax-funded universal program covered all seniors aged 70 and over (65 and over today). OAS helped to reduce poverty but was not sufficient to eliminate it. The solution was to create a program intended for workers, funded by contributions from employees and their employers, in an effort not only to reduce poverty levels but also to ensure that people would not experience a precipitous drop in their standard of living once they retired. In 1965, the federal government came to an agreement with the provinces to create the Canada Pension Plan (CPP), and Quebec launched its equivalent with the Quebec Pension Plan (QPP). Unlike OAS, the CPP and QPP are earnings-related income programs with mandatory contributions for all workers, meaning that only those who contribute will receive benefits. When the program was implemented, it was agreed that upon turning 65 a worker would have to have contributed for at least 10 years in order to be entitled to maximum benefits. This meant that during the first ten years of the CPP and the QPP, no one was entitled to receive the maximum pension.

In response to the pressing need to alleviate poverty among seniors, in 1967 the Government of Canada established the Guaranteed Income Supplement (GIS) as a top-up to OAS. Because this program was income-tested, only people with low incomes were eligible. The program was originally intended to be temporary but is still in effect today, and close to one third of Canada's seniors are receiving the GIS. These three publicly funded programs may be supplemented by private savings, such as the pension plans offered by some employers and registered retirement savings plans (RRSPs). With the introduction of these programs, which reached maturity in the mid-1990s, the proportion of seniors whose income fell below the low income cut-off dropped progressively and significantly, from approximately 30 percent in 1997 to less than 5 percent today.[8] However, as discussed below, this substantial decrease in poverty among the new cohorts of retirees does not equate to an age of prosperity for seniors.

Pensioners: From Poverty to Affluence?

The pension system was built on the desire to combat poverty among the older population, and this objective has been fulfilled to some extent. However, it does not mean that seniors are on easy street – simply that most of them are living above the low income cut-off. This can be explained partly by the low replacement rate offered by the QPP and the CPP, which aims to replace 25 percent of average income with a 40-year contribution period (starting in 2019, this is gradually being raised to reach 33.3 percent). Table 2.1 presents the average after-tax income per capita of Quebecers aged 65 and over and the average amounts received from OAS and the GIS for 2010. The data in this table are quite revealing with respect to the significant changes in income according to age and sex. Overall, average income is lower (albeit stable) for women, whereas it decreases with age for men. The income breakdown for seniors clearly shows the combined effect of OAS and the GIS, particularly for women aged 75 and over. Without this additional income, a significant number of women would have been below or very close to the low income cut-off for an individual – between $12,271 and $18,759

TABLE 2.1

Average after-tax income per capita, income from OAS and GIS by sex, Quebec, 2010 ($)

Income source	Male		Female	
	Age 65 to 74	75 and over	Age 65 to 74	75 and over
Average OAS benefit	5,500	6,000	5,700	5,900
Average GIS benefit	1,400	1,500	1,500	2,700
Average total after-tax income	31,900	26,500	23,200	23,400
Total income without OAS and GIS	25,000	19,000	16,000	14,800

Source: The data in this table are taken from Institut de la statistique du Québec (ISQ) (2013), *Revenu, faible revenu et inégalité de revenu: portrait des Québécoises et des Québécois de 55 ans et plus vivant en logement privé* (Quebec City: ISQ).

depending on the geographic area – in 2010.[9] It is worth remembering that approximately one third of seniors receive the GIS each year. It is obvious that without this program, the proportion of seniors living under the low income cut-off would be much higher.

Another way of analyzing seniors' incomes is to look at their distribution by income quintile.[10] This enables us to determine whether seniors are distributed equally across the different income levels or whether there are higher concentrations of them in the most impoverished segment of society, the middle class, or the highest-income category. Data from the Institut de la statistique du Québec reveal that, for 2011, more than half of people aged 65 and over were in the two lowest quintiles – the quintiles with the lowest income.[11] This indicates that financial security is rather precarious for many seniors and makes the case for income-security programs for the older population.

Seniors' Assets

In looking at how well-off seniors are, it is important to take elements other than income into account. For people aged 65 and over, data from Statistics Canada's Survey of Financial Security show that between 1999 and 2012, the net median value of their assets (for example, a house, savings, and a car) increased substantially: from $390,100 to $650,400 (+70 percent) for an economic family of two or more people and from $157,600 to $246,000 (+56 percent) for a single person.[12] However, this profile is somewhat misleading and conceals a reality that is more complex. These figures tend to be inflated by extreme upper values, such as the value of the assets of very wealthy people (mortgage-free houses and cottages, for example). It is therefore more appropriate to look at how wealth is distributed by income quintile, as we did above. Such an examination shows that wealth has not grown similarly among different income quintiles. The overall wealth held by families (all ages) grew by 73 percent during the 1999–2012 period. In the first (most affluent) quintile it rose by 80 percent, but in the last (poorest) quintile it rose by only 38 percent.[13]

Not All Seniors Are the Same: The Cases of Women and Immigrants
There are, of course, seniors in the upper income quintiles, and others with low incomes may actually have substantial assets. We do not mean to suggest that all older people are in dire financial straits, but it is important to recognize that seniors do not make up a homogeneous population and that

some groups are at greater risk of experiencing poverty than others. For example, women who live alone have always been at greater risk of falling below the low income cut-off. Although this situation has improved over the years, more than one quarter of such women (28.9 percent) were living below the low income cut-off in 2011. By way of comparison, the rate was 9.5 percent for the population as a whole for that year.[14] The proportion is similar for immigrants aged 65 and over who have been in Canada for less than 20 years.[15]

These two groups are disadvantaged from the standpoint of pension income under plans such as the CPP and QPP and private registered pension plans, since the amounts of such pensions are established on a contributory basis[16] – that is, based on a person's income level and the number of years he or she was in the labour force. Historically, women have been more likely to be employed part time and to be paid less, and to experience broken and incomplete careers. As a result, the pensions they have built have tended to be smaller than those of their male counterparts. Women are also at greater risk of ending up alone because their life expectancy is longer, a situation that eats away at their financial resources even if they are entitled to survivor benefits.

As for immigrants, they face numerous obstacles that jeopardize their financial security in old age. First, they are less likely to find full-time, permanent employment in the public sector or in a unionized position. Accordingly, their income from public and private pension plans tends to be lower than that of native-born Canadians.[17] Immigrants may also have more difficulty meeting the eligibility criteria for OAS (minimum of 10 years of residency in Canada, and 40 years to receive the maximum benefit). This applies in particular to recent immigrants taking advantage of the family reunification program to join their children who have settled in Canada. Because of this, they are almost completely dependent on their families for financial support. Canada has signed a number of international agreements under which pensions earned in a person's country of origin can be transferred, but they do not cover all immigrants.

Are We Heading toward Greater Volatility in Retirement Incomes?

Most of the current discussions around pension funding are centred on measures intended to avoid increasing the financial burden on the public purse. They include the promotion of private savings and the recent enhancement of the CPP and QPP. The objective of offering a better pension without increasing the fiscal burden may well be commendable, but all of these proposals ignore people who are not able to make an adequate contribution to such plans, placing them at risk of growing old in poverty. This focus on contributory plans is not unique to Canada; it can be seen in most countries that offer some form of old age pension.[18]

This transition is taking place alongside shifts observed in the workplace, as employers are increasingly tending to offer defined contribution plans. With this type of pension plan, the amount to be paid during the work year is known, but it is difficult to predict the benefits that an employee will receive at retirement. This stands in contrast to defined benefit plans, for which the benefit amounts are known in advance (as the name suggests). Defined contribution plans are similar to RRSPs in that all of the risks related to longevity or to sluggish (or even negative) rates of return are borne by the participant. The current fears that long-term economic growth will be slower and rates of return lower do not bode well for people whose savings are based solely on this type of plan.[19]

Conclusion

As a number of chapters in this book show, aging is a highly heterogeneous experience, but the picture conveyed by the media tends to be lacking in nuance. The same can be said about baby boomers' incomes in retirement. In short, there is a high level of diversity when it comes to employment and life circumstances and their impact on retirement income. In many ways, the factors that contribute to traditional socioeconomic disparities, such as gender, immigration, and occupational status, are just as important when people are retired as when they are in the labour force. The generalization that all baby boomers (and seniors as a whole) are affluent is therefore false.

Several of the issues discussed above raise serious questions about the impact of stock market volatility on the financial resources of the older population. Such volatility affects not only private investments but also a number of public and private pension plans. That is the main reason that Quebec and a number of other provinces have established boards or commissions of inquiry to look at pension benefits in recent years. Although the enhancement of the CPP and QPP represents a modest and positive step toward increasing the retirement income of Canadians in the future, the need for additional income for older pensioners who are less well-off remains.

Notes

1 Dominique Lamy (2013), "Boomers: riches comme Crésus?," *Conseiller,* June 25, <http://www.conseiller.ca/nouvelles/boomers-riches-comme-cresus-40931>, accessed March 14, 2017.

2 Ibid.

3 Valérie Lesage (2013), "Ces baby-boomers qui font (et défont) les tendances," *Les Affaires,* July 6, 10 (our translation).

4 "Baby-boomers: Les enfants gâtés de la retraite," *Libération,* June 15, 2010, 1.

5 Low income cut-offs after tax are income thresholds below which a family will likely devote a larger share of its income (20 percentage points more) than the average family does to the necessities of food, shelter, and clothing.

6 The low income measure is a relative measure that represents 50 percent of the median income adjusted to take household size into account.

7 Jenny R. Podoluk (1968), *Incomes of Canadians, 1961 Census Monograph* (Ottawa: Queen's Printer).

8 According to Statistics Canada data (last updated in 2016), CANSIM, *Table 206-0041, Low income statistics by age, sex and economic family type,* <http://www5.statcan.gc.ca/cansim/a26?lang=eng&id=2060041>, accessed February 28, 2017.

9 The low income cut-off varies according to the number of people in the household and the size of the community. See, for example, Statistics Canada (2015), *Table 1, Low income cut-offs (1992 base) after tax,* <https://www150.statcan.gc.ca/n1/pub/75f0002m/2015002/tbl/tbl01-eng.htm>, accessed February 28, 2017.

10 According to the Institut de la Statistique du Québec, the first step in determining the quintile limit is to categorize all incomes, from lowest to highest, for each reference group being examined. The next step is to select the income value under which the populations fall: 20 percent (lower limit), 40 percent (second limit), 60 percent (third limit), 80 percent (fourth limit), and 100 percent (upper limit). We used quintile limits to outline the degree of inequality for a particular income distribution. The smaller the difference in income between two quintile limits, the smaller the degree of inequality. Conversely, the greater the difference, the greater the degree of inequality. See Institut de la Statistique du Québec, <http://www.stat.gouv.qc.ca/statistiques/conditions-vie-societe/revenu/inegalite-revenu/def_quintile.htm>, accessed February 28, 2017.

11 Stéphane Crespo and Sylvie Rheault (2015), "Lien entre le revenu individuel et le faible revenu de la famille," *Données sociodémographiques en bref* (Quebec City: Institut de la statistique du Québec), Vol. 20, No. 1, 9–13. In 2011, the average income was $16,600 for the first quintile and $35,400 for the second, with 13.1 percent of seniors in the first and 40.5 percent in the second.

12 According to Statistics Canada data (last updated in 2014), CANSIM, *Table 2005–0002, Survey of Financial Security (SFS),* <https://www150.statcan.gc.ca/t1/tbl1/en/tv.action?pid=1110001601&request_locale=en>, accessed February 28, 2017.

13 Sharanjit Uppal and Sébastien LaRochelle-Côté (2015), "Changes in wealth across the income distribution, 1999 to 2012," *Insights on Canadian Society,* Ottawa, Statistics Canada Catalogue No. 75-006-X.

14 According to Statistics Canada data (last updated in 2013), CANSIM, *Table 202-0804, Persons in low income*, <http://www5.statcan.gc.ca/cansim/a05?lang=fra&id=2020804>, accessed February 28, 2017.

15 Lisa Kaida and Monica Boyd (2011), "Poverty variations among the elderly: The roles of income security policies and family co-residence," *Canadian Journal on Aging*, Vol. 30, No. 1, 83–100.

16 Patrik Marier and Suzanne Skinner (2008), "Orienting the public-private mix of pensions," in Daniel Béland and Brian Gran (eds.), *Public and Private Social Policy* (Basingstoke: Palgrave Macmillan), 45–69.

17 Derek Hum and Wayne Simpson (2010), "The declining retirement prospects of immigrant men," *Canadian Public Policy*, Vol. 36, No. 3, 287–305.

18 John Myles and Paul Pierson (2001), "The comparative political economy of pension reform," in Paul Pierson (ed.), *The New Politics of the Welfare State* (New York: Oxford University Press), 305–35.

19 Canadian Press (2016), "La nouvelle réalité économique commande de nouveaux réflexes, dit Carolyn Wilkins," *Le Devoir*, September 15, <https://www.ledevoir.com/economie/actualites-economiques/479975/la-nouvelle-realite-economique-commande-de-nouveaux-reflexes-dit-carolyn-wilkins>, accessed March 14, 2017.

3

Older Adults

Allergic to Social Change?

Julien Simard and Ignace Olazabal

The "Grey Army" and Its Anachronisms

In June 2016, the Brexit referendum brought to light an emerging inter-generational conflict in the United Kingdom: a significant proportion of people aged 65 and over voted for the United Kingdom to leave the European Union. Immediately after the plebiscite, numerous media commentators favourable to remaining in Europe attacked them overtly. A writer in the magazine *GQ*, whose readership is composed of trendy young business-men, opined, "Aside from a pathological preoccupation with immigration, the most pervasive reason for the grey army voting Leave is an inarticulate longing to return to the hazy memories of an idealised Britain that never was."[1] Many blogs and tweets contained heated remarks about older people, including diverse explanations, ranging from basic xenophobia to patho-logical nostalgia, for their referendum choices. Most of these discourses can be reduced to a profoundly ageist premise: in the vast field of politics, older adults are considered to be, by default, backward-looking and thus allergic to social change or "progress," represented in this case by remaining in the European Union. Our objective here is not to deny the fact that certain older Britons are, indeed, nostalgic, reactionary, or xenophobic, but to contest the generalization of these attitudes to the entire aging population.

Does Aging Imply Conservatism?

In light of these recent events, the myth that we wish to deconstruct in this chapter is that aging necessarily entails an aversion to social change and, as a corollary, an obstinate desire to maintain the political status quo. In short, this collective representation systematically associates aging with a political attitude generally labelled as "conservatism." This stereotype, which Neal E. Cutler identified in 1977 as "one of the most popular myths of American political folklore," has the direct effect of generalizing to the entire older population, in a given context, a collection of political attitudes and opinions often associated with the political right.[2]

Before proceeding, we would like to clarify the use of certain terms. The concept of conservatism is polysemic: in its broadest sense, the one that we have just used, it signifies "the systematic reflex of an individual or a group to support the status quo and the tendency to reject social, economic, or political change."[3] However, since conservative ideology historically developed in reaction to revolutionary and workers' movements of the last few centuries, it is often associated with the interests of privileged groups of the bourgeoisie, and thus with social conservatism. This leads us to a narrower definition of conservatism: "Support for reforms proposed by candidates of the right."[4] Among other attributes, the right is characterized by a preference for order, stability, and morality, as well as for material progress, capitalism, a strong attachment to the past, and elitism, along with pride in national identity.[5] Today, neoconservative and neofascist movements and individuals are the standard-bearers of some of these values; one example is the English Defence League in the United Kingdom.

Although the myth under discussion is complex and varied in its expressions, its essential structure is nonetheless based on a controversial understanding of aging – one often critiqued in a scientific context but just as present in social representations: that physiological aging is inexorably accompanied by a narrowing of attitudes and beliefs, especially ideological ones. This essentialist logic establishes that older persons' "senility" and "innate fear" of the unknown often lead them to political options on the right of the political spectrum, due to a presumed "anxiety in the face of change."[6] A current variant of the myth has it that older adults' political opinions are completely malleable and therefore easily swayed, as the same supposed senility would destroy their capacities for critical reflection. Who hasn't heard the clichés that "older adults vote for the 'best-looking' candidate" or for "those who bother to visit them in their retirement home"?

The supporters (both overt and discreet) of the myth discussed here generally claim that left-wing social change and youth are necessarily synonymous. A good illustration of this idea is a comment by a French sociologist, Jean-Claude Kaufmann, who wrote during the French presidential election of 2002 – when the extreme right had made it to the second round of the vote – "On one hand, there is youth, imbued with multiculturalism and dreaming of living life to the fullest. On the other is the new counter-revolution of the grey-haired."[7] A popular joke, attributed rightly or wrongly to Winston Churchill, claims that "a man under 30 who is not liberal has no heart and a man over 30 who is not conservative has no brain."[8] This particular vision transmitted by Kaufmann and Churchill stems principally from the Freudian theory of the life cycle.

Without getting into a detailed explanation here, the life cycle theory posits that the succession of roles adopted by the individual in social structures requires corresponding attitudinal and behavioural changes. From this comes the idea that aging individuals might be interested in preserving a social position "hard won" during their active working life, thus pushing them to favour the status quo. Of course, this is forgetting that a significant proportion of older adults do not reach enviable social positions as they age. However, the opposite explanation was also employed in an attempt to justify the thesis of increasing "rigidity" with age. In 1977, in the psychogerontological literature of the time, Cutler identified the argument that aging could induce a loss of status, in comparison to the period of active working life, that is difficult to recover after retirement. According to some authors, this situation could lead individuals to become frustrated, develop a rigid attitude, and opt for political conservatism.[9] Overall, these examples from psychosocial theories have been criticized for the same reason as the physiological theories: they reduce complex realities to simplistic, hasty, and excessive generalizations. What is true for some older adults is not necessarily true for others.

The Many Flaws in This Way of Thinking

More and more contemporary research debunks the idea of a simple, inevitable, and universal causal link between physical aging and conservatism (in both the broader and the narrower senses). Anne Muxel claims that analysis of political behaviour based on biological age lacks consistency and that one

must turn instead to social context, lived experience, and generational affili-
ation in order to fully understand the phenomenon.[10] There are, in fact,
many cleavages and social divisions in the "older population," such as those
of income, class membership, gender, and location – attributes that may
have a minor or major impact on political attitudes.[11] This is without even
considering the various life paths of individuals in a given society that is
itself undergoing constant change!

In short, to focus on biological age is to miss the forest for the trees. The
stereotype of aging leading inevitably to conservatism (in the broader or
narrower sense), everywhere and always, does not withstand empirical analysis. Although it is true that many individuals in the West may turn to
conservatism and the right as they age, we must nevertheless make some
distinctions and deconstruct the hasty generalizations about biological age.
In the view of Bernard Denni, who understands conservatism as support for
the moderate right, "The conservatism of seniors, therefore, is both a political reality and a sociological illusion."[12] It is this empirical complexity that
we will attempt to clarify briefly below. First, we examine some data from the
academic literature on electoral behaviour. We then describe the activities of
a group of aging women engaged in the fight for social justice, thus illustrat-
ing that there are certainly older adults who are working for left-wing, progressive social change. In doing so, we attack the two bases of the myth in
question: biological age as the cause of older adults' preference for the right,
and the systematic association of aging and promotion of the status quo.

What Does the Research Teach Us?

From the outset, we must recognize that the support of a significant number
of retired people and older adults for the right is a tangible reality in certain
contemporary political contexts. When we examine the statistics on the
electoral preferences of older citizens, we note that the majority of voters
from these age groups in a number of Western countries choose the right.[13]
Denni, in observing the electoral behaviour of the French in the second
round of presidential elections from 1965 to 2007, notes that older voters
"form a fairly homogeneous political group, characterized by political conservatism."[14] For example, during the 2007 French presidential election,
67.2 percent of those over 63 years of age voted for the right (Sarkozy) versus only 41.7 percent of those aged 18–30.[15]

Nevertheless, contrary to what one might initially expect, the explanation for older French voters' preference for the right is not so much their

biological age as such, but "the strong overrepresentation in that group of social, economic, and cultural characteristics – notably, property ownership, and a strong Catholic identity" – positively correlated with a right-wing political attitude in all age groups.[16] Similarly, Luc Rouban observes, in comparing two French departments with similar proportions of seniors (approximately 17 percent of the population in the 60 to 74 age range), that economic capital actually determines electoral preference.[17] The "sociological illusion" that Denni evokes resides in attributing this preference for the right to a direct effect of biological age – as do James Tilley and Geoffrey Evans without solid proof – rather than to a combination of varied and complex social characteristics and positions.[18]

In fact, analysis of the political behaviour of the new cohorts of retirees would indicate that, for France at least, the "right-wing position of those over 60, assumed until now to reflect increased conservatism with age, is not immutable."[19] The presumption is that generational renewal would cause older adults to gradually forsake the right, all other things being equal.[20] Furthermore, younger people may well be conservative, as Paul Light demonstrates when he notes that Ronald Reagan, the Republican (right-wing) candidate in the 1980 American presidential election, would never have been elected without the support of baby boomers, in their thirties at the time.[21] And this is not to mention the many "young people" who ardently supported the populist and xenophobic candidacy of Donald Trump in the 2016 American presidential election.

In short, the appeal of the right is not limited to a particular age group and is not absolute, even among older people, who are sometimes perceived as conservative by default in every historical period. In other words, whereas some studies show a certain preference for conservatism among older adults, depending on the context, others have shown that the political attitudes among older age groups are constantly changing. The use of biological age to explain political attitudes does not therefore withstand scrutiny, as electoral preferences are attributable to other factors.

Older Adults Committed to Social Change?

The fact that there are older adults on the left side of the political spectrum who become involved in various issues directly or indirectly related to the common good and the equitable redistribution of wealth contradicts the myth of an automatic relationship between aging and conservatism. Furthermore, limiting ourselves to quantitative analysis of electoral behaviour – that is, "formal" political participation – poses problems, since voting is a partial and incomplete indicator of individual and group political behaviour. Informal political participation consists of exerting "direct action on political powers through pressure tactics (petitions, demonstrations, and so on)."[22] Research by Achim Goerres reveals that participation by older adults in "unconventional" politics is increasing in a number of European countries, especially due to generational renewal.[23] This is a sign that political attitudes can change!

Closer to home, in Quebec, and in Canada more broadly, there is the example of the *Mémés déchaînées*, or Raging Grannies, a movement of older women developed around the peace movement but whose activism extends to a number of social justice issues. Dressed flamboyantly, the Grannies participate in all types of demonstrations. For these women, it would seem that maintaining the sociopolitical status quo is far from an option: indeed, the opposite is the case. The Grannies want to change things for those who come after them, an attitude recognized under the term "generativity," which is defined as the act of "guiding and caring for the next generation."[24] For example, the Grannies' manifesto stipulates that, in the context of the current environmental crisis, "as grandparents, we have a responsibility to the children and grandchildren of the future, and it is not too late for us to act."[25] This attitude toward social change is not limited to the Grannies but can be found to various degrees in the older population; one has only to lend an ear to realize this.

Conclusion

The idea that older adults should no longer vote or participate in political plebiscites is gaining ground in the media. In recent years, Quebec media personality and chef Daniel Pinard has repeated countless times on TV and radio, "It doesn't seem right to me that a person who has 8, 9, or 10 years left to live decides at the age of 70 what will happen to the children who come after."[26] After the vote on Brexit, in June 2016, a number of media outlets in the UK also demanded these sorts of measures. A *GQ* magazine journalist wrote, "We take pensioners' driving licenses away ... why not their right to vote?"[27] From this perspective, there is a presumption that seniors are, at best, supporters of the status quo and, at worst, completely disconnected from contemporary social realities, and that their political participation could only negatively affect future generations, as their anachronistic attitudes hinder the march of progress. In short, the myth that aging necessarily implies a preference for the status quo or conservatism persists and is increasingly evident in aging societies in which political crises may give rise to intergenerational conflicts. There is a need to attack this myth by using counter-examples and by furthering the recognition of older individuals and the value of their knowledge and experiences.

Notes

1   George Chesterton (2016), "We should ban older people from voting," *GQ*, June 14, <http://www.gq-magazine.co.uk/article/eu-referendum-old-people-shouldnot-vote>, accessed September 4, 2016.
2   Neal E. Cutler (1977), "Demographic, social-psychological, and political factors in the politics of aging: A foundation for research in 'Political Gerontology,'" *American Political Science Review*, Vol. 71, No. 3, 1018–19.
3   Philippe Boudreau and Claude Perron (2002), *Lexique de science politique* (Montreal: Chenelière/McGraw-Hill), 43 (our translation).
4   Bernard Denni (2011), "Le conservatisme des seniors," in Anne Muxel (ed.), *La politique au fil de l'âge* (Paris: Presses de Sciences Po), 128 (our translation).
5   Mokhtar Lakehal (2005), *Dictionnaire de science politique* (Paris: L'Harmattan), 148; Boudreau and Perron (2002), op. cit., 65.
6   Denni (2011), op. cit., 127 (our translation).
7   Quoted in Jean-Philippe Viriot-Durandal (2003), *Le pouvoir gris. Sociologie des groupes de pression de retraités* (Paris: Presses universitaires de France), 56 (our translation).
8   In the anglophone world, "liberal" is synonymous with "political left."
9   Cutler (1977), op. cit., 1019.
10   Anne Muxel (2011), *La politique au fil de l'âge* (Paris: Presses de Sciences Po).
11   Achim Goerres (2011), "Qu'est-ce qui pousse les personnes âgées à manifester?," in Anne Muxel (ed.), *La politique au fil de l'âge* (Paris: Presses de Sciences Po), 209.
12   Denni (2011), op. cit., 155 (our translation).
13   Some studies place the threshold for such age groups at 60 years of age, and others at 65.
14   Denni (2011), op. cit., 113 (our translation).
15   Ibid., 148.
16   Bernard Denni (2015), "Seniors et politique. Fracture générationnelle et révolution silencieuse?," in Jean-Philippe Viriot-Durandal, Émilie Raymond, Thibault Moulaert, and Michèle Charpentier (eds.), *Droits de vieillir et citoyenneté des aînés* (Quebec City: Presses de l'Université du Québec), 140 (our translation).
17   Luc Rouban (2012), "La droitisation de la campagne de Nicolas Sarkozy n'a pas convaincu les moins de 60 ans," *Le Figaro*, May 7, <http://elections.lefigaro.fr/presidentielle-2012/2012/05/07/01039-20120507ART FIG00694-le-vote-des-seniors-majoritairement-a-droite.php>, accessed August 12, 2016.
18   James Tilley and Geoffrey Evans (2014), "Ageing and generational effects on vote choice: Combining cross-sectional and panel data to estimate APC effects," *Electoral Studies*, Vol. 33, 19–27.

19 Viriot-Durandal (2003), op. cit., 64 (our translation).
20 Vincent Tiberj (2013), "Les temps changent, renouvellement générationnel et évolutions politiques en France," *Revue française de sociologie*, Vol. 54, No. 4, 741–76.
21 Paul Light (1988), *Baby Boomers* (New York: W.W. Norton & Co.).
22 Viriot-Durandal (2003), op. cit., 47 (our translation).
23 Achim Goerres (2009), *The Political Participation of Older People in Europe* (Basingstoke: Palgrave Macmillan).
24 Miya Narushima (2004), "A gaggle of raging grannies: The empowerment of older Canadian women through social activism," *International Journal of Lifelong Education*, Vol. 23, No. 1, 27.
25 Ibid., 29.
26 Radio-Canada (2016), "Vos vedettes sur le gril," broadcast of July 14, <http://ici.radio-canada.ca/premiere/premiereplus/humour/106769/vos-vedettessur-le-gril>, accessed August 4, 2016 (our translation).
27 Chesterton (2016), op. cit.

4

"That's Surprising, at Your Age!"
The Myth of Digital Disinterest

Kim Sawchuk, Line Grenier, and Constance Lafontaine

I am sitting in a café eating. A young couple in their twenties sits beside me. They ask me what I do. I reply that I am interested in digital media technologies and ageing. Without batting an eye, she comments: "Wow, that's surprising at your age!" I put my fork and knife down, stunned into silence. Suddenly, I realize that I have entered into a time of my life where expectations about my capacities, and my interests, are going to be associated with my grey hair and my changing appearance as "an older woman."

——— Notes, Kim Sawchuk, September 17, 2016, Amsterdam

Explaining the Myth

Myths about aging abound. What they have in common is that they can make an idea that is social and cultural appear natural. One of the prevailing and often unquestioned myths about aging that circulates in contemporary society – and is reflected in the above exchange – is that old age and new communications technologies are incompatible topics. This can be thought of as a manifestation of "digital ageism": a presumption that what is new and innovative and part of contemporary media culture is not of interest to people once they are associated with a certain age group – those belonging to older generations.

One central tenet of digital ageism is the assumption that older adults are not only incapable of learning how to use new media but, it follows, that they are disinterested in learning how to use them. Digital ageism promotes the idea that old age and new media are *innately* incongruous and associates youth with the values of a brave new digital world, for which young people are presumed to have a natural interest and aptitude. Having been raised with digital technologies, young people are often said to be *digital natives*, whereas seniors are regarded as *digital immigrants*.[1] This divide sets up age, or the appearance of age, as the determining predictor of interest in and ability to use technologies. The myth that older people and technologies are incongruous can also be understood as an extension of the wider belief that older people are "set in their ways" and incapable of coping with societal changes of all sorts. It relies on an assumption that digital technologies necessarily exert a positive impact on the everyday life of their users, and that for this reason digital technologies should be widely used.

This set of ageist assumptions and perceptions regarding new media can be found in casual conversation, in advertising, and in much of the social discourse on old age and new technologies. Older adults often appropriate these stereotypes, which may lead them to be reluctant to engage with technologies. Further, such myths generate patterns of exclusion and discrimination in society that have ramifications for older adults, for instance, in the workplace, where age discrimination is a salient form of discrimination.[2]

In this chapter, we discuss the myth of digital disinterest that has become associated with old age. We offer counter-examples and evidence drawn from years of research with older adults that we have conducted within the research group Ageing + Communication + Technologies (ACT) during collaborative digital media-making projects and studies on the transition from landlines to cell phones in Canada. As we have documented, adults in their sixties, seventies, eighties, and even nineties may develop an interest in new technologies, finding out more about them, and learning how to use them, and that aging and digital media need to be put into context.

Making Digital Content

The myth of digital disinterest raises a number of questions. How is interest expressed or manifested? Does non-use of technologies necessarily mean a disinterest in technologies? Five years ago, for example, we began digital literacy workshops in low-income housing (habitations à loyer modique, or HLMs) for older adults in Montreal. As we were setting up the project, we conducted door-to-door interviews with the residents. When asked if they were interested in learning digital technologies through workshops, the overwhelming majority answered "yes." Over half of the participants thought that digital technologies could have a significant impact on their lives. However, when asked "What, specifically, do you want to learn?" less than a third of the participants were able to answer the question. They wanted to take part in a networked society, but they weren't always sure what, specifically, this might entail. We also learned from this survey, and from the ensuing years of collaborations with people in HLMs, that although there is great interest in digital technologies among these seniors, their ability to translate their interest into learning and using digital technologies depends on a host of interrelated factors *beyond* their age. Socioeconomic class, education, and general literacy are important to take into account.[3] Indeed, we observed that such social barriers are notable obstacles for low-income seniors who want to begin using digital technologies. During workshops in HLMs, computers are provided only for a few hours. Yet, as our experience in offering workshops over the years indicates, practice and repeated use in a private setting are key to learning how to use technologies and assimilating them into daily life. Furthermore, if we consider the expense of high-quality devices and Internet service fees in Canada, we begin to understand that participating in the digital world remains an unrealistic proposition for some older adults. Many people see a drop in their income in their old age, as they rely on government pensions, and access may not be affordable. Despite a societal enthusiasm for digital technology, the fact remains that the opportunities for access are not the same for everyone.

A number of organizations, including community groups in Montreal, are seeking to harness popular interest in digital technologies and make them accessible to older adults. For example, groups such as Communautique, Yellow Door, and the Réseau d'information des aînés du Québec have set up projects, initiatives, or workshops to help fill some of older adults' needs in terms of access and skill learning.

At Ageing + Communication + Technologies, we have found that one pathway to encouraging older adults to engage with digital technologies is to provide reasons for digital engagement that are *meaningful* for them and worth their time, effort, and, in some cases, hard-earned dollars, rather than just going beyond the idea of "general interest." But meaningful engagement always depends on the confluence of a host of material, technical, social, and financial conditions.

In HLMs, but also with other groups of older adults, our research team has run workshops on various practices, including digital photography, music-making, photo scanning, and podcasting. Crucial to developing their interest in media-making with digital tools is ascertaining what they need and want, then making suggestions that do not force them to participate. It is important to set up an environment in which an appealing topic can be explored and participants' ideas and expertise can be shared, respected, and integrated into a co-creative process. In the workshop environments we have set up, participants are encouraged to be creative and not to fear making mistakes or breaking the device. They are asked to make a commitment to show up once a week and to socialize while working on their individual projects. Working together, or with "younger" facilitators, they are invited to teach each other, share skills, and critique the work so that they can make improvements if they want to. They are told to just try and not to worry about anyone judging the quality of their work. The emphasis is on experimentation through making and doing together. The workshops always conclude with a public presentation of their work, as this gives a timeline and an end goal. This encouraging and motivating approach offers another way to share results.

Not everyone will continue to create with digital technologies after the workshop. Not everyone will keep on using a tablet, laptop, or digital scanner. Some older participants come to the workshops, where equipment is made available, because they can't afford to buy it or have an apartment that is too small to clutter with devices. And like anyone, without practice, the skills they have learned may be forgotten. Some participants' interests may shift to something else. For others, engaging with a new technology represents a chance to get out of the house and try something different. For still others, as we have seen, interest in and engagement with digital technologies never cease, as these seniors become aware of the role that digital media play in their life as individuals and as members of communities and community groups.[4]

"I Love My Landline!" Octogenerians and Nonagenarians Speak

In 2012, we interviewed older adults living in a retirement home in an affluent area in Toronto.[5] Half of these adults were in their eighties, and the other half were in their nineties. When we interviewed them, it quickly became apparent that they were all very attached to their landline telephones and depended on them to maintain connections with family and friends locally

and internationally. Only a few used a cellphone. This low level of participation in cellphone culture would seem to confirm the myth that because
these 80- and 90-year-olds were born into the era of landline phones, the
cellphone was a foreign object to them and they had no interest in it.
But their reality is far more complex. Let's consider a few of the cases that
emerged during the interviews.

One woman recounted that she and her husband had bought a cellphone in later life, and she had given it up when he died. It had been used
to keep in contact with caregivers for emergency purposes. Another woman,
having given up her car and long trips in later life, felt that a cellphone was
no longer necessary for potential emergencies while on the road. In both
cases, the participants had used the cellphone at some point and decided
they no longer needed the technology. It was not just the cellphone that
was being abandoned, but the obligation to pay yet another monthly bill
for something that was not being used.

These women described how aging had changed many aspects of their
life circumstances. In tandem with these changes came a set of decisions
about what to keep, what to discard, and what activities to intensify: one
participant explained that she would rather spend her time volunteering at
the residence than using a device. These older adults discussed all the com-
plexities of their decision to keep their contract going or cut the cellular
cord. As we learned from these examples, aging alone does not explain the
low use of cellphones among these interviewees. Instead, their circumstances shifted as they aged, leading to the decision to give up the cellphone
at this point in their lives. Contrary to suppositions of the myth of digital
disinterest divided along the axes of age, the participants were capable of
learning. They became interested in these technologies for specific reasons
and with varying levels of intensity over time.

Even those who had never owned a cellphone expressed a relationship
with the device, but in terms tied to experience and circumstance. A woman
in her late eighties, who spoke candidly about her cognitive difficulties,
quizzed the interviewer at length about how a cellphone works and how it
differs from other forms of "wireless" devices, including the radio. Her difficult technical questions are a reminder that when cellphone users who are
at ease with digital technology turn on a device to make a call, they may not
know how it works in technical terms. Users, whatever their age, use the
devices to the extent of their knowledge, which may represent a fraction of
what that device can do. We discovered that those who had never owned a

cellphone themselves were interested in telling us how their presence, as well as that of other networked devices such as a laptop loaded with Skype, were changing the lives of those around them, including their children and grandchildren.

As our interviewees reminded us, as researchers we needed to adjust hasty and simplistic equations of *ownership* with *interest* and of *non-use* with complete and utter *disinterest* in the digital world. One may decide to continue not to use a device, or to occasionally use someone else's device. One may fall out of practice and then forget how to use it. One may decide that other expenses are more important than maintaining either an Internet connection or securing data over a cell phone. Thus, although age plays a role in their communicational and technological practices, it is not old age *per se* that led the participants in these studies to the abandonment of or disinterest in cellphones or computers, but changes in their life circumstances and their social networks.

The myth that we are contesting suggests that most older people are uninterested in digital technologies. Some of our other research, such as that related to Deafhood and aging, compels us to rethink how digital technologies focused on text and image are, to the contrary, of great interest and can be a source of increased social inclusion.[6]

Conclusion

In a German television skit that went viral in 2013, an older man prepares food with a younger woman, presumably his daughter. They stand back to back in the kitchen, chatting. He chops vegetables, she cooks at the stove. She asks him how he likes his new tablet. He replies that it's very useful. She turns around to see that he is using the tablet as a cutting board and then watches him place the device in the dishwasher, to the sound of canned laughter. In a user-made YouTube video from the same period, a toddler sits on a porch, with a magazine in her lap. She looks at it for a few moments and then, instead of turning the pages, as one would expect, she tries to zoom in on the image by making a pinching motion with her fingers.

In the videos, the older adult is depicted as naïve. He doesn't understand that the tablet is *not* a chopping block but a high-tech communications device. The toddler is puzzled. She doesn't comprehend that she can't make the images on the page move by swiping her fingers. The man is depicted as belonging to an era before the world of interactive networked digital devices. The girl is shown as an outsider to the era when publications were associated with paper and glossy magazines were sold on newsstands. These two videos speak to a set of intertwined myths about aging in the digital era and the presumption of intergenerational differences, divisions, and disconnections with current or past historical periods. The staged scenarios not only perpetuate a myth but sketch out one of the contours of digital ageism.

Everyone, young and old, cultivates interests throughout their lives, and these interests may shift over time. We all make decisions about which technologies we want to engage with and which we don't, and this is also true of new technologies. When a thirty-year-old shows disinterest in a technology or a social media platform – say, Facebook – it is framed as a reasoned personal choice. When a seventy-year-old shows a similar disinterest in Facebook, this same choice gets framed through a prism of old age. Non-use of technology becomes shorthand for a blanket rejection of and disinterest in all forms of digitized communication, and age becomes the cause and sole explanatory factor. Indeed, the myth of disinterest relies on the false premise that the "young" and "old" are homogeneous groups with respect to their interest in technologies and their engagement with a networked society. If we believe that older adults are necessarily disinterested in digital technologies, we miss out on understanding the nuanced and complex ways that we all engage with the digital world.

Notes

1   Marc Prensky (2001), "Digital natives, digital immigrants," *On the Horizon*, Vol. 9, No. 5, 1–6.
2   Martine Lagacé, Francine Tougas, Joelle Laplante, and Jean-François Neveu (2008), "Les répercussions de la communication âgiste sur le désengagement psychologique et l'estime de soi des infirmiers de 45 ans et plus," *Revue canadienne du vieillissement*, Vol. 27, No. 3, 285–99; Martine Lagacé, Francine Tougas, Joelle Laplante, and Jean-François Neveu (2010), "Communication âgiste au travail: une voie vers le désengagement psychologique et la retraite des infirmières d'expérience?," *Revue internationale de psychologie sociale*, Vol. 23, No. 4, 91–121.
3   Constance Lafontaine and Kim Sawchuk (2015), "Accessing InterACTion: Ageing with technologies and the place of access," in Jia Zhou and Gabriel Salvendy (eds.), *Human Aspects of IT for the Aged Population* (New York: Springer-Verlag).
4   Line Grenier and Kim Sawchuk (2017), "Regards croisés sur une mobilisation éclair. L'à-propos de la médiation et du vieillissement," *Recherches sociographiques*, Vol. 58, No. 1, 93–117.

5   Kim Sawchuk and Barbara Crow (2012), "'I'm G-Mom on the phone': Remote grand-mothering, cell phones and intergenerational dis/connections," *Feminist Media Issues*, Vol. 12, No. 4, 496–505.
6   Véro Leduc and Line Grenier (2017) "Signer/connecter. Enjeux croisés du vieillisse-ment, des technologies et de la sourditude," *Canadian Journal of Communication*, Vol. 42, No. 2, 213–33.

5

Grey-Haired Neurons

Does an Accurate Memory Have to Become a Memento of Younger Days?

Maxime Lussier, Manon Parisien, Nathalie Bier, and Sophie Laforest

Old age is a shipwreck.

——— *Charles de Gaulle* (our translation)

Is Aging an Illness?

One of the myths of popular culture is that if we live to be old enough, we'll inevitably become intellectually dependent on others. This myth harks back to the 1900s, when people thought that senility was a normal manifestation of aging that afflicted the mental capacities of the entire older population.[1]

Forgetfulness occurs at every age. However, these minor memory lapses, as they are called, assume a particular meaning for many older people. Although the fear of aging seems to diminish as we grow older, 54 percent of people report that they are very afraid of developing memory problems.[2] This could be a concern, as one study noted that people with very negative beliefs about aging are less likely to see their doctor when they experience problems.[3]

Over the past 15 years, there have been a great number of discoveries about the aging brain. Today, thanks to research and more accurate diagnoses, it's thought that people can live to be over 100 without necessarily developing major cognitive deficits. However, it's also a myth to believe that no cognitive changes occur with normal aging. Even in the absence of illnesses that affect the brain, what we might call normal aging is not entirely without changes on the cognitive level.

In this chapter, we describe the cognitive changes that we can expect to happen as we age and explain why they occur. Then, we show that there are a number of possible aging trajectories, and we look at various factors that influence the maintaining of cognitive health.

Does Everything Begin to Fall Apart as We Age?

The term "cognition" refers to the series of mental processes (attention, memory, language, visuospatial functions, and executive functions) that allow us to make decisions and accomplish our day-to-day tasks, ranging from the simplest (such as carrying on a conversation) to the most complex (filling out a tax return, for example). As we age, a number of so-called neurodegenerative illnesses may significantly impair our cognitive health. These include Alzheimer's disease in particular, but also other less common illnesses such as vascular dementia, frontotemporal dementia, and Lewy body dementia. Each of these forms of dementia affects cognitive health in different ways.

What cognitive changes can one expect to experience in the normal course of aging? First, all mental processes are not equally affected, as age-related neurophysiological changes are not uniformly distributed across the brain. Some processes become more altered as we age, whereas others remain intact and may even improve.

The speed at which we process information (that is, the pace of our mental operations) declines with age. It's as though the brain's "cruising speed" slows down a bit. This slowing affects all other cognitive capacities. That's why it may take longer to perform mathematical calculations or to come up with answers to a quiz. The attention required to accomplish simple tasks (such as listening to the radio) is only slightly affected, whereas the attention needed to perform complex tasks is significantly altered. Indeed, due to the decline in divided attention, it gradually becomes more difficult to focus the mind on two things at once, such as driving a car while having a conversation. Normal aging can also make us more susceptible to distraction – for example, when we have to carry on a conversation in the middle of a crowd. It can also become harder to handle several bits of information in succession (lessening of alternating attention), such as when one resumes working on a crossword puzzle during ads on TV.[4]

Furthermore, some types of memory are also affected in normal aging. Episodic memory – the memory of events that one can recount to others, such as memories of a trip or of what one ate the day before – is the type that is most affected in normal aging after 60 years of age.[5] For information to be remembered, it must go through three stages: encoding, storage, and retrieval. Encoding allows us to register something new, such as when one studies new subject matter for an exam. Storage allows us to retain the material studied for several days without having to review it. Finally, retrieval enables us to retrieve the answers when we need them. Information encoding and retrieval are particularly affected in normal aging, whereas the ability to retain information over time is fairly well preserved. In other words, if the information is properly recorded, it can be recovered (with the help of a clue if necessary), even in the case of information that was learned long ago. Problems in retrieving information are the main cause of the well-known phenomenon of "having a word on the tip of one's tongue," which happens more often as we grow older. It's also more difficult to remember to perform a task in the future (prospective memory), such as going to an appointment, as we age.

On a positive note, some cognitive capacities are better maintained. For example, the memory of motor learning (procedural memory)[6] is especially resistant to aging. This type of memory is said to be implicit, as it is not really conscious. It allows us to perform actions such as dressing, knitting, or cooking an egg without even thinking about them. So, there's some truth to the old adage that one never forgets how to ride a bicycle. Similarly, semantic memory remains quite strong as we age, which means that our mental stockpile of knowledge (what is the capital of Spain?) and our vocabulary (what does "cognition" mean?) continue to increase throughout our lives.[7] So, we shouldn't be surprised to hear centenarians talking about Twitter or Lady Gaga!

Why Does Our Memory Diminish with Age?

A number of factors contribute to the cognitive changes observed in normal aging. These include causes associated with cerebral functioning as well as causes that are separate from the efficient functioning of the brain. The brain changes throughout our lives. It develops quickly in our early years, and then grows little after the age of six, when it has reached 90 percent of its adult weight. Connections between neurons do, however, continue to become more and more complex, and it's now believed that the brain doesn't reach maturity until at least the age of 25.[8] But like all of the body's organs, the brain also ages. There is a gradual reduction in the amount of white matter and grey matter.[9] Some areas of the brain are especially prone to aging after age 70 – particularly the frontal lobes (responsible for controlling our attention during complex tasks) and the hippocampi (which are important for memory). One might think that this cerebral shrinkage is due to the death of a number of neurons, which are only rarely replaced by new neurons. However, research tends to show that there are also a reduction in the connections between neurons, a loss of efficiency in neuron networks (synapse contacts), and a lower concentration of neurotransmitters (substances that transmit messages between neurons).[10]

Of course, it's important to remember that these declines are subtle in the normal course of aging: we mustn't think that our brain looks like Swiss cheese! Nor is the brain a passive observer of its own aging process. It uses a number of strategies to adapt to this adversity: in particular, it reorganizes the roles of its various components to compensate for the weakest, it forms new neuron connections, and it decommissions inefficient connections.[11] That being said, the time does come when the brain's compensatory strategies fail to entirely offset the neurophysiological changes caused by aging. That's why there is indeed some gradual decline in cognitive capacities in normal aging.

On the other hand, different factors explain the changes in certain cognitive capacities as we grow older. For example, we know that aging is often accompanied by sensory losses (declines in sight and hearing). It has also been demonstrated that older adults with hearing problems find it harder to encode the information they hear into their memory.[12] Cognitive functioning also appears to be affected by social and cultural factors. For example, individuals are to some extent conditioned by their internalizing of negative stereotypes about aging. It has been shown that hearing ageist stereotypes leads to a decrease in memory performance among older adults.[13] Similarly, seniors with a strong sense of their personal efficiency and who have confidence in their intellectual capacities perform better in various memory tasks for this reason.[14] Our perception of aging can thus bring about changes in our efficiency, somewhat in the manner of a self-fulfilling prophecy.

Everyone Ages Differently

Although aging was once synonymous with senility, it's now believed that the aging process may be very different from one person to another. On the one hand, the media are full of examples of older people who remain intellectually vibrant and socially active, such as feminist and author Janette Bertrand (91 years old) and 80-year-old environmentalist David Suzuki. On the other hand, some older adults report that they feel less intellectually vigorous and prefer to avoid new or overly complex activities. Many studies have demonstrated that older people show significantly more heterogeneity in their cognitive performances than do young adults. Individual variability in performances in various intellectual tests gradually increases after age 65 and intensifies after age 75.[15] Why do some centenarians maintain their intellectual vigour, whereas other seniors, even younger ones, have more difficulty?

Researchers have identified a number of factors that can influence people's cognitive aging process. First, we know that a person's genetic background influences his or her risk of developing certain neurodegenerative illnesses. Physical health problems (including high blood pressure, high cholesterol, diabetes, and some cardiovascular illnesses) and mental health issues (such as symptoms of depression or anxiety) may also increase the likelihood of experiencing cognitive difficulties.[16] But the course of our lives and our lifestyle habits play a major role in how our genetic make-up expresses itself and may potentially delay or forestall the emergence of cognitive problems. Each person has a unique life journey, and aging can represent a greater opportunity to undergo a variety of life experiences.

A number of studies in fact show that academic background and type of employment can have a positive effect on cognitive vitality as we age. For example, a lower incidence of dementia among older adults was recently observed in England. The higher level of schooling from one generation to the next was identified as one of the most likely causes of this improvement.[17] Countless studies have also shown that practising physical activities or adopting healthy eating habits helps to maintain cognitive functioning as we grow older.[18] Similarly, several studies suggest that seniors who participate in intellectually or socially stimulating activities experience a slower cognitive decline in old age. Conversely, it is estimated that people who take part in few cognitively stimulating activities have a 2.6 times greater risk of developing Alzheimer's disease.[19]

How can our lifestyle habits influence the course of our cognitive aging? A number of researchers have hypothesized that good life habits help to increase our cognitive reserve. The term "cognitive reserve" refers to our "cerebral capital," which is different for everyone, and which enables us to combat the adversities of aging or neurodegenerative illness. In other words, with identical neurological damage, one person might have significant memory problems while another person might get away with minor repercussions.[20] On the neurological level, a greater cognitive reserve is associated with a neural network with denser connections that can tolerate more damage before performance is impaired.[21]

Conclusion

> The seeds of healthy aging are sown early.
> ———— Kofi Annan, 2001

The current state of knowledge tends to confirm that some gradual changes in cognitive faculties do indeed occur in normal aging. We need to remember, though, that this is different from pathological aging associated with neurodegenerative illnesses such as Alzheimer's disease. Moreover, the changes related to normal aging do not involve all of our cognitive faculties (vocabulary, for example, is preserved). The enormous heterogeneity of our individual trajectories in this respect should also be emphasized. Some factors that affect cognitive aging are beyond individual control (such as genetic make-up, social inequalities, poverty, and pollution). Researchers have, however, highlighted several factors that can influence cognitive aging. Unfortunately, in the wake of all the advertising targeted to seniors, it can be somewhat difficult to figure out what they are. As we wait for more detailed recommendations to come, the current scientific literature suggests that the best strategies for optimizing the cognitive aging process are to 1) control chronic illnesses such as diabetes and high blood pressure as best we can, 2) maintain healthy eating habits and have a regular physical activity regimen, and 3) practise cognitively or socially stimulating activities.

Which kinds of stimulating activities are best? Sudoku, playing music, taking a course, or learning a new language? The current state of knowledge does not enable us to make specific recommendations, as the literature offers no clear consensus on which types of activities are, or are not, considered stimulating.[22] So, it's important to choose activities that we find motivating and enjoyable so that we can naturally incorporate them into our routine. Finally, it's interesting to note that the cognitively or socially stimulating activities that we do after retirement are just as crucial to cognitive health as those that we did beforehand, if not more so.[23] So it's never too late to start!

Notes

1   Robert Katzman (2008), "The prevalence and malignancy of Alzheimer disease: A major killer," *Alzheimer's and Dementia*, Vol. 4, No. 6, 378–80.

2   CROP (2012), *Sondage sur le vieillissement de la population. Rapport préliminaire présenté à L'AQESSS*, April 30.

3   Catherine A. Sarkisian, Ronald D. Hays, and Carol M. Mangione (2002), "Do older adults expect to age successfully? The association between expectations regarding aging and beliefs regarding healthcare seeking among older adults," *Journal of the American Geriatrics Society*, Vol. 50, No. 11, 1837–43.

4   Julie A. Alvarez and Eugene Emory (2006), "Executive function and the frontal lobes: A meta-analytic review," *Neuropsychology Review*, Vol. 16, No. 1, 17–42.

5   Michael Rönnlund, Lars Nybert, Lars Bäckman, and Lars-Göran Nilsson (2005), "Stability, growth, and decline in adult life span development of declarative memory: Cross-sectional and longitudinal data from a population-based study," *Psychology and Aging*, Vol. 20, No. 1, 3–18.

6   James D. Churchill, Jessica J. Stanis, Cyrus M. Press, Michael Kushelev, and William T. Greenough (2003), "Is procedural memory relatively spared from age effects?," *Neurobiology of Aging*, Vol. 24, No. 6, 883–92.

7   Denis C. Park and Patricia Reuter-Lorenz (2009), "The adaptive brain: Aging and neurocognitive scaffolding," *Annual Review of Psychology*, Vol. 60, No. 1, 173–96.

8   Mariam Arain, Maliha Haque, Lina Johal, Puja Mathur, Wynand Nel, Afsha Rais, Ranbir Sandhu, and S. K. Sharma (2013), "Maturation of the adolescent brain," *Neuropsychiatric Disease and Treatment*, Vol. 9, 449–61.

9   David J. Madden, Julia Spaniol, Matthew C. Costello, Barbara Bucur, Leonard E. White, Roberto Cabeza, Simon W. Davis, Nancy A. Dennis, James M. Provenzale, and Scott A. Huettel (2009), "Cerebral white matter integrity mediates adult age differences in cognitive performance," *Journal of Cognitive Neuroscience*, Vol. 21, No. 2, 289–302.

10 Robert D. Terry and Robert Katzman (2001), "Life span and synapses: Will there be a primary senile dementia?," *Neurobiology of Aging*, Vol. 22, No. 3, 347–48; discussion, 353–54.

11 Park and Reuter-Lorenz (2009), op. cit.

12 Sandra L. McCoy, Patricia A. Tun, L. Clarke Cox, Marianne Colangelo, Raj A. Stewart, and Arthur Wingfield (2005), "Hearing loss and perceptual effort: Downstream effects on older adults' memory for speech," *Quarterly Journal of Experimental Psychology A*, Vol. 58, No. 1, 22–33.

13 Thomas M. Hess, Corinne Auman, Stanley J. Colcombe, and Tamara A. Rahhal (2003), "The impact of stereotype threat on age differences in memory performance," *The Journals of Gerontology, Series B: Psychological Sciences and Social Sciences*, Vol. 58, No. 1, P3–P11.

14 Marine Beaudoin and Olivier Desrichard (2011), "Are memory self-efficacy and memory performance related? A meta-analysis," *Psychological Bulletin*, Vol. 137, No. 2, 211.

15 Brent J. Small, Roger A. Dixon, and John J. McArdle (2011), "Tracking cognition-health changes from 55 to 95 years of age," *The Journals of Gerontology, Series B: Psychological Sciences and Social Sciences*, Vol. 66, Suppl. 1, i153–i161.

16 Philip B. Gorelick (2004), "Risk factors for vascular dementia and Alzheimer disease," *Stroke*, Vol. 35, No. 11, Suppl. 1, 2620–22.

17 Claudia Satizabal, Alexa Beiser, Vincent Chouraki, Geneviève Chêne, Carole Dufouil, and Sudha Seshadri (2016), "Incidence of dementia over three decades in the Framingham Heart Study," *New England Journal of Medicine*, Vol. 374, No. 6, 523–32.

18 Franceso Soli, Debora Valechi, Duccio Bacci, Rosanna Abbate, and Claudio Macchi (2011), "Physical activity and risk of cognitive decline: A meta-analysis of prospective studies," *Journal of Internal Medicine*, Vol. 269, No. 1, 107–17; Ilianna Lourida, Maya Soni, Joanna Thompson-Coon, Nitin Purandare, Iain A. Lang, Obioha C. Ukoumunne, and David J. Llewellyn (2013), "Mediterranean diet, cognitive function, and dementia: A systematic review," *Epidemiology*, Vol. 24, No. 4, 479–89.

19 Robert S. Wilson, P. A. Scherr, Julie A. Schneider, Y. Tang, and David A. Bennett (2007), "Relation of cognitive activity to risk of developing Alzheimer disease," *Neurology*, Vol. 69, No. 20, 1911–20.

20 Carol Brayne, Fiona Elaine Matthews, John H. Xuereb, J. C. Broome, J. McKenzie, M. Rossi, Paul G. Ince, Ian G. McKeith, John Lowe, Margaret Esiri, and John H. Morris (2001), "Pathological correlates of late-onset dementia in a multicenter community-based population in England and Wales," *Lancet*, Vol. 357, No. 9251, 169–75.

21 Yaakov Stern (2003), "The concept of cognitive reserve: A catalyst for research," *Journal of Clinical Experimental Neuropsychology*, Vol. 25, No. 5, 589–93.

22 Christopher Hertzog, Arthur F. Kramer, Robert S. Wilson, and Ulman Lindenberger (2009), "Enrichment effects on adult cognitive development," *Psychological Science in the Public Interest*, Vol. 9, No. 1, 1–65.

23 Allison A. Bielak, Tiffany F. Hughes, Brent J. Small, and Roger A. Dixon (2007), "It's never too late to engage in lifestyle activities. Significant concurrent but not change relationships between lifestyle activities and cognitive speed," *The Journals of Gerontology, Series B: Psychological Sciences and Social Sciences*, Vol. 62, No. 6, P331–P339.

Part 2
LIVING ENVIRONMENTS

6

Do Most Very Old Quebecers Live in Residential Long-Term Care Centres?

Anne-Marie Séguin, Isabelle Van Pevenage,
and Chloé Dauphinais

In the June 20, 2016 issue of *Le Journal de Montréal*, columnist Mathieu Bock-Côté offered the following provocative assessment of Quebec's residential long-term care centres (Centres d'hébergement et de soins de longue durée – CHSLDs):

> CHSLDs are places to park old people so they won't bother us any more as they approach the end of their lives. These days, old age is considered no longer a phase of life but a social problem that has to be solved or gotten rid of ... You wonder how an essentially prosperous society can leave a significant segment of its population in this condition.[1]

In 2010, according to the 2012–13 Report of the Auditor General of Quebec, 96.6 percent of Quebecers aged 65 and over were living at home or in seniors' residences, whereas only 3.4 percent were housed in institutions funded by the health and social services system.[2] The widespread myth that a large proportion of the senior population lives in CHSLDs is no doubt attributable, at least in part, to the fact that the various residential resources available to older adults are largely indistinguishable in people's minds and generally considered to be CHSLDs. This perception may also be fostered by the significant media coverage that these facilities receive.

Old age is generally viewed as a difficult phase of life characterized by health problems and synonymous with loss and disability. Data from major health surveys confirm that long-term disabilities and diseases increase with age; but does having a major long-term illness or disability make living in a CHSLD more likely? As we show below, the answer is no: older adults, even the very old, live in a variety of settings that provide a range of support and care services.

Health Problems among the Very Old

In 2010–11, 84 percent of Quebecers aged 85 and over reported living with at least one disability (mobility or vision problems, for example). Disabilities become increasingly frequent and severe at this age. For example, 25 percent of persons 85 and over reported having slight disability, 27 percent moderate disability, and 32 percent serious disability.[3] In addition, in Canada in 2014, an estimated 37 percent of women and 29 percent of men 85 and over suffered from dementia.[4]

As seniors begin to experience major health problems or severe – and, in many instances, multiple – disabilities, they must decide whether to stay at home or move to institutions offering residential environments more suited to their needs. That decision will be based on several factors, including the number of available spaces at various types of institutions, the seniors' financial resources, and the network of relatives and friends on whom they can rely.

A Diverse Range of Residential Environments

Despite this relatively bleak picture, the very old live in a variety of residential environments in Quebec: at home, in seniors' residences, and in intermediate resources (ressources intermédiaires, or RIs), family-type resources (ressources de type familial, or RTFs), and CHSLDs. To be admitted to an RI or a CHSLD, individuals must be assessed by an integrated health and social services centre, whether university affiliated (Centre intégré universitaire de santé et de services sociaux) or not (Centre intégré de santé et de services sociaux), which is the gateway for this type of accommodation. The eligibility criteria for these resources take into account the applicants' need for assistance in performing activities of everyday living, the state of their mental functions, and whether they suffer from behavioural disorders.[5] However, those who meet the criteria often face wait periods between the needs assessment and their admission to an RI or CHSLD, periods that vary by region and from one institution to another.

To dispel any confusion over the differences among the various residential resources available to Quebec seniors, these resources are briefly described below.

CHSLDs are intended for older adults whose health requires virtually constant monitoring and specialized medical care, and who, despite the support that relatives and friends may provide, can no longer live safely at home. Every CHSLD provides on-site medical care, medication management, hygiene care, and other specialized services (occupational therapy, physiotherapy, and so on). There are three types of CHSLD: public institutions, private institutions under agreement, and private institutions not under agreement. The first two categories operate under the same guidelines with the same level of public funding. Private institutions not under agreement are independent and self-governing private businesses licensed by the Ministère de la Santé et des Services Sociaux (MSSS, Quebec Ministry of Health and Social Services).

In March 2011, Quebec had 32,513 spaces in public CHSLDs, 6,554 in private CHSLDs under agreement, and 200 in private CHSLDs operated under public-private partnerships.[6] According to MSSS data, 15,364 residents aged 85 and over had been admitted to CHSLDs as of March 31, 2010, representing slightly less than 11 percent of the Quebec population in that age group.[7] Seniors suffering from dementia form a significant percentage of CHSLD residents. In Canada, in 2010–11, it was estimated that 42 percent of seniors 65 to 79 years of age living in residential long-term care centres suffered from dementia, with this proportion rising to 56 percent in the 80-and-over age group.[8] Lastly, the number of spaces of all types available in CHSLDs is inadequate to meet the needs. According to MSSS information, there were 3,551 pending applications for such spaces in June 2016.[9]

RIs are the second type of residential resource for older adults. These are private businesses associated with public health institutions, which are responsible for the quality of care provided in them. RIs offer an adapted living environment and support and assistance services for residents who, as a result of a moderate loss of autonomy, require help with activities of daily living and medical supervision, and are thus unable to live alone. Intermediate residences may include supervised apartments, rooming houses, foster homes, and group homes.

RTFs, or foster homes, are residences that accept up to nine persons who have been referred by a public institution in order to meet the needs of those individuals and to provide them with living conditions as similar as possible to those of a "natural" setting. These homes provide support, assistance, and supervision for residents experiencing a slight loss of autonomy.

In March 2011, Quebec had 5,570 spaces in intermediate resources and 976 spaces in family-type resources.[10] In other words, a tiny proportion of the 85-and-over age group was living in these two types of residential environments.

Seniors' residences, as defined by the Canada Mortgage and Housing Corporation, are dwellings that provide a number of rental units of various types: single rooms, rooms with two or more beds, studio apartments, and multi-room apartments. These residences offer meal services (which may be optional) and are occupied mostly by tenants aged 65 and over. They may include residential environments of different types ranging from small apartment buildings to large high-rises offering various levels of comfort and conveniences. Most seniors' residences provide services such as 24-hour monitoring, a dining room, and a common activity room. Some residences offer a broader range of services, either free of charge or for a fee, such as onsite medical services, a fitness room, and a hair salon. These residences generally do not accept persons with a moderate or severe loss of autonomy (requiring more than an hour and a half of daily care). However, some residences may accommodate a clientele requiring more intensive and specialized care.[11]

Subsidized housing projects, in which rents are based on household income and are at below-market levels, are also available for older adults. The rental units are essentially located in low-rent housing projects (managed by municipal housing authorities, cooperatives, or non-profit organizations) and in projects built under the AccèsLogis program. Most subsidized housing units inhabited by seniors 65 and over are located in projects reserved for retirees and pre-retirees. Most of these dwellings do not offer services apart from a common room for resident activities. There are exceptions to this rule, however, as some offer weekday lunch services and some activities.

The last type of residential environment, *the home,* may also take various forms: rental apartments, condos, houses, duplexes, and so on. Seniors may have been living in this home for many years or for a short period of time. The vast majority of older Quebecers and Canadians live at home.

In Quebec in 2010, 96.6 percent of adults 65 and over were living at home or in seniors' residences.[12] After the home, private seniors' residences are the second most popular living arrangement for older adults. There were 232,478 spaces in such residences in Canada in 2016, including 114,117 in Quebec.[13] The attraction rate among the population of seniors aged 75 and over is much higher in Quebec: 18.4 percent, compared with only 9.1 percent in Canada as a whole.[14] This difference may be attributable to rent levels, as the average rent for a studio apartment or individual room, including at least one meal a day, is $1,527 in Quebec, compared with $2,978 in Ontario (the highest), and $2,210 in Canada as a whole.[15] The data on subsidized housing occupied by older adults are more fragmentary. Around 2010, it was estimated that 37,403 senior households in Quebec were living in low-rent housing units and 10,952 in properties funded by the AccèsLogis program.[16]

Most Older Adults Strongly Prefer to Live at Home

Why do the vast majority of older adults, even the very old, want to live at home despite poor health and disabilities? The answer lies in the very nature of "home," which is not merely a physical place but also one that is rich with significance. The home is often shared with family members, or at least was in the past, which is one of the reasons for people's attachment to it. It is a place that contains meaningful objects and where people live according to their habits and routines. It is an environment where they can enjoy their privacy and lead their private lives. It affords a sense of security and control and is a place where people can make their own decisions about their day-to-day activities and how to go about them. Home is also a significant component of individual identity. By contrast, living in an RI, an RTF, or a CHSLD means having to abandon one's furniture or, in the best case, much of one's furniture and many personal belongings. It means having to forgo familiar habits and routines and to live by set meal times and menus, no longer being able to lock one's door, and so on. Although leaving home requires seniors to give up many things, this is less true for those entering a seniors' residence, as they may generally take some of their furniture and other familiar objects with them. In many instances, they can also maintain their privacy and a degree of control over their schedules and activities, over who enters their unit, and so on. These considerations and the fact that older people living in such residences have access to certain services (elevators, meals, activities, and so on) may explain why private residences appeal to seniors as a kind of compromise between home and an RI or a CHSLD when circumstances compel them to leave their home.

The attachment that many seniors feel for their homes must not, however, blind us to certain realities regarding the situations of older adults who continue living in their homes despite failing health and numerous disabilities.

Aging-in-Place Policies Are Underfunded

In 1979, the Quebec government adopted its first aging-in-place policy, under which families were identified as being responsible for their seniors. A succession of policies ensued: "Shift to Ambulatory Care" in 1989, "Home, the First Choice" in 2003, and "Aging and Living Together – At Home, in Your Community, in Quebec" in 2012. These government initiatives emerged from the general shift toward deinstitutionalization, based on the principle that older adults want to live at home as long as possible. The principle was undergirded by two other objectives: to cut government spending and to offset the negative effects of institutionalization (isolation, dependency, stagnation, passive acquiescence, and so on) on residents.

According to the policy statements, these aging-in-place policies were to be accompanied by increased budgets for home care and support. However, funding was not – and is still not – forthcoming, even though the CHSLD admission criteria are now more stringent and seniors' needs at home are growing. Conditions have also diversified insofar as healthcare needs following hospitalization and surgery have increased as a result of the shift to ambulatory care. Consequently, the minor rises in budgets allocated for home care are now essentially used to meet acute healthcare needs and not the home care needs of seniors with disabilities.[17] This explains why 43 percent of older adults with disabilities in Quebec have at least one need that is not being met in terms of activities of daily living and home living activities.[18] These issues were addressed in an in-depth survey report issued by the Quebec Ombudsman in 2012 after a large number of complaints were received from seniors and their families.[19] Those concerns re-emerged in a more recent annual report of the Quebec Ombudsman, who "remains particularly concerned about the difficulties people with reduced autonomy have in getting home support services."[20]

Is Home Always the First Choice?

Although many older adults love their homes and want to continue living there, some would like to move to another dwelling or neighbourhood or to be housed in a setting that more effectively meets their needs. For example, seniors living in uncomfortable housing (poorly heated, dilapidated, equipped with outdated sanitary facilities, and so on) located in an unsuitable environment (noisy, unsafe, hard to reach, and so on) may legitimately wish to be relocated. The housing may also be unsuited to the abilities of individuals who can no longer enjoy their living space for health reasons. Aging in place is not an option for those individuals, and especially not for seniors of modest financial means. Existing housing must therefore be improved and the adaptations necessary for an aging population must be made. Furthermore, the supply of housing options (CHSLDs, RIs, RTFs, and seniors' residences) must be adequate, affordable, and of sufficient quality to meet the needs of older adults who can no longer live at home and no longer wish to do so.

Conclusion

Not all very old Quebecers live in CHSLDs – far from it! This type of housing is an option for a very small percentage of older seniors. The very old, in fact, have quite different needs and resources in the areas of health, support, financial resources, and the networks of family and friends that they can mobilize. So, their residential choices are also quite varied.

With an aging population and longer life expectancies, increasing numbers of older adults will require support in staying at home in the final stages of their lives. Currently, that support is essentially being provided by family members and friends. Since, in the near future, adult children will be fewer in number and potentially scattered around the country and elsewhere, how will seniors with serious illnesses and severe disabilities be able to live at home? This situation, characterized by a shortage of public home care services and the shift to ambulatory care, has produced a number of undesirable and counterproductive effects. In crisis situations, for lack of alternatives, older adults tend to wind up in emergency departments and occupy hospital beds, which increases healthcare costs.

It is therefore important to provide seniors with various residential options that can meet their needs. Older adults are using many strategies to maintain their independence and continue living at home. However, when they can no longer do so, the present residential care system is incapable of rapidly taking them in and guaranteeing their comfort and dignity.

Notes

1 Mathieu Bock Côté (2016), "Les parcs à vieux," *Le Journal de Montréal*, June 20 (our translation).
2 Data from Auditor General of Quebec (2012), "Chapter 4: Residential Care Facilities," *Report of the Auditor General of Quebec to the National Assembly for 2012–2013.*

Functionally Dependent Seniors, 6. It should be noted here that institutions funded by the health and social services network include intermediate resources in addition to CHSLDs.

3   Chantale Lecours, Maxime Murphy, Gaëtane Dubé, and Marcel Godbout (2013), *Enquête québécoise sur les limitations d'activités, les maladies chroniques et le vieillissement 2010–2011. Utilisation des services de santé et des services sociaux des personnes de 65 ans et plus*, Vol. 3 (Quebec City: Institut de la statistique du Québec), 57.

4   Alzheimer Society of Canada (2016), *Prevalence and Monetary Costs of Dementia in Canada* (Toronto: Alzheimer Society of Canada).

5   The process involves "Iso-SMAF profiles," which are based on a scale from 1 to 14. Only individuals with profiles 10 to 14, and some presenting with profile 9, can be admitted to CHSLDs. See AQESSS – Association québécoise d'établissements de santé et de services sociaux (2013), *Le nouveau visage de l'hébergement public au Québec. Portrait des centres d'hébergement public et de leurs résidents* (Quebec City: AQESSS), <http://catalogue.iugm.qc.ca/GEIDEFile/30324.pdf?Archive=105021392320&File=30324_pdf>, accessed March 19, 2019.

6   Data from Auditor General of Quebec (2012), op. cit. For definitions of the various types of CHSLDs, see National Assembly of Quebec (2013), Committee on Health and Social Services, *The Living Conditions of Adults Living in Residential and Long-Term Care Centres*, consultation document (Quebec City: National Assembly of Quebec – Direction des travaux parlementaires, December), 6. These data exclude the number of spaces in private CHSLDs not under agreement.

7   Ministère de la Santé et des Services sociaux (2011), *Info-Hébergement* (Quebec City: Ministère de la Santé et des Services sociaux, September), 19, <http://collections.banq.qc.ca/ark:/52327/bs2066782>, accessed March 19, 2019.

8   Suzy L. Wong, Heather Gilmour, and Pamela L. Ramage-Morin (2016), "Alzheimer's disease and other dementias in Canada," *Health Reports*, Ottawa, Statistics Canada, Catalogue No. 82-003-X, Vol. 27, No. 5, 11–16.

9   Ministère de la Santé et des Services sociaux (2016), *Données sur les listes d'attente des CHSLD 2016–2017. Période 2*, <http://publications.msss.gouv.qc.ca/msss/document-001637/>, accessed September 10, 2016.

10   Auditor General of Quebec (2012), op. cit., 6.

11   CMHC – Canada Mortgage and Housing Corporation (2016), *Seniors' Housing Report – Canada Highlights* (Ottawa: CMHC).

12   Auditor General of Quebec (2012), op. cit., 6.

13   These figures include spaces in not-for-profit residences containing at least one unsubsidized unit.

14   The attraction rate is the ratio of the number of residents living in these residences to the number of individuals aged 75 and over in the population, multiplied by 100.

15   CMHC (2016), op. cit., 2–3.

16   Some households living in buildings funded under the AccèsLogis program may not receive the rent supplement and therefore pay higher rents than other residents: Patrik Marier and Anne-Marie Séguin (2015), "Aging and social assistance in the Provinces," in Daniel Béland and Pierre-Marc Daigneault (eds.), *Welfare Reform in Canada: Provincial Social Assistance in Comparative Perspective* (Toronto: University of Toronto Press), 349.

17   Jean-Pierre Lavoie, Nancy Guberman, and Patrik Marier (2014), *La responsabilité des soins aux aînés au Québec. Du secteur public au secteur privé* (Montreal: Institute for Research on Public Policy), No. 48, September.

18   Lecours et al. (2013), op. cit., 149.

19   Québec Ombudsman (2012), *Is Home Support Always the Option of Choice? Accessibility of Home Support Services for People with Significant and Persistent Disabilities* (Quebec City: Gouvernement du Québec).

20   Québec Ombudsman (2016), *2015–2016 Annual Report* (Quebec City: Gouvernement du Québec), 92.

Age-Friendly Cities

A Panacea for Aging in Place?

Meghan Joy, Patrik Marier, and Anne-Marie Séguin

The Myth

> Active ageing in supportive, enabling cities will serve as one of the most effective approaches to maintaining quality of life and prosperity in an increasingly older and more urban world.
>
> ───── World Health Organization, *Global Age-Friendly Cities: A Guide*[1]

The Age Friendly Cities (AFC) program grew out of a movement in the fields of gerontology and public health that stressed the importance of the immediate environment in improving senior citizens' quality of life. This initiative coincided with a renewal of interest in the social determinants of health, associated with a call to make cities better suited to active aging as a means of preventing certain health problems. A core intention of the AFC program is to move away from a negative understanding of population aging as a problem of costly "health deficits" to a positive approach that considers aging an opportunity to make local environments inclusive and healthy for everyone.[2] This change of perspective is crucial in a context in which the population is aging and people are living longer and prefer to age in their homes and communities for as long as possible. This context requires the implementation of a range of services, measures, and environmental adaptations that the AFC program strongly encourages municipalities to develop.

The World Health Organization (WHO) developed the AFC approach in 2007 and designed a comprehensive checklist that includes eight priority intervention areas: 1) outdoor spaces and public buildings planned with participation by senior citizens; 2) accessible and affordable transportation, including investments in walkability; 3) accessible and affordable housing; 4) social participation activities; 5) respect and inclusion, including eliminating ageism; 6) civic participation, particularly through volunteering and paid employment; 7) accessible communication and information sharing; and 8) community supports and services that encourage health promotion, including nutrition, recreation programming, and access to health services and home care.[3] In this sense, AFCs are situated as a solution to the everyday challenges experienced by senior citizens aging in place. This position is supported in Canada by the Public Health Agency and seniors' secretariats in several provinces, including Quebec and Ontario, that encourage local actors from municipal governments and not-for-profit organizations to engage in age-friendly efforts.

However, emerging research on AFC practices raises doubts about the program's ambitions, as its initiatives are small in scale and poorly funded.[4] AFCs appear not to be the panacea for aging in place that they claim to be. Understanding this myth, as well as the gap between AFC claims and practices, is crucial for moving forward in designing substantively age-friendly environments. To this end, in this chapter we analyze the AFC program in Quebec and Ontario, with a particular focus on implementation of the Toronto Seniors Strategy.

The Reality

The Province of Quebec and the City of Montreal
Quebec is the province that displays the most enthusiasm for the AFC program, which is the most visible and notable initiative of the province's Secrétariat aux aînés (Seniors' Secretariat). To date, more than 700 Quebec cities and towns are participating in the program. Each municipality has adopted five key objectives: 1) combatting ageism; 2) adapting the program's policies, services, and structures; 3) acting in a comprehensive and integrated fashion; 4) encouraging senior citizens' participation; and 5) relying on the collaboration and mobilization of the entire community.[5] Municipalities that join the program must also follow seven steps, including mandating someone to be responsible for the dossier concerning older adults, setting up a steering committee, and creating an action plan.[6] Although the

AFC approach clearly enhances the visibility of and knowledge regarding issues facing older adults across the province, the Quebec program falls short with regard to providing the necessary resources to meaningfully address the problems that seniors face.[7]

The Quebec program began allocating funds in 2009–10, with a commitment to providing $1 million per year for the development of municipal action plans, which led to a significant number of municipalities joining the AFC program.[8] In 2015–16 alone, a total of $1,180,000 was shared among 75 municipalities and regional county municipalities to enable them to develop or update their AFC plan. Most municipalities, with the exception of the largest urban centres, received sums ranging from $7,000 to $20,000.[9] Also in 2015–16, the Ministère de la Famille (Ministry of Families), within the context of the Québec Ami des Aînés (QADA, Quebec Friendly to Seniors) program, granted approximately $5.5 million for pilot projects, support for organizations, and research-action projects in Quebec regions. At the same time, the Ministry of Families allocated almost $10 million in grants for community initiatives in the context of the QADA – support for community actions – program.[10] Finally, since 2010, the department has allocated financial assistance for 137 projects totalling approximately $9 million, in the framework of the Québec-Municipalité amie des aînés (Quebec Municipalities Friendly to Seniors) infrastructure program, primarily for renovating buildings, upgrading infrastructure, improving street lighting, and developing different types of parks and pedestrian walkways.[11] These amounts may seem substantial, but they are modest in comparison to the cost of modifications to municipal infrastructure encouraged by the AFC program. For example, the cost of replacing traffic lights was estimated to be $11,500 per intersection in Montreal in 2012.[12]

In the case of large cities such as Montreal, the Quebec government allocated significant sums for the AFC program, but these sums also proved to be insufficient in view of the needed interventions. For example, in the spring of 2016, the Quebec government granted $3.4 million to Montreal under the QADA, Infrastructures Québec-Municipalités, and AFC programs. This sum was intended for hiring 26 new community workers to work with vulnerable older adults, updating the municipal action plan, and supporting community actions for seniors.[13] For its part, Montreal announced a financial commitment for 2016–18 of $4.5 million for projects for seniors and people with reduced mobility. Several Montreal boroughs have also developed initiatives that are not included in this amount. For example, as part of the AFC program, the Villeray–Saint-Michel–Parc Extension Borough has developed recreational activities for older adults, supported some 40 seniors' organizations and clubs, organized approximately 30 cultural events for those aged 50 and older, and offered a shuttle service in the Saint-Michel neighbourhood to facilitate transportation for older adults.[14]

When the sums allocated to support various AFC initiatives are compared to the annual operating budget of the City of Montreal, which was $5.2 billion in 2017, the modesty of the resources devoted to making the city better adapted to the realities of aging becomes obvious.[15] There is a need to be cautious here, however, because merely examining the funds directly associated with the AFC program does not enable us to fully assess a city's commitment to seniors. For example, the City of Montreal's contribution to financing the costs of operating adapted transport on its territory has grown much faster than that of the Quebec government, in order to respond to the needs of a rapidly increasing clientele. This type of service is essential to maintaining the mobility of many individuals with severe disabilities, a large proportion of whom are seniors.[16]

Before analyzing AFCs in Ontario, it is important to note that municipalities in Quebec and Ontario are allocated different responsibilities by their respective provincial governments. In Quebec, these exclude the fields of social and health policies, whereas in Ontario, municipalities are called upon to intervene in these areas.

The Province of Ontario and the City of Toronto

Like Quebec, Ontario has designated the AFC approach as a major priority, coordinated in this case by the Ontario Seniors' Secretariat (now the Ministry for Seniors and Accessibility). This commitment includes the preparation of an information guide associated with a grant program offering $500 to $8,000 to not-for-profit organizations and local administrations to develop and implement the approach.[17] In 2013, the Toronto City Council unveiled its Toronto Seniors Strategy (TSS), which offered general recommendations and detailed specific measures that the city intended to take, based on the eight priorities of the AFC approach.[18] Although the city's commitment to understanding and responding to the changing needs of its aging population through the TSS should be applauded, there is a troubling lack of resources devoted to the program.

The TSS was passed by City Council without a formal budget, and there is no dedicated office or core staff to coordinate and enforce implementation of the strategy. This is particularly challenging in a large city with a substantial bureaucracy and service system. Inaction is all the more likely in a context in which each of the city divisions promising to initiate age-friendly projects is receiving no targeted funding support through the TSS. Although several city divisions support AFC initiatives, other divisions are reluctant to admit that they serve senior citizens for fear of further service demands. The causes of the inadequate funding for implementing AFCs in Toronto are related to a complex mix of political ideology and institutional structures. The idea that the state should keep taxes as low as possible is dominant in Toronto and impedes investment in public services. This situation is exacerbated by the city's dependence on property taxes as the principal source of revenue, which is particularly problematic because the federal and provincial governments have transferred more physical infrastructure and service responsibilities to the local level of government in the last few decades.[19] This context is highly relevant for AFCs because the devolution has occurred in several domains that are on the WHO AFC checklist, such as affordable housing and public transit. For example, for its aging population, Toronto is attempting to adjust to new demands on its adapted public transportation service, Wheel-Trans, by encouraging senior citizens to use regular public transit. However, the transit agency lacks the funds to make public transport entirely accessible, as it is directed by the municipal council year after year to limit its budget.

This difficult situation for Toronto, and for other large cities (such as Montreal), appears to be ignored by the federal and provincial governments in their promotion of AFCs. There is an assumption that large cities will make up for resource challenges through their partnerships with not-for-profit organizations, universities, and businesses. Although these partnerships certainly result in interesting local projects, they cannot make up for decades of underinvestment in physical and social infrastructure that now needs to be upgraded and enhanced to promote the accessibility and affordability required in the AFC checklist. Small-scale funding support for pilot projects and information guides is inadequate for implementation of an effective AFC in Toronto. As such, the recommendations highlighted in the TSS are small in scale and do not support the large-scale service and infrastructure changes required to meet the needs of Toronto's seniors. Extraordinarily, the TSS makes little mention of the need for Wheel-Trans improvements and investments despite increasing demand from senior citizens who require the service to access city life.

In a context in which revenue is scarce, the TSS represents a strategy that targets seniors with the most acute health challenges who use Toronto's emergency services, such as ambulances, shelters, social housing, and long-term care. Municipal public servants are struggling to provide the long-term care supports needed for an aging population with mental health and addiction challenges who are now living permanently in Toronto shelters. Similarly, local not-for-profit organizations are increasingly being contracted by the province to take charge of medicalized home support to senior citizens living in the community. As local actors provide more emergency health and social services due to the inadequate funding of healthcare and social welfare at other levels of government, they struggle to fund health-promotion work that improves local environments. This focus directly challenges the claim that AFCs are moving from a negative to a positive approach to aging. In this context, city staff and not-for-profit organizations have little time to partner on AFC work, including developing meaningful relationships with senior citizens' groups to ensure their active and ongoing involvement in political decision-making.

Conclusion

Research on AFC initiatives in Quebec and Ontario, including in Montreal and Toronto, challenges the myth that AFCs are a panacea for the everyday problems experienced by senior citizens aging in place in urban environments. Although the AFC program has provided a strong impetus toward raising awareness of seniors' needs across municipalities, and has an impressive checklist in this regard, the means deployed to achieve the large-scale objectives of the program are insufficient. The financial commitments granted to local actors as part of AFC initiatives have consisted primarily of short-term support to prepare an action plan and targeted project-based funding thereafter. Larger systemic funding gaps are being overlooked by Canada's federal government as well as by provincial governments in Quebec and Ontario. Moreover, these governments and the WHO itself ignore historical and contemporary trends in public sector restructuring through which more responsibility for physical infrastructure and social services has been transferred to municipalities and not-for-profit organizations without providing them with adequate resources. In fact, AFCs may represent a continuation of these restructuring trends while, ironically, allowing other levels of government to claim that they support senior citizens. The AFC myth therefore offers a potentially powerful political payoff. To meet the everyday needs of senior citizens, the gap must be exposed between the benefits and improvements foreseen by implementation of the program as currently defined and the reality of senior citizens aging in place in all their diverse identities, as well as of the not-for-profit organizations and city staff supposedly enabled to support them.

Although this research raises many challenges to the implementation of AFCs, the program should not be cast aside as purely symbolic, as the movement to improve access to services and amenities for senior citizens through democratic decision-making is imperative to enhancing quality of life as the population ages. It is important to shed light on the problems with putting the program into practice in order to provide a guide for how to move forward to support a substantial AFC. We must not assume that once a city embarks on becoming age-friendly, the work is done and senior citizens are socially included and have an improved quality of life. Canadian municipalities have limited resources at their disposal, and achieving meaningful policy outcomes at the scale presented in the AFC checklist requires considerable participation and funding from the federal and provincial governments. An AFC is impossible without higher levels of investment in physical infrastructure, healthcare, and social services. Further research is needed on how to achieve large-scale intergovernmental AFCs in Canada.

Notes

1   World Health Organization (2007), *Global Age-Friendly Cities: A Guide* (Geneva: WHO Press), 75, <http://www.who.int/ageing/publications/Global_age_friendly_cities_Guide_English.pdf>, accessed July 31, 2017.

2   Stephen Golant (2014), *Age-Friendly Communities: Are We Expecting Too Much?* (Montreal: Institute for Research on Public Policy), *Insight*, No. 5, 1–20.

3   Ibid.

4   Andrew Scharlach (2012), "Creating aging-friendly communities in the United States," *Ageing International*, Vol. 37, No. 1, 25–38; Tine Buffel, Chris Phillipson, and Thomas Scharf (2012), "Ageing in urban environments: Developing 'age-friendly' cities," *Critical Social Policy*, Vol. 32, No. 4, 597–617; Jo-Anne Everingham, Andrea Petriwskyj, Jeni Warburton, Michael Cuthill, and Helen Bartlett (2009), "Information provision for an age-friendly community," *Ageing International*, Vol. 34, No. 1/2, 79–98.

5   Gouvernement du Québec (2009), *Municipalité amie des aînés: favoriser le vieillissement actif au Québec* (Quebec City: Gouvernement du Québec), 15–21.

6   Ibid.

7   Juliette Rochman and Diane-Gabrielle Tremblay (2010), "Services et seniors: l'impact du programme MADA sur le développement des services municipaux communautaires et privés au Québec," *Gérontologie et société*, Vol. 33, No. 135, 285–339.

8   Gouvernement du Québec (2009), *Plan budgétaire* (Quebec City: Finances Québec), Section E, 17.

9   According to data from the Quebec Ministère de la Famille (last updated in 2016), *Projets financés – 2015–2016, Municipalités en démarche MADA*, <https://www.mfa.gouv.qc.ca/fr/aines/mada/liste-mada/Pages/projets-finances-2015-2016.aspx>, accessed March 14, 2017.

10 According to data from the Quebec Ministère de la Famille (last updated in 2016), *QADA, soutien aux organismes communautaires – Projets 2015–2016*, <https://www.mfa.gouv.qc.ca/fr/aines/quebec_ami_des_aines/Pages/projets-2015-2016-soutien-actions-communautaires.aspx>, accessed July 31, 2017.

11 Website of the Ministère de la Famille (last updated in 2017), "Programme d'infrastructures Québec-Municipalités – Municipalité amie des aînés," <https://www.mfa.gouv.qc.ca/fr/aines/mada/Pages/programme_infrastructure.aspx>, accessed March 14, 2017.

12 Pierre-André Normandin (2012), "Feux de signalisation: les coûts de la réfection augmentent de 3 millions," *La Presse*, April 10, <http://www.lapresse.ca/actualites/montreal/201204/09/01-4513737-feuxde-signalisation-les-couts-de-la-refection augmentent-de-3 millions.php>, accessed February 23, 2017.

13 Website – Portail Québec – Services Québec (2016), *Politique Vieillir et vivre ensemble, chez soi dans sa communauté, au Québec – Plus de trois millions de dollars pour améliorer les conditions de vie des personnes ainées de la région de Montréal*, April 10, <http://www.fil-information.gouv.qc.ca/Pages/Article.aspx?idArticle=2404104348>, accessed March 14, 2017.

14 Ville de Montréal website, *Municipalité amie des ainés – MADA*, <http://ville.montreal.qc.ca/portal/page?_pageid=8638,95977675&_dad=portal&_schema=PORTAL>, accessed July 31, 2017.

15 Ville de Montréal website (2016), Communiqués, *Montréal amie des aînés et accessibilité universelle – La Ville de Montréal réaffirme son engagement envers les aînés et les personnes ayant des limitations fonctionnelles en attribuant une somme de 4.5 M$ à des projets leur étant destinés*, June 29, <http://ville.montreal.qc.ca/portal/page?_pageid=5798,42657625&_dad=portal&_schema=PORTAL&id=27148>, accessed March 14, 2017; Ville de Montréal (2016), *Budget de fonctionnement en bref, 2017* (Montreal: Ville de Montréal), <http://ville.montreal.qc.ca/pls/portal/docs/page/service_fin_fr/media/documents/Budget2017_bref_fr.pdf>, accessed July 31, 2017.

16 Société de transport de Montréal – STM (2015), *Mémoire de la STM. Présenté dans le cadre des consultations prébudgétaires 2015–2016 du ministère des Finances du Québec*, 12–13, <https://www.stm.info/sites/default/files/pdf/fr/stm-memoire_budget-quebec-2015-16_public.pdf>, accessed July 31, 2017.

17 Ontario Government (2013), *Finding the Right Fit: Age Friendly Community Planning* (Toronto: Queen's Printer for Ontario); Ontario Government (2015), *Seniors*

Community Grant Program, website – Government of Ontario (Ontario Seniors Secretariat), online: <http://www.seniors.gov.on.ca/en/srsorgs/scgp.php>, accessed July 31, 2017.

18   City of Toronto (2013), *The Toronto Seniors Strategy: Towards an Age-Friendly City* (Toronto: City of Toronto).

19   Meghan Joy and Ronald K. Vogel (2015), "Toronto's governance crisis: A global city under pressure," *Cities*, Vol. 49, 35–52.

8

Seniors and Their Cars

Choice or Necessity?

Paula Negron-Poblete and Anne-Marie Séguin

Les personnes âgées accros à l'auto (Seniors: addicted to their cars)
—————— title of an article in *Le Soleil*, January 23, 2012[1]

In the media and in the literature on daily mobility, the prevalence of car use among seniors is often mentioned. A large majority of senior citizens are said to have driver's licences and to get around mostly by car. Losing their licence is therefore viewed as a pivotal and difficult event for older adults.

But is this actually the case? Is car use really that common among seniors? To answer this question, we begin with some data on the number of people who hold driver's licences, broken down by age and gender. We then identify the factors likely to contribute to car use among older adults. Next, we take a closer look at the Montreal region and the transportation choices available there. We do this for the region as a whole and for three smaller areas, each representing a different urban setting, with a view to determining whether the type of built environment has an impact on the mode of transportation chosen.

Car Use among Older Quebec Adults

Few data are available for Quebec as a whole that can be used to better understand the place of the car in people's lifestyles. There are, however, data on the number of people who have a driver's licence.[2] Without a licence, people become dependent on others for a ride or are forced to use other means of transportation. According to data from the Société de l'assurance automobile du Québec, the number of driver's licences in the province has risen by 1.5 percent per year since the late 1970s, an indication of how widespread the car has become as a way for people to get around.[3] Seniors are part of this trend. In 2015, the vast majority of older people were able to drive themselves: in fact, 69 percent of those aged 65 and older held a driver's licence.[4] In comparison, the proportion for Quebecers aged 16 and up as a whole was 77 percent – only 8 percent higher than for seniors alone.

During the five-year period from 2010 to 2015, the proportion of people aged 65 and over who held a driver's licence rose by 29 percent. The increase was particularly striking for the 85–89 age group (52 percent) and for those aged 90 and over (99 percent). During that same period, the corresponding percentage increase for the Quebec population as a whole was only 4.4 percent. In 2015, 37,968 Quebecers aged 85–89 held driver's licences and 7,475 aged 90 and over did so, accounting for 32 percent and 12 percent, respectively, of seniors in those age groups. However, these statistics do not reflect a number of major gender-based differences. In Quebec, 58 percent of older women hold driver's licences, compared with 83 percent of older men. This gender-based difference can be observed at the national level in Canada, as well as in other countries. In light of this difference, it is not surprising that women are more likely to avail themselves of active transportation and public transit.[5] Even seniors who no longer have a driver's licence may rely on a car as their primary means of transportation, but as passengers. This situation is particularly true of older women, who are driven around by someone else, in many cases their spouse. The experts nonetheless anticipate that the gap between women and men drivers may decrease as the baby boomers reach retirement age, given the higher proportion of women drivers in that generation.[6]

Factors Conducive to Car Use among Seniors

In a study on older drivers in Canada and the United States, better health was identified as one of the factors contributing to the rapid growth in the number of older drivers, and particularly of very old drivers.[7] Another factor behind the widespread car use among seniors is the lack of alternative means of transportation that meet their mobility needs. In Canada and the

United States, car use is especially prevalent in rural areas, given the virtual absence of alternative forms of transportation.[8] In such areas, seniors who no longer possess the capacity and the skills needed to operate a motor vehicle find their mobility compromised, unless they have someone they can count on to drive them around. In metropolitan areas in Canada, higher housing density and a greater mix of activities (stores, services, community organizations), along with better public transit services, should encourage more frequent use of other means of transportation.[9] The Quebec data from 2014 confirm these observations. The proportion of people aged 65 and over who hold driver's licences does in fact vary by administrative region. The lowest proportions of seniors with driver's licences are observed on the Island of Montreal (53 percent), in Laval (66 percent), and in the Capitale-Nationale region (68 percent), all of which are urban areas.[10] The highest proportions are in the Laurentians (76 percent) and Centre-du-Québec (75 percent) regions, which are predominantly tourist and rural areas, respectively.

There is one other factor that can help to explain why seniors in metropolitan areas, and the younger ones (age 65–74) in particular, are so fond of their cars: more and more older adults are living in the suburbs, which are designed on the premise that people will be driving (exclusively residential areas, dead-end streets, concentration of businesses and services in shopping malls, and so on).[11] For many people residing in the suburbs, it is not really possible to get around without a car.

The unfavourable conditions that older adults face in getting from place to place also contribute to car use among this group. In some cases, there are no sidewalks, or sidewalks may not be properly maintained or cleared of snow. There may be no benches to sit on to rest, or not enough time to cross the street, or public transit may be inadequate or poorly designed. These and other factors discourage walking and the use of public transit.[12] Moreover, a significant number of Quebecers aged 65 and over suffer from disabilities: more than one third of them report disabilities related to mobility and agility.[13] Having to walk to a particular destination or to a bus stop or subway station can be a demanding and sometimes perilous undertaking for seniors with reduced mobility (see Chapter 19, "Do Older Adults Have All the Time in the World?"). What is more, most older adults have less energy, and they need to take this into consideration. Under these circumstances, having a car offers an attractive way to preserve their energy for their activities rather than using it simply to get from point A to point B.

The lifestyles of many seniors may also explain why car use is so prevalent. Today's seniors (baby boomers in particular) enjoy better health than previous generations and participate in many activities that take place outside the home, such as shopping, social and cultural activities, sports, volunteer work, and employment. Being in control of their mobility is therefore essential to their quality of life, and a car can give them greater freedom of movement, particularly in places where public transit is poor or nonexistent and parking is easy to find.[14]

Overview of Seniors' Mobility Practices in the Montreal Region

Given the lack of data on seniors' transportation choices for Quebec as a whole, we will focus on the Montreal metropolitan region, for which data are available. This area provides a good opportunity to look at the means of transportation that older adults choose given the diversity of urban environments and the wide variety of transportation options available. Data from the 2013 Montreal region Origin-Destination Survey highlight the dominance of the car in the Montreal metropolitan region.[15] In fact, 85 percent of seniors aged 65–74 and 68 percent of those aged 75 and over live in a household in which they have access to at least one car, compared with 89 percent for the 18–64 age group. Driver's licences are held by 83 percent of people in the 65–74 age group and by 57 percent of those aged 75 and over, compared with 87 percent of people aged 18–64. Older men are significantly more likely (87 percent) to have a driver's licence than are older women (61 percent).

Based on this portrait, it is obvious that car travel is by far the primary means of transportation used by seniors. For the 65–74 age group, 64 percent of trips are as car drivers and 16 percent are as car passengers. The figures for walking and public transit are 10 percent and 8 percent, respectively. Among those aged 75 and over, the proportion of seniors driving themselves falls, accounting for 57 percent of trips, with other means of transportation picking up the slack: being driven by someone else (20 percent of trips) and walking (12 percent). Public transit use remains stable, at 8 percent of total trips. In a place such as the Montreal metropolitan region, why is public transit use so low? To shed some light on this question, we decided to take a close look at three different areas – an inner-city neighbourhood and two suburbs – to determine whether the local transportation services that are offered and the type of urban setting have an impact on the means of transportation chosen.

Different Habits in Different Areas

The three areas studied are Rosemont (an inner-city neighbourhood), Pont-Viau–Laval-des-Rapides (a first-ring suburb), and Saint-Eustache (a more distant suburb). All three areas have substantial numbers of residents aged 65 and over: 16 percent in Rosemont, 20 percent in Pont-Viau–Laval-des-Rapides, and 14 percent in Saint-Eustache. What hypotheses can be formulated about these three areas? Living in a densely populated neighbourhood with mixed land use, such as Rosemont, which offers good public transit services and many nearby destinations, should encourage people to avoid driving and to rely on walking and public transit. Conversely, living in a suburban area such as Pont-Viau–Laval-des-Rapides or Saint-Eustache should strongly encourage car use, as these areas are characterized by low housing density with businesses and services developed around travel by car.[16]

A comparison of the means of transportation that seniors use in these three areas yields three findings (see Figure 8.1). First, it is clear that in Saint-Eustache the car is the predominant means of transportation used by seniors aged 65–74 (93 percent) and by those 75 and over (95 percent). The same holds true, albeit to a lesser extent, in Pont-Viau–Laval-des-Rapides (88 percent and 86 percent of trips for the corresponding age categories). Cars are less pre-eminent in Rosemont (60 percent in the 65–74 age group and 57 percent among those aged 75 and over). These figures confirm that the type of urban environment has an impact on the means of transportation that seniors use.

Second, public transit is not heavily used by older adults. In Rosemont, where public transit services are better than in the other two areas, public transportation accounts for only 16 percent of the trips made by seniors. In the other two areas, only marginal use is made of this means of transportation, which accounts for a maximum of 5 percent of trips (including 0 percent of seniors aged 75 and over in Saint-Eustache).

Third, the extent to which seniors use walking as a way to get around varies significantly in the different areas. In Rosemont, walking accounts for 21 percent of the trips made by people aged 65–74 and 23 percent for those aged 75 and over, but for only 7 percent of trips made by seniors living in Pont-Viau–Laval-des-Rapides and for between 3 percent and 4 percent of trips for those living in Saint-Eustache. In the latter two areas, walking is therefore insignificant as a means of transportation.

There are essentially two explanations for the low level of public transit use by seniors in these three areas. First, public transit services, particularly

FIGURE 8.1

Modal choice among seniors in Rosemont, Pont-Viau–Laval-des-Rapides, and Saint-Eustache, 2013

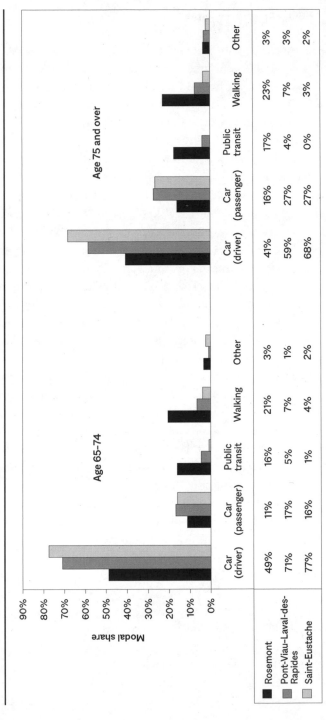

	Car (driver)	Car (passenger)	Public transit	Walking	Other	Car (driver)	Car (passenger)	Public transit	Walking	Other
		Age 65–74					Age 75 and over			
Rosemont	49%	11%	16%	21%	3%	41%	16%	17%	23%	3%
Pont-Viau–Laval-des-Rapides	71%	17%	5%	7%	1%	59%	27%	4%	7%	3%
Saint-Eustache	77%	16%	1%	4%	2%	68%	27%	0%	3%	2%

Source: 2013 Montreal region Origin-Destination survey, version 13.2b. Data treatment by authors.

in Saint-Eustache and to a lesser extent in Pont-Viau–Laval-des-Rapides, are limited and essentially geared towards people who commute to work (peak-hour routes to places of employment or intermodal stations). In other words, public transportation does not provide accessibility to destinations that might be of interest to older citizens. The second explanation likely has to do with a failure to ensure that public transit services – specifically, the level of service and the types of vehicles used – are in line with seniors' needs and capabilities. This may be why, despite the high level of service offered in Rosemont, seniors there are not overly inclined to take public transit, even when the urban environment is conducive to walking.

Conclusion

The mobility practices of seniors do not differ radically from those of younger adults in Quebec: for this age group, as for the others, the car plays a key role in daily mobility. There is nonetheless a change in mobility practices among some seniors as they grow older and turn to other means of transportation. They become passengers, or they choose to walk, or, less frequently, they turn to public transit. However, not all environments are conducive to use of the latter two modes. The circumstances in low-density rural areas and the outskirts of urban areas (inadequate or no public transit, long distances between destinations) are such that seniors, like younger adults, are highly – if not totally – dependent on driving. They therefore need to hang on to their driver's licences and own a car for as long as possible in order to preserve their mobility. This means that a substantial portion of their income, which for many older people is quite modest (see Chapter 2, "Living on Easy Street? The Myth of the Affluent Senior"), must go toward keeping a car on the road.

Our analysis indicates that car use among seniors is widespread. However, it seems that many areas do not offer much in the way of alternatives, giving seniors little choice if they wish to remain mobile. In other words, older adults' reliance on their cars may be a matter of the conditions in the areas in which they live. This dependency is a source of concern in a political context in which governments are strongly encouraging seniors to grow old in their own communities and in which many of them wish to do so. Without a car, will they be able to preserve their right to mobility as they age? Only the political will to adapt residential environments and transit services will be able to reduce the degree to which older adults living in many areas of Quebec rely on their cars.

Notes

1   Annie Morin (2012), "Les personnes âgées accros à l'auto," *Le Soleil,* January 23.
2   However, it must be recognized that a person may have a licence but drive very little, if at all.
3   SAAQ – Société de l'assurance automobile du Québec (2015), *Données et statistiques 2013* (Quebec City: SAAQ), 3.
4   Data taken or calculated by the authors from the following sources: SAAQ – Société de l'assurance automobile du Québec (2016), *Bilan 2015 et dossier statistique. Accidents, parc automobile, permis de conduire* (Quebec City: SAAQ); ISQ – Institut de la statistique du Québec (2015), *Le bilan démographique du Québec. Édition 2015* (Quebec City: ISQ).
5   Marie-Hélène Vandersmissen (2012), "Mobilité et espaces d'activité des 65 ans et plus dans la région de Québec," in Paula Negron-Poblete and Anne-Marie Séguin (eds.), *Vieillissement et enjeux d'aménagement: regards à différentes échelles* (Quebec City: Presses de l'Université du Québec), 31–65.
6   Martin Turcotte (2012), "Profile of seniors' transportation habits," *Canadian Social Trends,* Ottawa, Statistics Canada, Catalogue No. 11-008-x, 3–16.
7   Bonnie M. Dobbs (2012), "The new older driver in the United States and Canada: Changes and challenges," in Joseph Coughlin and Lisa D'Ambrosio (eds.), *Aging America and Transportation: Personal Choices and Public Policy* (New York: Springer), 119–36.
8   Meghan Stromberg (2007), "Growing old in a car-centric world," *Planning,* Vol. 73, No. 10, 6–11.
9   Turcotte (2012), op. cit.
10 Data calculated by the authors from the following sources: SAAQ (2016), op. cit.; ISQ – Institut de la statistique du Québec, accessible at <http://www.stat.gouv.qc.ca/docs-hmi/statistiques/population-demographie/structure/index.html>, accessed March 10, 2017. We did not include calculations for the Nord-du-Québec region, which presents an exceptional situation.
11 Anne-Marie Séguin, Philippe Apparicio, and Paula Negron (2013), "La répartition de la population âgée dans huit métropoles canadiennes de 1981 à 2006: un groupe de moins en moins ségrégué," *Cybergeo: European Journal of Geography,* No. 639, <https://journals.openedition.org/cybergeo/25860>.
12 Paula Negron-Poblete (2015), "Se déplacer en banlieue lorsqu'on est une femme âgée: une mobilité sous contraintes," in Sébastien Lord, Paula Negron-Poblete, and Juan Torres (eds.), *Mobilité et exclusion, quelles relations?* (Montreal: Presses de l'Université Laval), 193–224.
13 Chantale Lecours, Maxime Murphy, Gaëtane Dubé, and Marcel Godbout (2013), *Enquête québécoise sur les limitations d'activités, les maladies chroniques et le vieillissement, 2010–2011. Utilisation des services de santé et des services sociaux par les personnes de 65 ans et plus,* Volume 3 (Quebec City: Institut de la statistique du Québec).
14 Sébastien Lord, Florent Joerin, and Marius Thériault (2009), "La mobilité quotidienne de banlieusards vieillissants et âgés: Déplacements, aspirations et significations de la mobilité," *The Canadian Geographer/Le Géographe canadien,* Vol. 53, No. 3, 357–75; Kevin DeGood (2011), *Aging in Place, Stuck without Options: Fixing the*

Mobility Crisis Threatening the Baby Boom Generation, Transportation for America, <http://t4america.org/maps-tools/seniorsmobilitycrisis2011>, accessed March 10, 2017.

15 The 2013 Origin-Destination survey for the Montreal region was carried out by the Agence métropolitaine de transport (AMT). The survey collected data on various aspects of daily mobility in the region. For further information on the survey, see AMT – Agence métropolitaine de transport (2015), *L'enquête origine-destination 2013. Mobilité des personnes dans la région de Montréal* (Montreal: AMT – Secrétariat à l'Enquête Origine-Destination). Unless otherwise indicated, all data presented in the rest of this chapter come from this survey.

16 Vandersmissen (2012), op. cit.; Lord et al. (2009), op. cit.; Negron-Poblete (2015), op. cit.

9

Challenging the Myth of Older Homelessness as Chronic Homelessness

Victoria Burns

When you think of older people experiencing homelessness (OPEH), what images come to mind? Perhaps a homeowner, a businessperson, your own grandparent, or you, yourself, doesn't spring to mind? This is because of the widespread assumption that the majority of OPEH are chronically homeless – that they have been homeless for extended periods of time. The reality is that older people experiencing homelessness form an incredibly diverse population, including people who have had relatively stable employment, families, and housing for a good part of their lives. Drawing on existing literature and findings from a qualitative study focusing on 15 people who were homeless for the first time after the age of 50, I aim to reveal the complexity of the phenomenon of older homelessness and to challenge the myth of older homelessness as chronic homelessness.[1]

Understanding Homelessness and, Particularly, Older Homelessness

There are an estimated 150,000 to 235,000 people experiencing homelessness (PEH) in Canada, with 4 percent to 49 percent of this population said to be composed of older people.[2] This significant divergence can be explained by the lack of consensus among researchers, practitioners, and policy makers on the definition of PEH and the age at which they may be characterized as "older." According to Canadian institutions, individuals are considered to be older once they reach the age of 65 – the legal retirement age, at which they may be eligible for social benefits and programs reserved for seniors. However, according to the academic literature, PEH should be considered older from age 50 on, due to the health risks and reduced life expectancy found among this group.[3]

The most conservative estimates of homelessness come from government sources that employ a narrow definition, such as the one used by Statistics Canada, which counts only people in emergency shelters.[4] Many of the highest estimates are provided by nongovernmental sources that attempt to take into account the complexity and rapid growth of homelessness.[5] A group of Canadian researchers recently developed a national definition of homelessness that includes four different housing situations: 1) living on the street or in places not designed for human habitation; 2) using emergency shelters; 3) being lodged temporarily (for example, living in temporary housing or "couch surfing"); and 4) living in precarious lodging or dwellings that do not meet public health and safety standards.[6] The Quebec government has also recently adopted a broader definition and plans to use a comprehensive strategy and a variety of approaches to counter this phenomenon, including integrated emergency resources, housing, health services, and social services.[7]

In the past decade, policy makers have been demanding reliable estimates of the number of PEH before taking action. Many statistics have thus recently been produced for American and Canadian cities, including Toronto, Vancouver, and Montreal, using the "point-in-time" (PIT) method, which enables PEH to be counted on a given day.[8] According to the latest Montreal PIT result, there were 3,016 PEH in Montreal on the night of March 24, 2015.[9] Among these individuals, 41 percent were 50 years of age or older (compared to 39 percent between the ages of 31 and 49 and 19 percent who were 30 years old or younger). Moreover, 49 percent of emergency shelter users were 50 or older, and a number of them were experiencing homelessness for the first time.[10] Despite the increased use of PIT counts, this method has been criticized for underestimating invisible homelessness (the large number of people residing in temporary or unsafe housing).[11]

What Do We Know about Older People Experiencing Homelessness?

The scientific research, including some Canadian studies, suggests that older homelessness, like homelessness at other stages of life, is a complex phenomenon caused by individual circumstances (such as mental or physical health issues or family breakups) combined with structural factors (a short-age of housing or adequate employment).[12] These studies also distinguish between two different pathways leading to later-life homelessness: 1) that of adults with a long history of marginality, which is characterized as chronic homelessness; and 2) that of individuals who recently became homeless for the first time in their lives.[13] Although the numbers of both groups are grow-ing in Canada, contrary to popular belief, only 2 percent to 4 percent of the entire PEH population are chronically homeless, with this group historically being composed of single men with mental health or addiction problems. Men in this group are also often the most visible and are seen as major users of public services.[14] These characteristics help to explain why, in the past decade, chronic homelessness has been prioritized in research, policies, and interventions, and why other subgroups, including the growing group of older people experiencing homelessness for the first time in later life, have been largely neglected. In an effort to address this issue, I conducted a quali-tative study to explore the experiences of 15 individuals in this situation aged 50 or older in Montreal.[15] The participants' demographic characteris-tics are as follows:

- 15 participants: 8 men, 7 women
- $^{13}/_{15}$ born in Quebec, $^{12}/_{15}$ francophones, $^{15}/_{15}$ Caucasians
- $^{11}/_{15}$ have a high school education or more
- $^{4}/_{15}$ were homeowners at some point
- $^{7}/_{15}$ lived in the same housing for more than 20 years
- $^{5}/_{15}$ had stable careers for more than 20 years
- $^{8}/_{15}$ are single and have never married; $^{1}/_{15}$ is a widower; $^{6}/_{15}$ are divorced
- $^{10}/_{15}$ have children
- Monthly income from $513 to $2,000; monthly rent from $200 to $705.

Two Different Pathways into Homelessness: Gradual and Rapid

Although the experience of each participant in the study is unique, I identi-fied two main trajectories into homelessness: one gradual and one rapid. The individuals whose pathway was gradual described having had a number of years of instability in their personal lives, employment, and housing. Despite some long-standing difficulties, these people managed to stay in housing for a good part of their lives. In contrast, those who experienced rapid trajectories spoke of a long history of housing and employment stability. It was only later in life that these individuals experienced a series of significant social and personal losses that drove them to homelessness, with no major warning signs. Here are two examples of pathways into homelessness: one gradual, and the other rapid. (Pseudonyms are used to protect the participants' anonymity.)

Anna, 61 Years Old, Gradual Trajectory

Anna was born in Montreal. Single and childless, she lived in a subsidized apartment for 22 years before becoming homeless. Although she was a university graduate, she had been unable to work full time for thirty years because of mental health problems. Due to her long-term disability status, she had been receiving $770 a month, and she paid $300 a month for housing. When asked what led her to homelessness, she described the poor maintenance of her apartment, as well as conflicts with the owner and her neighbours, which she found increasingly difficult to handle with age. To stretch her budget, for many years she had been sharing some meals with a neighbour. However, when a disagreement led to a total breakdown of their relationship, it became more difficult for her to stretch her budget to pay her rent and make ends meet. Her physical health also deteriorated, and she lacked the energy to deal with her apartment, which was no longer in good condition. She turned to a number of community organizations but did not get the help she needed to keep her apartment, as she explains:

> Well, I went to an organization for them to help me manage my budget, and I was put on a waiting list. They didn't call me. Because I still had a lot of pretty well thought-out ideas, I put together a letter, mentioning all the steps I'd taken to work out a solution and offered that to the board of directors. To make them understand that it was out of my control, that it wasn't because I wanted to fuck with them, as they say in the building.

She wanted to leave her apartment but felt trapped, as she did not have the means to pay for an apartment in the private rental market and the wait list for subsidized housing was five to seven years. She reached out to many community resources for help, but to no avail, and she was completely exhausted: "After 22 years, I was a wreck ... psychologically and physically ... I was exhausted." In danger of being evicted, she turned to an emergency women's shelter.

David, 70 Years Old, Rapid Trajectory

David, born in Montreal, was a university-educated father of two. He recently lost his wife and retired from a 40-year professional career. He attributed his homelessness to a combination of losses, including his retirement, followed by the sudden deaths of his wife, his daughter, and his mother over a five-month period. As he explained, these losses triggered a relapse into alcoholism after more than 30 years of sobriety:

> Everything happened at the same time. Two and a half years ago, three people died, one after the other. My mother died first, then my oldest daughter was the second to die, and then there was my wife. All that in five months. It took a month, let's say, before it all started. It was stupid of me to retire.

After the death of his wife, David isolated himself from his friends and family – in short, from everything that reminded him of her. He no longer felt at home in his apartment because the place reminded him of his deceased wife. He was late paying his rent and his bills and ultimately had to sell his possessions in order to make ends meet. In two years, he went from a stable situation – living in the same apartment with his wife for 27 years and having run a successful business from home – to living as an unemployed widower in a shelter.

The 15 participants in the study identified various personal and social factors, as well as problems related to their environment, as explanations for their rapid or gradual paths to homelessness. Those with gradual pathways tended to identify conflicts with the management of their housing as a main trigger of homelessness, whereas individuals with rapid pathways were more likely to refer to intense social losses. For all participants, poverty, a lack of appropriate and affordable housing, or the poor conditions of their lodging were key contributors to their homelessness. Even though most participants had worked during their lifetimes, the majority (10 out of 15) had incomes below the poverty level.[16] A number of participants had to allocate a sizeable portion of their income, sometimes as high as 80 percent, to rent. Many of those whose trajectories were gradual lived in insalubrious and unsafe housing. According to the Canadian definition of homelessness, which includes those at risk and living in precarious lodging, a number of participants were technically experiencing homelessness before actually losing their housing.[17] In other words, they were among the hidden homeless, a population that remains largely invisible to researchers, decision makers, and practitioners.

Responding to the Needs of Older People Experiencing Homelessness: Challenges and Issues

Homeless older people with complex health and social service needs are often confronted with additional obstacles blocking their access to stable and appropriate housing. Those who need intensive care are frequently excluded from long-term care residences due to alcohol or behavioural problems.[18] Many emergency shelters are not designed to adapt to the requirements of residents with age-related mobility (obligation to leave the shelter during the day; absence of elevators) or health issues.[19] Even when older adults are able to transition to autonomous housing, their concerns about living alone without specialized support contribute to their sense of instability and make it more difficult for them to remain independent.[20] In other words, it is unlikely that they will remain stable in autonomous lodging if support services are not provided, as older people are more inclined than other age groups to be socially isolated and to require additional care.[21]

How, then, can we respond to the housing needs of older people experiencing homelessness? Rapid rehousing programs, such as Housing First, largely funded by the federal government under the Homelessness Partnering Strategy[22] and drawn upon by a number of communities across Canada, have proved efficient in quickly moving people into scattered-site permanent supportive housing.[23] This type of program raises concerns for older people experiencing homelessness due to their additional need for support, which is not always considered in these initiatives.[24] Also, given the incredible diversity and growing size of this population, new ideas and varied and innovative housing solutions must be found to respond to its complex health and social needs.

Conclusion

Despite the increasing number of older people experiencing homelessness, there is a tendency not to recognize the heterogeneity of this population. In this chapter, I have shown that there is considerable diversity among homeless older people in terms of gender, age, socioeconomic situation, life experiences, and pathway into homelessness. The tendency to homogenize this group can also be observed for the population of older people in general; this homogenization, in turn, contributes to various types of social exclusion.[25] How can we better document and acknowledge the heterogeneity of older people experiencing homelessness? I would posit that it is crucial to conduct research on this group, which is as yet rather small, with a partici-patory orientation. Older people experiencing homelessness must be given a voice in developing solutions adapted to their *multiple and complex* needs. Furthermore, for these strategies to work, public perceptions of homeless-ness as a stigma must be changed. I hope that this chapter makes a modest contribution to such a change by giving a voice and a human face to older people experiencing homelessness, a population that must be recognized so that it does not continue to grow, silent and invisible.

Notes

1   Victoria Burns (2016), "Oscillating in and out of place: Experiences of older adults residing in homeless shelters in Montreal, Quebec," *Journal of Aging Studies*, Vol. 39, 11–20; Victoria Burns (2015), "Oscillating in and out of place across housed-homeless trajectories: Experiences of newly homeless older adults in Montreal, Quebec," PhD dissertation, Social Work, McGill University.

2   Stephen Gaetz, Jesse Donaldson, Tim Richter, and Tanya Gulliver (2013), *The State of Homelessness in Canada 2013* (Toronto: Canadian Homelessness Research Net-work Press), <http://homelesshub.ca/sites/default/files/SOHC2013.pdf>, accessed March 8, 2017; Gordon Laird (2007), *Shelter: Homelessness in a Growth Economy: Canada's 21st Century Paradox* (Calgary: Chumir Ethics Foundation); Eric Latimer, James McGregor, Christian Méthot, and Alison Smith (2015), *Dénombrement des personnes en situation d'itinérance à Montréal le 24 mars 2015* (Montreal: Ville de Montréal).

3   Amanda Grenier, Rachel Barken, Tamara Sussman, David Rothwell, Valérie Bourgeois-Guérin, and Jean-Pierre Lavoie (2016), "A literature review of homeless-ness and aging: Suggestions for a policy and practice-relevant research agenda," *Canadian Journal on Aging/La Revue canadienne du vieillissement*, Vol. 35, No. 1, 28–41.

4   Havi Echenberg and Hilary Jensen (2008*), Defining and enumerating homelessness in Canada* (Ottawa: Library of Parliament).

5   Gaetz et al. (2013), op. cit.; Gouvernement du Québec (2014), *Ensemble, pour éviter la rue et en sortir: Politique nationale de lutte à l'itinérance* (Quebec City: Gou-vernement du Québec), <http://publications.msss.gouv.qc.ca/msss/fichiers/2013/13-846-03F.pdf>, accessed March 8, 2017.

6   Ibid.

7   Gouvernement du Québec (2014), op. cit.

8   Gaetz et al. (2013), op. cit.; Employment and Social Development Canada (2016), *Guide to Point-in-Time Counts in Canada of the Homelessness Partnering Strategy* (Ottawa: Government of Canada).

9   Latimer et al. (2015), op. cit.

10   Ibid.

11   Réseau d'aide aux personnes seules et itinérantes de Montréal (RAPSIM) (2016), *L'itinérance à Montréal, au-delà des chiffres* (Montreal: Réseau d'aide aux personnes seules et itinérantes de Montréal).

12 Gaetz et al. (2013), op. cit.; Lynn McDonald, Julie Dergal, and Laura Cleghorn (2007), "Living on the margins: Older homeless adults in Toronto," *Journal of Gerontological Social Work,* Vol. 49, No. 1–2, 19–46; Grenier et al. (2016), op. cit.; Jean Gagné and Mario Poirier (2013), "Vieillir dans la rue," *Relations,* No. 767, September, 33–35; Burns (2016), op. cit.; Victoria Burns, Amanda Grenier, Jean-Pierre Lavoie, David Rothwell, and Tamara Sussman (2012), "Les personnes âgées itinérantes – invisibles et exclues, une analyse de trois stratégies pour contrer l'itinérance," *Frontières,* Vol. 25, No. 1, 31–56.

13 McDonald et al. (2007), op. cit.

14 Gaetz et al. (2013), op. cit.

15 Burns (2015), op. cit.; Burns (2016), op. cit.

16 Centre d'étude sur la pauvreté et l'exclusion (2009), *Prendre la mesure de la pauvreté* (Quebec City: Gouvernement du Québec).

17 Gaetz et al. (2013), op. cit.

18 Maureen Crane and Anthony M. Warnes (2007), "The outcomes of rehousing older homeless people: A longitudinal study," *Ageing and Society,* Vol. 27, No. 6, 891–918.

19 Burns (2015), op. cit.; Burns (2016), op. cit.

20 Ibid.; Crane and Warnes (2007), op. cit.

21 McDonald et al. (2007), op. cit.; Crane and Warnes (2007), op. cit.; Burns (2016), op. cit.; Laura Hecht and Bonita Coyle (2001), "Elderly homeless: A comparison of older and younger adult emergency shelter seekers in Bakersfield, California," *American Behavioral Scientist,* Vo 45, No. 1, 66–79; Burns et al. (2012), op. cit.

22 Government of Canada website, "The Homelessness Partnering Strategy," <https://www.canada.ca/en/employment-social-development/programs/communities/homelessness.html>, accessed March 8, 2017.

23 Paula Goering, Scott Veldhulzen, Aimee Watson, Carol Adair, Brianna Kopp, Eric Latimer, Geoff Nelson, Eric MacNaughton, David Streiner, and Tim Aubry (2014), *National At Home/Chez Soi Final Report* (Calgary: Mental Health Commission of Canada), <http://www.homelesshub.ca/resource/national-homechez-soifinal-report#sthash.WyFxyqbj>, accessed March 8, 2017.

24 Burns et al. (2012), op. cit.; Burns (2015), op. cit.

25 Michèle Charpentier, Nancy Guberman, Véronique Billette, Jean-Pierre Lavoie, Amanda Grenier, and Ignace Olazabal (eds.) (2010), *Vieillir au pluriel. Perspectives sociales* (Quebec City: Presses de l'Université du Québec).

10

Are Penitentiaries Suitable Places for Older Inmates?

Michel Gagnon and Michel Dunn

Let's put seniors in prisons and criminals in seniors' homes.
——— Yves Carignan, "Un échange Prison contre CHSLD"[1]

Description and Origin of the Myth

The prison world is no doubt quite a mystery to most of us. The many movies and television shows set in prisons certainly pique the imagination, even though they often stray from reality. Understandably, however, they instill fear, and we tend to think that no one would willingly dare to consider spending time behind bars. Yet sometimes we hear that prison inmates are apparently treated better than are seniors in CHSLDs (centres d'hébergement de soins de longue durée, or residential long-term care centres). At least, those are the kinds of comments one reads on the Web or hears on call-in radio programs; this is the "Club Fed" myth (an allusion to Club Med holiday resorts). Some people even sarcastically suggest that their elderly parents should be placed in prisons and older inmates in CHSLDs.[2]

Why is this such a persistent myth? The first question might be whether the people who propagate it know much about prison life and, in particular, the living conditions of incarcerated seniors.

A report prepared for Public Safety and Emergency Preparedness Canada and the Correctional Service of Canada in 2005 provided a detailed survey of existing research findings on public perceptions of prison life. One of the report's principal findings was that "most participants admitted that they had little real idea of what inmates do all day in prison ... most participants admitted that they could only guess at what inmates do all day."[3] The researchers also found that the public generally believes prison life is easy. Without being provided any details about penitentiaries, people were asked whether conditions in those institutions were too harsh, about right, or too comfortable. Most responded that they were too comfortable, although they could not give reasons for their answers. Without knowing what actually happens in prisons, the public thus tends to imagine that inmates are treated too well.

But what causes this confusion? According to the same report, based on a thorough review of all surveys addressing the issue, the media were identified as the general public's primary source of information. "When asked to identify their main source of information about the correctional system, responses were evenly divided between newspaper stories and television news. This may well explain many of the misperceptions or stereotypes held by the public."[4] An article titled "Yoga et Zumba pour les détenus" (Yoga and Zumba for inmates), written by Marc-André Gagnon and published in the *Journal de Québec* on May 24, 2016, is a clear example of the type of media discourse that shapes the public's perception of prison as being too comfortable.[5]

Two Worlds Similar in Some Respects and Totally Different in Others

Here, we lift the veil on what actually goes on behind prison walls and examine the situation of older inmates in order to determine if their daily lives are similar to those of CHSLD residents. To make as accurate a comparison as possible with the situation of seniors who enter CHSLDs, we decided to focus on the experience of inmates who were already older at the time they were incarcerated.

We start by defining the two worlds. The mission of a CHSLD is "to offer, on a temporary or permanent basis, an alternative environment, lodging, assistance, support and supervision services as well as rehabilitation, psychosocial and nursing care and pharmaceutical and medical services to adults who, by reason of loss of functional or psychosocial autonomy can no longer live in their natural environment, despite the support of their families and friends."[6] In Canada, a penitentiary is a place of imprisonment, operating under federal government authority, to which the Correctional Service of

Canada confines persons who are required to serve sentences of two years or more "by exercising reasonable, safe, secure and humane control."[7]

A significant difference between these two types of institutions is immediately apparent: a CHSLD provides appropriate services to seniors, whereas a penitentiary protects the public by controlling incarcerated persons, regardless of their age, and no type of service suited to the needs of older inmates is offered. Older persons confined in penitentiaries are naturally presumed to have committed offences for which they have forfeited their right to freedom for periods of varying length, but their sentences should not preclude their right to safety or to bodily integrity.[8]

The Perspective of Territorial Exclusion

All too often, as some people advance in age, they experience situations of exclusion that affect their living conditions. Those situations may shape various aspects of everyday life, including perceptions and judgments expressed about seniors and aging; seniors' relationship to territory; their economic conditions; and the quantity and quality of care and services they receive. In the scientific literature, many authors have addressed these situations from the standpoint of exclusion, and it is from this perspective, particularly that of territorial exclusion, that we propose to analyze the myth that people are treated better in prisons than in CHSLDs.[9]

The myth that inmates live *la dolce vita* in prison may thus be considered from the standpoint of territorial exclusion. The focus here is how seniors who experience difficult situations as their territory shrinks to the size of a CHSLD are treated compared to seniors who are incarcerated in an equally restricted territory, that of a prison.

What is meant by "territorial exclusion?" This form of exclusion "is manifested in a reduction of geographic freedom, a confinement to isolated spaces ... a loss of control over one's living environment."[10] The degree to which this definition conjures up the situations of both older inmates and seniors living in CHSLDs is surprising, although some situations are specific to the territory of the prison.

The Abrupt Shift from Freedom to Prison

This morning, I was at home, in my house, surrounded by my loved ones and all my possessions ... This evening, I am confined to a cage, alone, and my only possessions are the clothes on my back. Those simple sentences, which any newly incarcerated person might say, accurately sum up the radical break from previous circumstances that occurs when one enters prison.

When severe disruptions (such as disease, death, or divorce) occur, normal life is seriously jeopardized, and we may even go so far as to question the meaning of life. But when such a destructive event occurs in one aspect of our lives, other, more stable, aspects come to the rescue, reassuring us and helping us find meaning and direction in life. However, for older persons who are suddenly incarcerated, everything collapses simultaneously, leaving them with no connection to their previous lives.[11]

Shock Amplified by Lack of Support

Imagine that you are 50, 60, 65, or even 75 years old and that you have been yanked from your familiar environment (home, neighbourhood, city, family and friends) and confined in a hostile environment – a maximum-security institution if you have been sentenced to life imprisonment. You have your cell, which measures little more than three by two metres and comes with steel doors or bars, stone walls and barbed-wire fences, armed guards, and cellmates (inmates) whom you have never met and may seem very threatening. You have now lost all your familiar bearings. Older inmates find themselves in a state of shock, and they experience strong feelings of loneliness, powerlessness, fear, despair, extreme sadness, and depression that, in many instances, may cause withdrawal and suicidal ideation.[12]

It might be tempting for some to liken the shock of incarceration to the one that seniors feel when they suddenly find themselves in a CHSLD following a stroke or serious fall that leaves them partially paralyzed. There are, indeed, some similarities in the feelings experienced in either situation, but seniors who find themselves in a CHSLD, regardless of the level of stress they feel, are being welcomed to a place where they are offered assistance, support, rehabilitation, and psychosocial, nursing, pharmaceutical, and medical care. In addition, the CHSLD environment has been designed for people who, like them, suffer from severe illnesses and disabilities.

Older inmates, on the other hand, have no one to hold their hand or to comfort and reassure them. In this territory, which is characterized more by control than assistance and support, physical and psychological violence are omnipresent in the form of round-the-clock surveillance, body and cell searches, rough physical intervention by guards, and shouting, verbal abuse, and assaults among inmates. All the inhabitants of this world are permanently on the defensive.

An Obstacle-Strewn Territory

Prisons were designed for younger, not older, people. Correctional personnel receive no training on issues relating to the problems of aging, and the vast majority of employees do not want to "take care" of older inmates. They see themselves as prison guards, not personal care attendants. There are also no attendants to assist older inmates with limited mobility with getting out of bed, washing, and dressing – not to mention the lack of a minimum level of resources, such as the additional blankets, mobility aids, and other accessories provided in CHSLDs.

Older inmates understand from the moment they arrive that their new territory will test them. They must share a minuscule cell with an often-younger cellmate who is disinclined to sympathize with an "old man's" problems. In that limited space, power relationships are frequently established that disadvantage the older inmate. CHSLDs are not ideal places, of course, but they are designed for an older, vulnerable clientele and are staffed accordingly.

Old prison buildings, made of steel and concrete, are always cold, damp, and inadequately lit. The noise of doors, loudspeakers, and arguments among inmates and between inmates and guards is constant and deafening. Moments of calm that might alleviate stress are few and far between.[13]

For inmates with mobility issues, their small space shrinks even further: the excessive number of stairways in prisons impedes their mobility and prevents them from going out into the yard and taking part in activities that might otherwise help relieve some of their distress. Many older inmates are thus confined to their cells, which only further exacerbates their territorial exclusion. Inmates with mobility problems may even find it difficult to get to the infirmary, a fact that undermines access to essential health services for aging persons. What would happen if a serious situation arose? There are no doctors on site to care for them.[14] The literature also indicates that older inmates are likely to experience regular ageism, intimidation, taunts, ridicule, humiliation, manipulation, harassment, and assaults.[15]

Impact of Confinement Conditions

What is the measurable impact of these difficult conditions of confinement on older inmates? Like many seniors, aging inmates are likely to have health problems associated with stroke, diabetes, arthritis, asthma, high blood pressure, and other conditions. What is alarming is that many inmates begin to experience these chronic health problems at the age of 50.[16] Consequently, the lower threshold used to define the older prison population is 50 years of age, not 65.[17]

A study conducted in Canadian penitentiaries in 2013 showed that the average age of inmates who had died from natural causes was 60.[18] As we know that the life expectancy of Canadians is 79 years for men and 83 years for women, we may assume that this fact is related to the harmful conditions of prison life for older inmates.[19] Another study shows that nearly one in two inmates experiences psychiatric problems.[20]

One national survey in the United States found that typical inmates in their fifties have the physical appearance and accompanying health problems of someone at least 10 years older.[21] This finding shows just how hard prison living conditions are.

It is therefore clear, in the present circumstances, that prison sentences for the commission of offences do not merely represent a loss of freedom for older persons. They also impose very difficult conditions that exacerbate the health problems associated with aging without guaranteeing the care needed to address those problems.

Conclusion

Although CHSLDs are far from ideal places in which to live, they clearly cannot be compared to prisons, which are not designed to meet the needs of older inmates. On the contrary: prisons are inappropriate places for persons suffering from the chronic disabilities and ailments that generally come with aging. This situation is concerning because no one, especially in Canada, should be faced with such a reality. Like many researchers, we believe that the solution entails an informed and responsible awareness of the current vulnerability of our older prison inmates.[22]

It is also clear to us that life in a CHSLD raises issues of isolation, care, and living conditions for seniors whose physical and mental abilities have declined. We therefore believe that comparing the living conditions of older inmates with those of CHSLD residents will not help us find solutions to their respective problems. Instead, our best chance to improve the lives of older people is to encourage researchers and decision makers to address both realities and to combine the efforts of all stakeholders involved. In our view, this joint effort must shape the future and the development of an inclusive and pluralistic society.

Notes

1 Yves Carignan (2011), "Un échange Prison contre CHSLD," *Blogue en plan*, February 4, <http://www.yvescarignan.com/2011/02/>, accessed February 20, 2017 (our translation).

2 Ibid.

3 Julian V. Roberts (2005), *Literature Review on Public Opinion and Corrections: Recent Findings in Canada*, Report for the Correctional Service of Canada, Ottawa, March 31, 3, <https://www.csc-scc.gc.ca/text/pa/ev-pblc-op/public_opinion_e.pdf>.

4 Ibid., 11.

5 Marc-André Gagnon (2016), "Yoga et Zumba pour les détenus," *Journal de Québec*, May 24, <http://www.joumaldequebec.com/2016/05/24/yogaet-zumba-pour-les -detenus>, accessed February 20, 2017.

6 *Act respecting health services and social services*, updated to November 1, 2016, s. 83, <http://legisquebec.gouv.qc.ca/en/pdf/cs/S-4.2.pdf>, accessed February 20, 2017.

7 Mission statement of the Correctional Service of Canada (2017), <https://www.csc -scc.gc.ca/publications/005007-3002-eng.shtml>, accessed February 20, 2017.

8 *Solosky v. The Queen* (1979), 50 CCC (2d) 495.

9 Nancy Guberman and Jean-Pierre Lavoie (2012), "Politiques sociales, personnes âgées et proches aidants au Québec: sexisme et exclusion," *Canadian Woman Studies/Les Cahiers de la femme*, Vol. 29, No. 3, 61–70; Thomas Scharf and Norah Keating (eds.) (2012), *From Exclusion to Inclusion in Old Age: A Global Challenge* (Bristol: Policy Press); Véronique Billette and Jean-Pierre Lavoie (2010), "Introduction. Vieillissements, exclusions sociales et solidarités," in Michèle Charpentier, Nancy Guberman, Véronique Billette, Jean-Pierre Lavoie, Amanda Grenier, and Ignace Olazabal (eds.), *Vieillir au pluriel. Perspectives sociales* (Quebec City: Presses de l'Université du Québec), 1–22; Jean-François Bickel and Stefano Cavalli (2002), "De l'exclusion dans les dernières étapes du parcours de vie. Un survol," *Gérontologie et société*, Vol. 3, No. 102, 25–40.

10 Billette and Lavoie (2010), op. cit. (our translation).

11 Elaine Crawley and Richard Sparks (2006), "Older men in prison: Survival, coping and identity," in Alison Liebling and Shadd Maruna (eds.), *The Effects of Imprisonment* (Cambridge: Willan Publishing), 348, 349. In this paragraph, we present a brief summary of the situation described by Crawley and Sparks, who, in turn, drew on the remarks of Stanley Cohen and Laurie Taylor (1972), *Psychological Survival* (Harmondsworth: Penguin), 53. We suggest that the reader consult these authors for a clear understanding of the seriousness of the specific moment when previous life ends.

12 Ronald H. Aday (2003), *Aging Prisoners, Crisis in American Corrections* (Westport: Praeger), 114.

13 All the facts cited in this paragraph are noted in the annual reports of the Correctional Investigator of Canada published from 2010 to 2014. Office of the Correctional Investigator of Canada (2010, 2011, 2012, 2013, 2014), *Annual Reports of the Office of the Correctional Investigator* (Ottawa), <https://www.oci-bec.gc.ca/cnt/rpt/index -eng.aspx>, accessed February 20, 2017.

14 Office of the Correctional Investigator of Canada (2014), *Annual Report 2013–2014* (Ottawa), 19, <https://www.oci-bec.gc.ca/cnt/rpt/pdf/annrpt/annrpt20132014-eng. pdf>, accessed February 20, 2017: "Most federal penitentiaries lack 24/7 health care staffing."

15 Office of the Correctional Investigator of Canada (2011), *Annual Report 2010–2011* (Ottawa), 21–22, <https://www.oci-bec.gc.ca/cnt/rpt/pdf/annrpt/annrpt20102011 -eng.pdf>, accessed February 20, 2017.

16 Aday (2003), op. cit., 16.

17 Ibid.

18 Office of the Correctional Investigator of Canada (2014), op. cit., 29.

19 Life expectancy figures according to Statistics Canada data published in 2012, <https://www150.statcan.gc.ca/n1/pub/91-215-x/2012000/part-partie2-eng.htm>, accessed February 20, 2017.

20 Susan Baidawi, Shelley Turner, Christopher Trotter, Colette Browning, Paul Collier, Daniel O'Connor, and Rosemary Sheehan (2011), "Older prisoners: A challenge for Australian corrections," *Trends and Issues in Crime and Criminal Justice*, Australian Government, Australian Institute of Criminology, No. 426, August; Aday (2003), op. cit.

21 Aday (2003), op. cit.

22 Ibid.; Crawley and Sparks (2006), op. cit.

Part 3
DIFFERENT AGING EXPERIENCES

11

Older Adults Living with Mental Health Problems

"Nothing More Can Be Done with Them"

Ginette Aubin and Bernadette Dallaire

My mother is 70 years old. After several bouts of depression, she was placed in a psychiatric hospital at her request. She was treated only with drugs and, when released, given a prescription for her rheumatism. The doctor whom I spoke to about her therapy told me that at 70 years of age, it was too late for my mother, and that it was now only a matter of geriatrics.

———— Experts' answers to questions on the "Psychologies" website[1]

Some people continue to have preconceptions about older adults, believing that they are "rigid and inflexible" in their attitudes and behaviours, and that therefore their condition cannot be expected to improve or change.[2] Such beliefs are even more prevalent with respect to adults who, in addition to being older, live with mental health problems. An illness such as depression, accompanied by symptoms of insomnia, sadness, and weight loss, is often downplayed and considered something that is to be expected as people age.[3] Such mental health problems may be perceived as a weakness or flaw for which the person is responsible – as something that must be hidden or gotten rid of in order to avoid embarrassing or disgracing his or her family.[4]

Moreover, behaviours that include talking to oneself or interacting with others in an unusual way contribute to the perception that people with such issues are "not all there."[5] Observing behaviours of this kind can confirm or amplify such beliefs by reinforcing fears and prejudices. These representations may also be internalized by seniors, who therefore do not want to be associated with mental illness. People experiencing mental health problems are uncomfortable and ashamed about it, and they sometimes deliberately avoid seeking help.[6] Furthermore, some older adults may believe that it is too late to start a treatment such as psychotherapy.[7] At the same time, some practitioners fear that speaking about recovery when patients present functional and cognitive loss may give false hope to them and their family members.[8] Attitudes of this kind are even more pronounced when it comes to older people with serious mental health problems such as schizophrenia.[9]

Believing that seniors with mental health problems have few needs is singularly unhelpful. This view seems to be substantiated by the all-too-common sight of older adults sitting passively in front of the television set in the common area of their residential care home. In these and similar settings, everything is organized and planned and the daily lives of the residents are managed by others, leaving them with little power over their own lives.[10] Inactivity, passivity, and lack of initiative typify their days.[11] It must not be forgotten, however, that these traits are neither voluntary nor normal among older people; rather, they are the outcome of several factors, including the fact that, in most cases, they did not choose their environment and living conditions. To these factors must be added the internalization of negative beliefs about themselves, which further amplifies their stigmatization (being socially identified or labelled in negative terms). Older people like these are therefore faced with two forms of stigmatization: they are both "old" and "crazy."[12]

What Do We Know about Seniors Living with Mental Health Problems?

Some seniors with mental health issues may have had them since earlier in their lives and have undergone one or more acute episodes (requiring hospitalization, for example). When they have recovered, or when treatment has mitigated their symptoms, many resume their previous roles and activities (including work, recreation, and contributing responsibly to society) – in some cases by adapting their roles and activities to their new circumstances. The trajectories of older adults with mental disorders thus cover a wide spectrum, ranging from severe disability and acute social isolation to a level of social functioning and integration similar to that of their fellow citizens.[13] Others may have received their first diagnosis at a more advanced age and now have to deal with new mental health problems such as depression or anxiety disorders (e.g., generalized anxiety, anxiety attacks, or panic attacks). Still others will never consult healthcare professionals for such problems, even though their symptoms are serious and sometimes lead to self-neglect and even suicidal ideation or acts.[14]

Regardless of the chronological course of a given mental health problem or the stage of life at which it emerges, its effects, such as sadness, passivity, and loss of pleasure, are not "normal" states or traits of aging.[15] In many instances, these effects stem from environmental factors, including living conditions and caregivers' lack of knowledge, with the result that older adults become isolated and do not have access to services that might benefit them.[16] The problems experienced by older adults may also be related to the distress of different kinds of mourning – due not only to the loss of those dear to them, but to loss of their independence and their separation from a home that they liked or that was meaningful to them or from a lifestyle (see Chapter 22, "How Older Adults Experience Bereavement").[17] Poverty, extreme vulnerability, loss of dignity and self-esteem, loss of empowerment, broken social ties, and the internalization of negative labels are thus all factors that can affect these seniors' everyday experience.[18] Recent advances in research, however, show that it is both possible and necessary to go beyond such negative views.

Steps to Take

Aging with a mental health problem does not always equate with functional decline or with treatment in a psychiatric or geriatric institution.[19] We now know more about how seniors with mental health problems feel about their specific needs in various spheres of life (e.g., accommodation, care, services, and social contacts) – needs that differ significantly from those of younger people.[20] The needs most frequently cited by older people in both urban and rural settings include having meaningful activities, a social network, and support for their families. The need for services, especially counselling, psychotherapy, and physical care, was also identified as among the most important.[21] The studies that led to these findings concluded that new strategies must be developed to better address seniors' needs and aspirations.[22]

To deal with these issues, the Mental Health Commission of Canada has made a number of recommendations about mental health services for older adults.[23] The recommendations focus on a number of priorities, including

1) promotion of mental health; 2) prevention and early identification of mental health problems; 3) establishment of an integrated mental health service system with due regard for seniors' medical, functional, and psycho-social needs; and 4) implementation of principles and guidelines that priori-tize older adults' self-determination and social inclusion, and the belief that they have the ability to achieve wellness, respect, and equity. Recognition of the lifetime accomplishments and contribution to society of older people is one of the core values upon which these recommendations are based. There-fore, interventions with the general population are recommended, with a focus on aspects such as public awareness about the myths and stigmatiz-ation surrounding aging and mental illness. The commission also recom-mends that practitioners receive specific training.

With respect to the individual needs of older adults living with mental health problems, the recommendations include interventions aiming to sup-port the social participation of seniors insofar as they wish to become in-volved. These interventions include helping seniors to develop social skills and adopt strategies to improve memory, organizational proficiency, and building a positive self-image.[24] The research findings show that older adults can learn new things, and that doing so improves their social functioning and integration into the community.[25]

Other innovative interventions currently being developed are based on individual and personalized assistance with social participation and on sen-iors' participation in group workshops, available through community and health and social services networks, to enhance the process of community inclusion.[26] Alongside these efforts, new research is emerging on older adults with serious mental health issues, an area that was largely neglected until only a few years ago.[27] A number of these pioneering studies are based on the "recovery" approach. Mental health recovery, which was in-itially developed for other age groups, requires a transformation of rela-tionships between individuals and their environments. Recovery means embarking on a process that is focused not on problems but on the renewal of one's vision of oneself and one's life. This approach also promotes princi-ples that foster an enhanced quality of life in the community: 1) empower-ment – the ability to take independent action, which means having choices, the power to make decisions, and the ability to apply these decisions in everyday life, particularly in one's living environment; and 2) social inclu-sion, if desired, which means belonging to networks of relatives, friends, and neighbours with whom one can take part in activities, play positive roles, obtain support, and be appreciated.[28]

The mental health field also includes an important prevention and promotion component, which has become a reality in recent years thanks, in part, to the adoption of campaigns to counter the stigmatization both of mental illness and of seeking help to address it. These awareness campaigns, and their messages along the lines of "Seeking help is okay, positive, brave, normal, and nothing to be ashamed of," have been aimed primarily at young people and members of the labour force. However, the "Let's Talk" campaign has not yet asked seniors to do the talking.[29]

The current silence that surrounds our older fellow citizens is, we feel, a message in itself. It is a message in which the "social invisibility" of seniors with regard to mental health is rooted in beliefs that conflate two worlds, each of which is symbolically loaded with taboos and apprehensions: mental illness and the image of a "nutcase" on the one hand, and stereotypes about old age and "old people" on the other.

In this context, increasing efforts are being made by a growing number of diverse groups to combat stigmatization and exclusion in society. However, the challenges involved in accessing services and resources, and in social inclusion and recovery, apply particularly to older adults with mental health problems. That being the case, how can practitioners, families, citizens, and communities support these individuals? The (few) existing studies show that, like their young and not-so-young counterparts, seniors with mental health problems not only can develop or revive the skills needed for everyday interactions but can also find or recover the desire to reach out to others and play a larger role in the community. To promote and support this aspiration to reforge such social ties, the various categories of actors in the immediate circle of these seniors (families, neighbourhoods, and public, private, and community organizations) must, in return, develop or provide as much as they can of the physical, material, and human support required.[30] The bottom line is that everyone needs to be mobilized to establish ways and means that are truly inclusive for these older adults. Such an effort could include measures that focus specifically on mental health issues, as well as programs, services, and interventions of a more general nature, such as combatting isolation and ensuring access to transportation and affordable housing.

Nothing More to Be Done – Really?

We have found that older adults with mental health problems are living in a society that all too often seems to ignore them. What can we say about this invisibility? The suffering senior holds a mirror up to us, and when we look into it, what we see is not a stranger but our own potential future – another "older" self that we do not wish to see because we find it painful or frightening. Yet, we need to learn how to look these fellow citizens fearlessly in the eye and recognize their resilience, strengths, abilities, and, especially, their desire to enjoy a better quality of life and to age in a better way ... *together with the rest of us.* We now have a much clearer idea about what needs to be done to embrace them. We can – if we want to – recognize that, contrary to common assumptions, there is definitely much that "can be done" with these older men and women. Are we up for the challenge?

Notes

1   Experts' answers to questions on the "Psychologies" website: <http://www.psychologies. com/Therapies/Toutes-les-therapies/Psychotherapies/Reponses-d-expert/70-ans -est-ce-trop-tard-pour-entreprendre-une-therapie>, accessed March 13, 2017 (our translation).

2   Charlotte Herrick, Lynne Pearcey, and Candace Ross (1997), "Stigma and ageism: Compounding influences in making an accurate mental health assessment," *Nursing Forum*, Vol. 32, No. 3, 21–26; World Health Organization and World Psychiatric Association (2002), *Reducing Stigma and Discrimination against Older People with Mental Disorders: A Technical Consensus Statement* (Geneva: Department of Mental Health and Substance Abuse, WHO).

3   Kareen Nour, Bernadette Dallaire, Alan Regenstreif, Mona Hébert, and Nina Moscovitz (2010), "Santé mentale et vieillissement. Problèmes, répercussions et services," in Michèle Charpentier, Nancy Guberman, Véronique Billette, Jean-Pierre Lavoie, Amanda Grenier, and Ignace Olazabal (eds.), *Vieillir au pluriel. Perspectives sociales* (Quebec City: Presses de l'Université du Québec), 135–60.

4   Elizabeth Flanagan and Larry Davidson (2009), "Passing for 'normal': Features that affect the community inclusion of people with mental illness," *Psychiatric Rehabilitation Journal*, Vol. 33, No. 1, 18–25.

5   Ibid.

6   Daniel Jimenez, Stephen Bartels, Veronica Cardenas, and Margarita Alegría (2013), "Stigmatizing attitudes toward mental illness among racial/ethnic older adults in primary care," *International Journal of Geriatric Psychiatry*, Vol. 28, No. 10, 1061–68.

7   Daniela Gonçalves, Carlos Coelho, and Gerard Byrne (2014), "The use of healthcare services for mental health problems by middle-aged and older adults," *Archives of Gerontology and Geriatrics*, Vol. 59, No. 2, 393–97.

8   Roderick McKay, Regina McDonald, David Lie, and Helen McGowan (2012), "Reclaiming the best of the biopsychosocial model of mental and 'recovery' for older people through a 'person-centred' approach," *Australasian Psychiatry*, Vol. 20, No. 6, 492–95.

9   Paul Meesters, Max Stek, Hannie Comijs, Lieuwe de Haan, Thomas Patterson, Piet Eikelenboom, and Aartjan Beekman (2010), "Social functioning among older community-dwelling patients with schizophrenia: A review," *American Journal of Geriatric Psychiatry*, Vol. 18, No. 10, 862–78.

10 Gunilla Martinsson, Ingegerd Fagerberg, Christina Lindholm, and Lena Wiklund-Gustin (2012), "Struggling for existence – Life situation experiences of older persons with mental disorders," *International Journal of Qualitative Studies on Health and Well-Being*, Vol. 7, <https://www.ncbi.nlm.nih.gov/pmc/articles/PMC3371755/>.

11 Monica Nordström, Anna Dunér, Elisabeth Olin, and Helle Wijk (2009), "Places, social relations and activities in the everyday lives of older adults with psychiatric disabilities: An interview study," *International Psychogeriatrics*, Vol. 21, No. 2, 401–12.

12 Bernadette Dallaire, Michael McCubbin, Mélanie Provost, Normand Carpentier, and Michèle Clément (2010), "Cheminements et situations de vie des personnes âgées présentant des troubles mentaux graves: perspectives d'intervenants psycho-sociaux," *La Revue canadienne du vieillissement / Canadian Journal on Aging*, Vol. 29, No. 2, 267–79.

13 Meesters et al. (2010), op. cit.

14 Nour et al. (2010), op. cit.

15 Philippe Thomas and Cyril Hazif-Thomas (2008), "Les nouvelles approches de la dépression de la personne âgée," *Gérontologie et société*, Vol. 3, No. 126, 141–55.

16 Stephen Bartels (2011), "Commentary: The forgotten older adult with serious mental illness: The final challenge in achieving the promise of Olmstead?," *Journal of Aging and Social Policy*, Vol. 23, No. 3, 244–57; Marja Depla, Ron de Graaf, Jooske van Busschbach, and Thea Heeren (2003), "Community integration of elderly mentally ill persons in psychiatric hospitals and two types of residences," *Psychiatric Services*, Vol. 54, No. 5, 730–35.

17 Jacqueline Corcoran, Emily Brown, Megan Davis, Michelle Pineda, Jessica Kadolph, and Holly Bell (2013), "Depression in older adults: A meta-synthesis," *Journal of Gerontological Social Work*, Vol. 56, No. 6, 509–34.

18 Martinsson et al. (2012), op. cit.; Bernadette Dallaire, Michael McCubbin, and Mélanie Prévost (2010), "Vieillissement et trouble mental grave: questions de représentations, questions d'intervention," in Martine Lagacé (ed.), *L'âgisme: comprendre et changer le regard social sur le vieillissement* (Quebec City: Presses de l'Université Laval); Lydia Ogden (2014), "Interpersonal relationship narratives of older adults with schizophrenia-spectrum diagnoses," *American Journal of Orthopsychiatry*, Vol. 84, No. 6, 674–84.

19 Bartels (2011), op. cit.

20 Michel Bédard, Carrie Gibbons, and Sacha Dubois (2007), "The needs of rural and urban young, middle-aged and older adults with a serious mental illness," *Canadian Journal of Rural Medicine*, Vol. 12, No. 3, 167–75.

21 Shuli Futeran and Brian Draper (2011), "An examination of the needs of older patients with chronic mental illness in public mental health services," *Aging and Mental Health*, Vol. 16, No. 3, 327–34.

22   Including Bédard et al. (2007), op. cit., and Futeran and Draper (2011), op. cit.
23   Penny MacCourt, Kimberley Wilson, and Marie-France Tourigny-Rivard (2011), "Guidelines for comprehensive mental health services for older adults in Canada," Calgary, Mental Health Commission of Canada, <https://www.mentalhealth commission.ca/sites/default/files/2017-09/mhcc_seniors_guidelines_0.pdf>, accessed March 13, 2017.
24   Stephen Bartels and Sarah Pratt (2009), "Psychosocial rehabilitation and quality of life for older adults with serious mental illness: Recent findings and future research directions," *Current Opinion in Psychiatry*, Vol. 22, No. 4, 381–85.
25   Ibid.
26   Ginette Aubin, Manon Parisien, Pierre-Yves Therriault, Kareen Nour, Véronique Billette, Anne-Marie Belley, and Bernadette Dallaire (2015), "Développement de programmes visant à soutenir l'autonomie de l'intégration dans la communauté d'aînés ayant une problématique de santé mentale," *Vie et vieillissement*, Vol. 13, No. 1, 11–16; Ginette Aubin, Manon Parisien, Norma Gilbert, Bernadette Dallaire, Véronique Billette, and Julie Beauchamp (2019), "The Count Me In! Program: An Innovative Approach to Supporting Community Participation for Seniors Living with Psychosocial Difficulties," *Canadian Journal of Community Mental Health*, Vol. 38, No. 1, 61–65.
27   Dallaire, McCubbin, and Prévost (2010), op. cit.; Bartels and Pratt (2009), op. cit.; Stephanie Daley, David Newton, Mike Slade, Joanna Murray, and Sube Banerjee (2013), "Development of a framework for recovery in older people with mental disorder," *International Journal of Geriatric Psychiatry*, Vol. 28, No. 5, 522–29.
28   Dallaire, McCubbin, and Prévost (2010), op. cit.; Daley et al. (2013), op. cit.
29   We are referring here to the slogan used in a recent Canada-wide campaign sponsored by a well-known private foundation.
30   Joy Baumgartner and Jonathan Burns (2014), "Measuring social inclusion – A key outcome in global mental health," *International Journal of Epidemiology*, Vol. 43, No. 2, 354–64; Sean Kidd, Tyler Frederick, Lesley Tarasoff, Gursharan Virdee, Steve Lurie, Larry Davidson, David Morris, and Kwame McKenzie (2016), "Locating community among people with schizophrenia living in a diverse urban environment," *American Journal of Psychiatric Rehabilitation*, Vol. 19, No. 2, 103–21.

12

Aging with Intellectual and Developmental Disabilities
The Myth of the Eternal Child

Daniel Dickson

> Although little attention has been paid to the matter thus far, it is fairly clear today that the aging of people with PDD (pervasive developmental disorders) and their family members must be taken into consideration when defining service offerings. When parents die or are no longer able to take care of their child, it creates another major transition period entailing special needs.[1]
>
> ——— Québec Ombudsman, *Services for Young People and Adults with a Pervasive Developmental Disorder,* 2012

The Presentation of the Myth

Disability is something we are commonly thought to age into. Indeed, familiar narratives of aging into functional decline dominate popular discourse and obscure the divergent narratives of those who age *with* disability. In particular, this perpetuates the exclusion of people with intellectual and developmental disabilities (IDD) who have historically been marginalized through exclusionary practices such as institutionalization. At the root of this exclusion lies the notion that people with IDD are incapable of appropriate social functioning, propelled by the myth that these individuals age as "eternal children." This myth, based on the fallacy that people with IDD never develop beyond childhood, is evident in exclusionary practices that have limited their access to key areas of social citizenship such as employment and education.

In Quebec, these exclusionary practices have begun to be challenged by progressive policies that have ended the era of institutionalization and attempted to root out stigmatization and discrimination. At the same time, owing to dramatic improvements in life expectancy resulting from healthcare advancements and deinstitutionalization, Canadians with IDD are increasingly living into older age. However, provincial programs to increase social participation have focused almost exclusively on children and young adults, to the detriment of older adults with IDD. As the epigraph to this chapter shows, older adults with IDD have long been overlooked in the social services landscape, in part because they are seen as frozen in a state of dependence and reliance on their families. Moreover, in a social services context dominated by narratives of austerity, older adults with IDD are often the first victims of service cuts, as evidenced by recent developments in Quebec.[2] The prevailing sentiment seems to be that governments are willing to invest in social services for people with IDD only when there is a chance that they can contribute meaningfully to the economy through participation in the labour force. Although this strategy may ultimately lead to greater social participation for all people with IDD, it does nothing to overcome current barriers to participation for older adults with IDD, including pervasive stereotypes such as the eternal child myth.

How does this myth affect the intersection of aging and disability? Does it keep people with IDD from having an authentic and complete experience of older adulthood? To address these questions, I review the existing literature on this myth and apply the concepts therein to the specific case of older adults with IDD in Quebec.

The Myth of the Eternal Child

The myth of the eternal child originates from the broader stereotype of disability as a personal tragedy, in which the social exclusion of people with disabilities is justified by their perceived incapacity to perform tasks deemed integral to social functioning.[3] For people with IDD, this inadequacy is tied to the perception of low intelligence. This negative social construct is the foundation of the eternal child myth, which, like other stereotypes – such as the "village idiot" and the "dumb ox" – imposes a negative social role by emphasizing a perceived inability to adapt to or participate in social life within the larger community.[4] The social exclusion that results from this perceived inadequacy informs a system of disability services that act to create and legitimize the dependency of individuals with IDD.[5] In fact, the stereotype is attached to a long, culturally embedded history that is disconnected from the effects of specific impairments on an individual's capacity for social functioning.

The eternal child myth has persisted historically because centuries of exclusion through institutionalization – along with misdiagnosis and limited medical understanding – meant that children with IDD almost never survived to old age.[6] Institutionalization occurred early in life, when children were removed from their parents – voluntarily, or occasionally by government order – and placed in rural institutions, hidden away from the public eye, where they endured abhorrent conditions, various forms of abuse, and invasive medical practices such as overmedication and sterilization.[7] Thus, the myth may have originated because people with IDD were effectively made invisible throughout their lives. Indeed, prior to the late 1980s old age was not even broadly recognized as a separate stage of adult development for people with IDD.[8] Obviously, this dark era of institutionalization created the conditions for misconceptions, misunderstandings, and myths to emerge. Moreover, medical and social services systems authorized these exclusionary practices, thereby validating the public perceptions of abnormality and deviance that are the foundation of reductive stereotypes.

Recent advances in social integration – through deinstitutionalization and increased access to social functions such as education and employment – have acted to raise the visibility of people with IDD. Similarly, increased income-support funding and quality-of-life improvements in the areas of nutrition, living conditions, and access to health services have resulted in a sharp rise in life expectancy for people with IDD over the past three decades.[9] More policies have emerged to promote social inclusion and active participation among Canadians with disabilities since their full citizenship was legislatively enshrined in the *In Unison* report of 1998.[10] Despite these advances, however, the eternal child myth persists in modern social constructs of IDD, as is evidenced by research in numerous areas.

First, the myth is evident in cultural representations in which characters with IDD are commonly portrayed as innocent and child-like, awkward and asexual, and ultimately made different by their dependence on others. Portrayals of IDD in popular movies such as *Forrest Gump* (1994) and *Rain Man* (1988) have demonstrated elements of the eternal child stereotype: the asexual and isolated Forrest, and Raymond the antisocial, autistic savant who proves incapable of functioning outside of the institution.[11] This is not to suggest that these characteristics cannot occur among individuals within the diverse population of people with IDD, just as they do within other identity categories. Instead, the point of identifying common disability stereotypes in popular media is to examine how these representations reinforce and lend credibility to the myths from which they are derived. Indeed, both of the movies mentioned above received the Academy Award for best picture despite their reductive, stereotypical portrayals of characters with IDD. Recent movies have offered more nuanced portrayals of IDD, such as Louise Archambault's *Gabrielle* (2013), in which the title character's autonomy is thematically explored through her pursuit of a romantic relationship with another adult with IDD. However, although Archambault explicitly critiques the attitudes that inform social exclusion, she overlooks the eternal child myth by framing the title character's reluctant dependence on neurotypical adults as her major crisis.

Beyond fictional representation, the eternal child myth is also apparent within the education, employment, and health and social services sectors. It is especially evident when statistical metrics such as IQ, brain age, and autonomy measurements are used to justify the exclusion of people with IDD from access to more general services. These services see independence as the end result of personal development – of growth out of childhood. This service focus is consistent with the theory of successful aging, which emphasizes maintaining independence by avoiding disability and disease, maintaining high cognitive and physical function, and engaging actively with life.[12] Within this context, all people with IDD are bound from birth to be deemed unsuccessful in these critical hallmarks of personal development. Therefore, social services seemingly exist not to target barriers to inclusion but to show compassion for those who will never live a truly fulfilled life. This may help to explain why, despite policies attempting to increase their inclusion, people with IDD are still largely absent from social functions such as education, employment, and political participation.[13] Thus, the act of socially constructing people with IDD as eternal children both allows for their exclusion and legitimizes exerting control over them.

Deconstructing the Myth

Older adults with IDD are a relatively new population in terms of visibility and social acceptance. Academic studies addressing this growing population have only recently emerged in the fields of social work, sociology, psychology, and public policy. These studies provide important evidence that contradicts the eternal child myth and disrupts the universality of the "aging into disability" narrative of decline in older adulthood.

One promising area of research has demonstrated how the idea of successful aging is incompatible with the experiences of older adults who are aging *with* disabilities. This work has been heavily influenced by the understanding that what "disables" an individual has more to do with cultural expectations, social constructs, or myths about disability than with the specific impairments experienced by disabled individuals. In other words, this social model sees disability as the disadvantage imposed upon individuals with one or multiple impairments by barriers that deny them true inclusion in society.[14] From this foundation, successful aging has been critiqued for overgeneralizing the experiences of older adults. By generalizing the numerous intersectional identities that exist within the broader category of "older adult," public policies promote the exclusion of older adults with disabilities.[15] Given that one of the key goals of successful aging is to encourage participation in activities of daily life, accounting for the identities of older adults with IDD could enrich this theory and expand its application. In order for this to occur, however, a broader understanding of what is unique to the experiences of older adults with IDD must spread to challenge powerful stereotypes.

Social inclusion requires allowing older adults with IDD to be visible and have a voice. To this end, new participatory research strategies seek to involve older adults with IDD in sharing their unique experiences while simultaneously testing existing theories related to aging and disability. The added benefit of these strategies is that they enable study participants from underresearched populations to have input into the project design, analysis, and dissemination of findings. In one recent study, older adults aging with disabilities were asked to create photo-novels to express what social participation meant to them.[16] The project sought to directly explore the similarities and differences among these unique experiences of aging and to compare them with common stereotypes or myths. The participants identified numerous activities that they engaged in – often with accommodations to overcome barriers – that represented meaningful social participation to them, deconstructing the myth of the disengaged older adult. Moreover, they indicated that over the course of their lives, they had developed effective strategies for dealing with the stigmatization associated with dependency, which they identified as the biggest factor in their marginalization as older adults with lifelong disabilities.[17] As a result, their narratives directly contradict the notion that dependency impedes personal growth or development, and they thus pose a significant challenge to the eternal child myth.

Similarly, research focused on the experiences of older adults with IDD within specific social services settings has found evidence that individuals develop strategies to deal with stigma over the lifecourse. One important study found that older adults with IDD are, on average, more independent and competent than younger adults with IDD, thus requiring less assistance from support staff, even though their age is often used as an excuse to exclude them from services targeting personal growth and development.[18] Again, an important implication of this evidence is that significant social adaptation and personal growth occurs among this population over the course of their lives, contradicting the eternal child stereotype. To specifically address this stereotype, an exhaustive study on service delivery in Australia, the UK, and the United States finds that person-centred planning has the potential to overcome the biases that characterize older adults with IDD as wholly dependent.[19] This same study concludes that planning is more likely to be successful when significant flexibility is provided to match tools and resources with intended outcomes and staff are trained to specifically confront stereotypes when they interact with the public.[20] Once again, this research emphasizes the involvement of older adults with IDD in establishing priorities and choosing outcomes for the services that they receive in order to better serve their unique requirements and debunk the persistent myths that act against their inclusion.

Conclusion

The biggest obstacle to pursuing successful person-centred outcomes for older adults with IDD may be resource scarcity in the social services system. This is not to suggest that person-centred care is too expensive to implement. On the contrary, it is already a significant element of health and social service planning at various levels of government in Canada. To address the root of exclusion of people with IDD, however, it is necessary to take aim at the logic that makes it possible, and therein lies the problem. The logic of exclusion is deeply embedded in political institutions, social service structures, and broader attitudes, as is evidenced by the persistence of the eternal child myth. Disrupting this logic is a monumental task, particularly in relation to other social service priorities.

People with IDD make up only 0.4 percent of the Canadian population 65 years and older.[21] This equates to approximately 23,000 Canadians, and likely fewer than 10,000 Quebecers. Many within this small population are survivors of institutions, carrying a legacy that uniquely influences the types of services and supports that they require relative to future cohorts of older adults with IDD.[22] Therefore, it might be difficult to rationalize significant government expenditure to address the problem of exclusion for this specific population, even though prominent officials have identified the need.[23] Perhaps rather than increasing services and supports under the logic of the existing paradigm, what is required is an investment in *increasing* the autonomy of this vulnerable group when it comes to shaping their collective narrative. If the myths and stereotypes that act to constrain their social opportunities are debunked, older adults with IDD may one day come to be recognized and celebrated as equal partners in the mosaic of intersecting identities under the umbrella of aging and the Quebec identity more generally.

Notes

1   Québec Ombudsman (2012), *Services for Young People and Adults with a Pervasive Developmental Disorder: From Government Commitment to Cold Hard Facts* (Quebec City: Direction des communications, 2012), 62.

2   In 2017, CBC reported that a Montreal rehabilitation centre cut day program services for over 100 adults, targeting all clients who were over 55 years of age because they were "without any hope of improvement." See <https://www.cbc.ca/news/canada/montreal/outcry-over-service-cuts-for-severely-disabled-unreasonable-says-health-authority-senior-manager-1.4418696>.

3   Michael Oliver and Colin Barnes (2012), *The New Politics of Disablement* (New York: Palgrave Macmillan).

4   Wolf Wolfensberger (2000), "A brief overview of social role valorization," *Mental Retardation*, Vol. 38, No. 2, 105–23.

5   Oliver and Barnes (2012), op. cit., 137.

6   Nancy Breitenbach (2001), "Ageing with Intellectual disabilities; Discovering disability with old age: Same or different?," in Mark Priestley (ed.), *Disability and the Life Course: Global Perspectives* (Cambridge and New York: Cambridge University Press).

7   Raymond A. Lemay (2009), "Deinstitutionalization of people with developmental disabilities: A review of the literature," *Canadian Journal of Community Mental Health*, Vol. 28, No. 1, 181–94.

8   Alan Walker and Carol Walker (1998), "Normalisation and 'normal' ageing: The social construction of dependency among older people with learning difficulties," *Disability & Society*, Vol. 13, No. 1, 126.

9   Shahin Shooshtari, Saba Naghipur, and Jin Zhang (2012), "Unmet healthcare and social services needs of older canadian adults with developmental disabilities," *Journal of Policy and Practice in Intellectual Disabilities*, Vol. 9, No. 2, 81.

10 Michael J. Prince (2009), *Absent Citizens: Disability Politics and Policy in Canada* (Toronto: University of Toronto Press).

11   Fiona Whittington-Walsh (2002), "From freaks to savants: Disability and hegemony from the Hunchback of Notre Dame (1939) to Sling Blade (1997)," *Disability & Society*, Vol. 17, No. 6, 695–707.

12   John W. Rowe and Robert L. Kahn (1997), "Successful aging," *The Gerontologist*, Vol. 37, No. 4, 433–40.

13   Prince (2009), op. cit.

14   Oliver and Barnes (2012), op. cit.

15   Meredith Minkler and Pamela Fadem (2002), "'Successful aging': A disability perspective," *Journal of Disability Policy Studies*, Vol. 12, No. 4, 229–35.

16   Emilie Raymond and Amanda Grenier (2015), "Social participation at the intersection of old age and lifelong disability: Illustrations from a photo-novel project," *Journal of Aging Studies*, Vol. 35, 190–200.

17   Ibid., 198.

18   Walker and Walker (1998), op. cit.

19   Christine Bigby (2004), *Ageing with a Lifelong Disability: A Guide to Practice, Program, and Policy Issues for Human Services Professionals* (London and New York: Jessica Kingsley).

20   Ibid., 57–59.

21   Statistics Canada (2015), *Developmental Disabilities among Canadians Aged 15 Years and Older, 2012*, <http://www.statcan.gc.ca/daily-quotidien/151203/dq151203b-eng.htm.>

22   Lemay (2009), op. cit.

23   Quebec Ombudsman (2012), op. cit.

13

Older Adults Are Not Affected by HIV/AIDS
The Origins and Consequences of a Misconception

Isabelle Wallach

I went to my nurse practitioner for my annual physical and at the end
of the exam I asked her if she was going to give me an HIV test. The nurse
practitioner laughed and said "Why would you want an HIV test?"

———— Joanne Altschuler and Anne Katz, "'Of course it's relevant!'
A Focus Group Study of Older Adults' Perceived Importance
of HIV/AIDS Prevention Education."[1]

One Myth Can Mask Another: The Assumed Asexuality of Older Adults

The above quotation – from a study on the perceived importance of HIV
prevention among older adults – illustrates just how many people, including
professionals, genuinely believe that older adults are unaffected by HIV/
AIDS. As reflected in the nurse practitioner's attitude and comments, even
today most people find it incredible or ridiculous that older adults might
behave in ways that could lead to HIV infection and that they should therefore follow safe-sex practices. What behaviours are we talking about here?
For a start, the idea that older adults are sexually active is still not commonly
acknowledged, even though attitudes are beginning to change.[2] People find
it even harder to believe that older adults engage in risky sexual behaviour
– new partners, multiple partners, extramarital relations, paying for sex, or
engaging in sex under the influence of drugs or alcohol – all of which are

forms of contact that increase the risk of being unaware of their partners' HIV status (HIV positive, negative, unknown) or of simply not using a condom. Believing the myth that HIV does not affect older adults means also believing that older men will not have sex with other men, even though gay men make up one of the groups most seriously affected by the virus.

Why is aging perceived to imply asexuality or being capable only of a faithful, romantic heterosexual relationship? The commonly held view that older adults are not sexually active is based mainly on a set of stereotypes that reinforce the belief that sexuality and aging are incompatible. The fact is that there are still prejudices regarding old age, which is associated with fragility, dependence, illness, and passivity, whereas being sexually active is generally associated with conceptions of youth, performance, vitality, health, and passion.[3] The contrast between these stereotypes contributes significantly to the belief that older adults, unless they are in excellent physical shape, cannot continue to have a sex life.

The second reason for the continued belief in the myth of asexuality in older adults is the association between a desirable appearance and sexuality. Being attractive is seen as an external sign of internal sexuality, which implies that only those who are desirable are inherently interested in sex.[4] And because society today tends to place a premium on bodies that meet ideals of youthful beauty and disparages those that show signs of aging, older bodies are labelled as undesirable and older adults are excluded from the sphere of sexual activity.[5]

There is one more factor that contributes to the dissociation between sexuality and aging, and that is the traditional social construct of sexuality as a natural and universal phenomenon whose primary goal is procreation. This ideal, which originates in the earliest writings of sexologists and in Judaeo-Christian morality, further strengthens the association between sexuality and youth.[6]

Where does the normative view of sexuality for older adults – supposedly within the framework of a monogamous and heterosexual marital relationship – come from? Its source may be the hierarchical system of sexual values in Western societies. In this hierarchy, proper, normal, or natural sexuality is considered, among other things, to be heterosexual, marital, monogamous, and non-commercial, whereas bad, abnormal, or unnatural sex would include homosexual, extramarital, or casual sex with multiple partners, and prostitution.[7] Because the idea that older adults have an active sex life remains disturbing, it is no doubt easier to think that their sexuality is based on emotional ties with few sexual connotations.

Unsafe Practices and New HIV Infections: A Reality That Also Affects Older Adults

Data from many different sources are challenging the myth that HIV does not affect older adults. Worldwide, more than four million people aged 50 and older currently have HIV, a prevalence that has doubled since 1995.[8] These figures include people who contracted HIV when younger and have aged with it, as well as those who were infected after the age of 50. In Quebec, one quarter (24.5 percent) of those newly diagnosed with HIV in 2014 were 50 years of age and older.[9] The belief that it is unnecessary to have older adults undergo an HIV test is therefore groundless. Not only that, but HIV-infected adults who remain untreated are at higher risk of illness and develop AIDS more quickly, and proportionately more of them die than younger people, making it all the more important for them to have an HIV test as quickly as possible.[10]

As noted above, the myth that older adults are not affected by HIV is based on a set of beliefs that need to be deconstructed. To start with, it is important to understand that older people have a sex life and that many continue to engage in sexual activity to an advanced age. According to recent surveys conducted in the United States and Europe, between one half and three quarters of 60- to 69-year-old adults, and approximately one quarter of those 70 and over, are sexually active with a partner.[11] According to another American study, between 20 percent and 30 percent of men and women in their 80s are sexually active.[12]

The belief that older adults do not engage in unsafe sexual practices has also largely been debunked by the findings of research into the sexuality of older adults. Many seniors look for new partners, sometimes online, which is conducive to risky sexual behaviour.[13] A study of older Canadians wintering in Florida (snowbirds) found that only 14 percent of those who had new sexual partners used condoms.[14] Moreover, a significant minority of older men and women have multiple sexual partners, and several studies have reported non-exclusive sexual relations among older populations.[15] Although data on the subject are scarce, a study of heterosexual men aged 60 to 84 revealed that many were clients of prostitution, and over half of them did not use a condom when engaging in such sexual activities.[16]

Drug abuse involving intravenous injection as a source of infection and alcohol abuse leading to unsafe sexual behaviours have been reported in several studies on older adults.[17] For older women, drinking can also make them more willing to comply with the desires of their male partners who refuse to use condoms, which corroborates how difficult it is for older women to assert themselves and challenge their partners about their previous risky practices.[18] And, of course, homosexuality is a reality among older men, including among those who have not come out of the closet because of the stigmatization they were subjected to in their youth. Gay men continue to engage in sex as they get older and remain at risk of HIV infection.[19]

When Misconceptions Affect the Attitudes of Professionals and the Services They Provide

The myth that HIV does not concern older adults has many repercussions, in terms not only of the risk of new infections but also of the need to care for older adults with HIV. We can begin by pointing out that this myth and the misconceptions associated with it are what lie behind the absence of prevention efforts that specifically target older adults.[20] Several studies have shown that health professionals tend not to raise issues of sexuality and sexual health with their older patients, because of their embarrassment about discussing such subjects with a population that is perceived to be asexual, because of their lack of knowledge about this field, or because they think that the risk of HIV infection decreases with age.[21] And yet, these older people would appear to be willing to discuss sexuality with their health professional, although they may be ill at ease with raising the issue in the conversation because they are afraid of being perceived negatively.[22] This failure to communicate about HIV may explain why older adults lack information about the pathology of HIV infection, and particularly about their risk of becoming infected, and why they tend not to use condoms, especially menopausal women who believe that they can no longer become pregnant.[23]

The myth that there is no HIV among older people has another consequence: the invisibility of older adults living with HIV, one of the major repercussions of which is the scarcity of social and health services for them.[24] Professionals working with older clients do not consider HIV to be a necessary component of their field of expertise, and organizations and health services that specialize in HIV are only beginning to become aware that their clientele is aging. The resources available for HIV-infected older adults are accordingly almost nonexistent at a time when this population is facing multiple health and psychosocial support needs, primarily because of isolation and the lack of informal (other than professional) support for them.[25]

Conclusion: The Urgency of Recognizing the Risks of HIV Infection among Older Adults

To conclude, the myth that older adults are unaffected by HIV persists, even among health professionals. As we have seen, this myth is based on a series of misconceptions about the sexuality of older people, who are depicted as necessarily monogamous, marital, heterosexual, and romantic – misconceptions that mask the reality of some seniors' unsafe sexual behaviours. Far from being inconsequential, such erroneous beliefs make it more difficult for older adults to receive information about HIV, which delays testing and, consequently, diagnosis and treatment. This myth, and the ensuing lack of prevention, also contribute to the reduced use of condoms by older adults, particularly women, who tend to feel that the virus is not a concern for them. The belief that there is no HIV risk for older adults makes those living with this infection more invisible and represents a barrier to providing them with appropriate services. It would therefore appear urgent to deconstruct this myth and make older adults, health professionals, and social services aware of the reality in order to curb new infections and improve the quality of life of older adults living with HIV.

Notes

1 Joanne Altschuler and Anne Katz (2015), "'Of course it's relevant!': A focus group study of older adults' perceived importance of HIV/AIDS prevention education," *Qualitative Social Work*, Vol. 14, No. 5, 695.
2 Several authors have referred to current cultural trends in which some new and more restrictive social and medical standards describe sexuality among older adults as essential for successful and healthy aging. See, for example, Linn Sandberg (2015), "Sex, sexuality and later life," in Julia Twigg and Wendy Martin (eds.), *Routledge Handbook of Cultural Gerontology* (New York: Routledge).
3 Merryn Gott (2005), *Sexuality, Sexual Health and Ageing* (Berkshire: Open University Press).
4 Ibid.
5 Laura Hurd Clarke (2011), *Facing Age: Women Growing Older in Anti-Aging Culture* (New York and Plymouth: Rowman & Littlefield).
6 Gott (2005), op. cit.
7 Gayle S. Rubin (1993), "Thinking sex: Notes for a radical theory of the politics of sexuality," in Henry Abelove, Michele A. Barale and David M. Halperin (eds.), *The Lesbian and Gay Studies Reader* (London: Routledge).
8 Mary Mahy, Christine S. Autenrieth, Karen Stanecki, and Shona Wynd (2014), "Increasing trends in HIV prevalence among people aged 50 years and older: Evidence from estimates and survey data," *AIDS*, Vol. 28, No. 4, S453–S459.

9   Raphaël Bitera, Micheline Fauvel, Michel Alary, Cécile Tremblay, Raymond Parent, Diane Sylvain, and Maureen Hastie (2015), *Programme de surveillance de l'infection par le virus de l'immunodéficience humaine (VIH) au Québec: rapport annuel 2014, Messages clés et sommaire* (Quebec City: Institut national de santé publique).

10 Kelly A. Gebo (2006), "HIV and aging," *Drugs and Aging*, Vol. 23, No. 11, 897–913.

11 Stacy T. Lindau, L. Philip Schumm, Edward O. Laumann, Wendy Levinson, Colm A. O'Muircheartaigh, and Linda J. Waite (2007), "A study of sexuality and health among older adults in the United States," *New England Journal of Medicine*, Vol. 357, No. 8, 762–74; Nathalie Bajos and Michel Bozon (2011), "Les transformations de la vie sexuelle après cinquante ans: un vieillissement genré," *Genre, sexualité et société*, No. 6, Autumn, <http://gss.revues.org/index2165.html>, accessed March 7, 2017.

12 Vanessa Schick, Debby Herbenick, Michel Reece, Stephanie A. Sanders, Brian Dodge, Susan Elizabeth Middlestadt, and J. Dennis Fortenberry (2010), "Sexual behaviors, condom use, and sexual health of Americans over 50: Implications for sexual health promotion for older adults," *Journal of Sexual Medicine*, Vol. 7, Suppl. 5, 315–29.

13 Sheyna S. R. Alterovitz and Gerald A. Mendelsohn (2013), "Relationship goals of middle-aged, young-old, and old-old Internet daters: An analysis of online personal ads," *Journal of Aging Studies*, Vol. 27, No. 2, 159–165. See also Victor Minichiello, Gail Hawkes, and Marian Pitts (2011), "HIV, sexually transmitted infections, and sexuality in later life," *Current Infectious Disease Reports*, Vol. 13, No. 2, 182–87.

14 Katie Mairs and Sandra L. Bullock (2013), "Sexual-risk behaviour and HIV testing among Canadian snowbirds who winter in Florida," *Canadian Journal on Aging/ La Revue canadienne du vieillissement*, Vol. 32, No. 2, 145–58.

15 Ramani Durvasula (2014), "HIV/AIDS in older women: Unique challenges, unmet needs," *Behavioral Medicine*, Vol. 40, No. 3, 85–98; Lindau et al. (2007), op. cit.; Schick et al. (2010), op. cit.; James R. Fleckenstein and Derrell W. Cox (2015), "The association of an open relationship orientation with health and happiness in a sample of older US adults," *Sexual and Relationship Therapy*, Vol. 30, No. 1, 94–116; Sue Malta and Karen Farquharson (2014), "The initiation and progression of late-life romantic relationships," *Journal of Sociology*, Vol. 50, No. 3, 237–51.

16 Christine Milrod and Martin Monto (2016), "Condom use, sexual risk, and self-reported STI in a sample of older male clients of heterosexual prostitution in the United States," *American Journal of Men's Health*, Vol. 10, No. 4, 296–305.

17 Marcia M. Neundorfer, Phyllis Braudy Harris, Paula J. Britton, and Delores A. Lynch (2005), "HIV-risk factors for midlife and older women," *The Gerontologist*, Vol. 45, No. 5, 617–25; Robin J. Jacobs, Michael N. Kane, and Raymond L. Ownby (2013), "Condom use, disclosure, and risk for unprotected sex in HIV-negative midlife and older men who have sex with men," *American Journal of Men's Health*, Vol. 7, No. 3, 186–97.

18 Trish Morison and Catherine M. Cook (2015), "Midlife safer sex challenges for heterosexual New Zealand women re-partnering or in casual relationships," *Journal of Primary Health Care*, Vol. 7, No. 2, 137–44; Diane Zablotsky and Michael Kennedy (2003), "Risk factors and HIV transmission to midlife and older women: Knowledge, options, and the initiation of safer sexual practices," *Journal of Acquired Immune Deficiency Syndromes*, Vol. 33, S122–S130.

19 Shari Brotman, Bill Ryan, and Robert Cormier (2003), "The health and social service needs of gay and lesbian elders and their families in Canada," *The Gerontologist*, Vol. 43, No. 2, 192–202; Douglas Kimmel, Tara Rose, and Steven David (eds.) (2006), *Lesbian, Gay, Bisexual and Transgender Aging* (New York: Columbia University Press).

20 Nathan L. Linsk, Jane P. Fowler, and Susan J. Klein (2003), "HIV/AIDS prevention and care services and services for the aging: Bridging the gap between service systems to assist older people," *Journal of Acquired Immune Deficiency Syndromes*, Vol. 33, S243–S250.

21 Emily Haesler, Michael Bauer, and Deirdre Fetherstonhaugh (2016), "Sexuality, sexual health and older people: A systematic review of research on the knowledge and attitudes of health professionals," *Nurse Education Today*, Vol. 40, 57–71.

22 Jessica L. Tillman and Hayley D. Mark (2015), "HIV and STI testing in older adults: An integrative review," *Journal of Clinical Nursing*, Vol. 24, No. 15–16, 2074–95; Altschuler and Katz (2015), op. cit.

23 Susan J. Henderson, Lisa B. Bernstein, Diane Marie St. George, Joyce P. Doyle, Anuradha Paranjape, and Giselle Corbie-Smith (2004), "Older women and HIV: How much do they know and where are they getting their information?," *Journal of the American Geriatrics Society*, Vol. 52, No. 9, 1549–53; Schick et al. (2010), op. cit.; Mairs and Bullock (2013), op. cit.; Minichiello et al. (2011), op. cit.

24 Teresa Fritsch (2005), "HIV/AIDS and the older adult: An exploratory study of the age-related differences in access to medical and social services," *Journal of Applied Gerontology*, Vol. 24, No. 1, 35–54; Charles Furlotte, Karen Schwartz, Jay J. Koornstra, and Richard Naster (2012), "'Got a room for me?' Housing experiences of older adults living with HIV/AIDS in Ottawa," *Canadian Journal on Aging/La Revue canadienne du vieillissement*, Vol. 31, No. 1, 37–48.

25 Isabelle Wallach and Shari Brotman (2013), "Ageing with HIV/AIDS: A scoping study among people aged 50 and over living in Quebec," *Ageing and Society*, Vol. 33, No. 7, 1212–42; Isabelle Wallach, Xuân Ducandas, Michel Martel, and Réjean Thomas (2016), "Vivre à l'intersection du VIH et du vieillissement: Quelles répercussions sur les liens sociaux significatifs?," *Canadian Journal on Aging/La Revue canadienne du vieillissement*, Vol. 35, No. 1, 42–54.

14

Aging, Sexuality, and the "Cougar" Myth

Milaine Alarie

Even today, there is still some cultural unease about older people's sexuality, given that aging has traditionally been associated with asexuality. Popular assumptions regarding human sexuality are influenced not only by ageism but also by sexism, which means that women are particularly affected by ageist normative expectations regarding appropriate sexual desire and behaviour. Among the phenomena that challenge the cultural opposition between aging and (women's) sexuality are age-hypogamous intimate relationships – that is, relationships in which the woman is older than her male partner. Women who date younger men are often referred to as "cougars," a term that surfaced in popular language about 20 years ago.[1] This topic has garnered particular media attention in recent years with movies such as *Prime* (2005) and *Adore* (2013) and television shows such as *Cougar Town* (2009–15). There is also a proliferation of books (for instance, *Cougar: A Guide for Older Women Dating Younger Men*, 2002) and dating websites (such as cougarlife. com) for individuals seeking an age-hypogamous intimate relationship.

Cultural Representations of the "Cougar"

Although many people see the "cougar" image as a symbol of female sexual emancipation, others point out that the cultural representations of women who date younger men disseminated in the media are not always positive or inclusive.[2] For example, these women are often portrayed as hypersexual or somewhat aggressive in their approach to seduction. The cultural representation of the age-hypogamous relationship formation process as one that is inherently driven by the woman implies that it is unthinkable for a man to genuinely desire an older woman. In fact, "cougars" are sometimes depicted as being dangerous for younger men. The negative or humorous connotations associated with the image of the confident and sexually assertive "cougar" also suggest that it is abnormal for middle-aged or senior women to think of themselves as sexual subjects and inappropriate for them to take the lead in the relationship formation process.

"Cougars" are also frequently portrayed as being financially secure. This suggests that it is impossible for a man to be interested in a woman whose body shows clear signs of aging without her having to buy his affection or invest in her physical appearance in order to look younger. In fact, women who are interested in younger men are commonly depicted as clinging desperately to their youth. Some cultural representations of age-hypogamous intimate relations suggest that not all older women may legitimately date a younger man; only women who can successfully maintain a youthful physical appearance – women in their early forties, trim, energetic, and with dyed hair – are portrayed as being socially acceptable "cougars."[3]

Lastly, these relationships are also frequently portrayed as temporary flings or as doomed to failure. It is often suggested that a man is unlikely to develop romantic feelings for an older woman or wish to build a serious relationship with her. In short, although these representations may challenge the notion that middle-aged and senior women are asexual, they also reinforce many preconceptions about women's worth and the acceptability of their sexuality as they age.

Social Norms and Double Standards: The Origins of the Myth

There is no question that sexual practices and relationships have evolved considerably in recent decades in North America. Factors that have contributed to this change include women's integration into the labour force, their increasing financial independence, numerous legal changes such as those related to divorce and women's financial rights, new reproductive technologies, and the rapid growth of the pornography industry.[4] Changes in sexual and marital practices have also been influenced by the evolution of social norms, such as the growing acceptance of sexual diversity, the waning importance of virginity before marriage, and recognition of the legitimacy of female sexual desire and pleasure.[5]

Although women today benefit from a sexual freedom that was not as socially accepted for their counterparts in previous generations, women's sexuality continues to be subject to greater social control than men's, and gendered sexual double standards still exist. These provide men with greater sexual freedom in terms of the number of sexual partners they can have and the contexts in which they can have sex (one-night stands, "friends with benefits" relationships, and so on). In other words, women are more likely to be judged negatively than men for similar sexual experiences.

Sexual double standards are also influenced by ageism, which allows middle-aged and senior men to explore their sexuality more freely than women of the same age.[6] Middle-aged and senior women's sexuality and intimate relationships are further constrained by the dominant cultural script regarding men's and women's value as intimate partners, which suggests that women's worth is first and foremost determined by their physical appearance, whereas men's worth is based on their socioeconomic status.[7] Considering that women's beauty has traditionally been associated with youth and that personal income tends to increase with age, the message conveyed is that women lose value as they age, whereas men gain value as they age. Consequently, although many can conceive of a middle-aged or senior man as desirable and having an active sex life, they struggle to think the same of a woman of a similar age.

This cultural script affects the dating market and complicates middle-aged and – especially – senior women's dating choices. Several studies show that, on average, the older the man, the wider the gap between his age and the age of what he considers to be the ideal partner.[8] These preferences affect men's partnering choices; a man who marries in his twenties does so, on average, with a woman one year his junior, but this gap increases to from 9 to 12 years for a man who marries in his sixties.[9] Coupled with the fact that men's life expectancy is shorter than women's, these preferences contribute to the imbalanced male-female ratio among middle-aged and older people in the dating market, a phenomenon particularly pronounced among seniors.[10] Despite the imbalanced sex ratio among middle-aged and senior single people, the fact is that the vast majority of middle-aged women and a considerable proportion of senior women have an active sex life.[11] It is also important to note that, far from being victims of an unfair dating market, some middle-aged and senior women *prefer* being single.[12]

The cultural fascination with women who have intimate relationships with younger men cannot be explained simply by a cultural unease around age-discrepant relationships, given that relationships in which the man is older than his female partner are common and generally well received. It could be argued that these women have a hold on the collective imagination because they are perceived as defying many preconceived notions and social norms regarding women's – especially older women's – sexuality in a number of ways. Indeed, "cougars" are imagined as 1) destabilizing the cultural script according to which women become less physically attractive as they age and lose value in the dating market; 2) challenging the cultural script that encourages women to play a more passive role in the relationship formation process and let men take the lead; 3) defying cultural norms by openly expressing their sexuality at an age when they are expected to present themselves as asexual; and 4) ignoring the cultural imperative for women to be – or at least seek to be – in a stable, long-term intimate relationship rather than exploring their sexuality without looking for love or long-term commitment.

Age-Hypogamous Intimate Relationships: Beyond the Myth

There are currently very few studies on age-hypogamous intimate relationships, and fewer still on senior women in this type of relationship. However, we know that age-hypogamous marital relationships are not that common. According to Canadian census data, only 6 percent of marriages and common-law unions consist of a woman four or more years older than her spouse.[13] However, the average age gap between a husband and wife in a first marriage has narrowed in the past decade, from about four years to two, both in Canada and the United States.[14] Moreover, the percentage of marriages in which the woman is at least four years older than her spouse rose from 6.3 percent in 2000 to 7.8 percent in 2015 in the United States, suggesting that this kind of relationship has recently become more common.[15]

In terms of the conjugal choices of Canadian seniors, studies show a decrease over the past 30 years in the proportion of couples with a large age gap; 40 percent of senior couples in 1981 consisted of partners with an age difference of three years or less, and this proportion increased to 49 percent in 2011. That said, among age-discrepant couples, men are much more likely than women to be the older partner. For example, in 23 percent of couples consisting of at least one senior in 2011, the man was at least seven years older than his partner, whereas the woman was older by seven or more years in only 3 percent of cases.[16]

However, these data reflect only unions officially recognized by the government; many couples do not declare themselves as "common-law spouses," especially partners in a new relationship, who do not live together, or who are not as committed to their relationship. If we consider all types of intimate relationships (from one-night stands to marriages or common-law unions), American data show that approximately 13 percent of the middle-aged women reported having a sexual partner who was at least five years their junior in the previous 12 months, compared with 34 percent of women who had a sexual partner at least five years older than them.[17]

North American studies also show that the odds of a woman becoming involved in an intimate relationship with a younger man increase with age.[18] Women in their fifties are therefore more likely to engage in an age-hypogamous intimate relationship than are women in their thirties. There are several possible explanations for this phenomenon: could the imbalanced sex ratio among single people in their fifties and seniors prompt some women to choose a younger man because there are few single men their own age? Is it possible that, as they age, some women become more aware of the gendered double standards around sexuality and so choose to engage in experiences typically reserved for men? Does the importance that women place on certain traits (such as socioeconomic status, good health, and physical appearance) in a man change with age? Do some women simply have a greater affinity for younger men?

With regard to the socioeconomic profile of women who tend to choose a younger male partner, a study based on American data shows that there is a negative statistical relationship between a woman's income and the likelihood that she will choose a sexual partner at least five years younger.[19] This suggests that, contrary to what some might believe, women's affluence is not a major factor affecting their ability to attract younger men. The same study also shows that middle-aged women who were previously married or in a common-law relationship and are now divorced, separated, or widowed are more likely than others to be involved in an intimate relationship with a man at least 10 years younger. It would therefore appear that the experience of marriage or common-law union affects middle-aged women's choices in terms of partner age.

A recent study conducted among Canadian women aged 30 to 60 who are dating younger men shows that, contrary to common cultural representations of "cougars," very few of these women perceive themselves as seductresses who actively pursue younger men.[20] In fact, most respondents report that their younger partners were the ones who approached them and actively tried to seduce them, not the other way around. Lastly, another recent study reveals that more than half of the intimate relationships in which the woman is at least five years older than her partner lasted at least two years, and that approximately 43 percent of those women were in fact married to – or cohabiting with – their younger partner.[21] Therefore, contrary to what is suggested by the cultural representations of age-hypogamous intimate relationships, these relationships are often serious and can be long-lasting.

Conclusion

Over the past two decades, much has been written about women who have intimate relationships with younger men. Through their dating choices, these women reject some of the gendered norms regarding sexuality, relationship formation, and partner selection. They also challenge the dominant cultural narrative according to which women's value as a partner decreases with age. For these reasons, some view "cougars" as symbols of women's sexual empowerment, whereas others see them in a negative light. Ultimately, although some issues around age-hypogamous intimate relationships remain unexplored, existing studies show that cultural representations of the "cougar" are not based on reality; rather, they reflect ageist and gendered double standards regarding sexuality and intimate relationships.

Notes

1   Rosemary-Claire Collard (2012), "Cougar figures, gender, and the performances of predation," *Gender, Place and Culture: A Journal of Feminist Geography*, Vol. 19, No. 4, 518–40; Beth Montemurro and Jenna Marie Siefken (2014), "Cougars on the prowl? New perceptions of older women's sexuality," *Journal of Aging Studies*, Vol. 28, No. 1, 35–43.

2   Collard (2012), op. cit.; Betty Jo Barrett and Dana S. Levin (2014), "What's love got to do with it? A qualitative grounded theory content analysis of romance narratives in the PG era of World Wrestling Entertainment (WWE) programming," *Sexuality and Culture*, Vol. 18, No. 3, 560–591; Betty Kaklamanidou (2012), "Pride and prejudice: Celebrity versus fictional cougars," *Celebrity Studies*, Vol. 3, No. 1, 78–89; Rose Weitz (2010), "Changing the scripts: Midlife women's sexuality in contemporary U.S. film," *Sexuality and Culture*, Vol. 14, No. 1, 17–32.

3   Weitz (2010), op. cit.

4   See Liza Mundy (2012), *The Richer Sex: How the New Majority of Female Breadwinners is Transforming Sex, Love, and Family* (New York: Simon & Schuster); Laurence Charton (2008), "Conjugalité," in Joseph J. Lévy and André Dupras (eds.), *Questions de sexualité au Québec* (Montreal: Liber); Hélène Belleau (2004), "Être parent aujourd'hui: la construction du lien de filiation dans l'univers symbolique de la parenté," *Enfances, Familles, Générations*, No. 1, Fall, 11–21; Joseph J. Lévy (2008), "Contraception," in Joseph J. Lévy and André Dupras (eds.), *Questions de sexualité*

au Québec (Montreal: Liber); David Allyn (2000), *Make Love, Not War: The Sexual Revolution, an Unfettered History* (Boston: Routledge).

5   See Bob Altemeyer (2001), "Changes in attitudes toward homosexuals," *Journal of Homosexuality*, Vol. 42, No. 2, 63–75; Joseph J. Lévy (2008), "Conduites sexuelles," in Joseph J. Lévy and André Dupras (eds.), *Questions de sexualité au Québec* (Montreal: Liber); Paula Kamen (2000), *Her Way: Young Women Remake the Sexual Revolution* (New York: New York University Press).

6   Laura M. Carpenter, Constance A. Nathanson, and Young J. Kim (2006), "Sex after 40? Gender, ageism, and sexual partnering in midlife," *Journal of Aging Studies*, Vol. 20, No. 2, 93–106.

7   Cheryl Brown Travis, Kayce L. Meginnis, and Kristin M. Bardari (2000), "Beauty, sexuality, and identity: The social control of women," in Cheryl Brown Travis and Jacquelyn W. White (eds.), *Sexuality, Society, and Feminism* (Washington: American Psychological Association).

8   Bram P. Buunk, Pieternel Dijkstra, Douglas T. Kenrick, and Astrid Warntjes (2001), "Age preferences for mates as related to gender, own age, and involvement level," *Evolution and Human Behavior*, Vol. 22, No. 4, 241–50.

9   Paula England and Elizabeth Aura McClintock (2009), "The gendered double standard of aging in US marriage markets," *Population and Development Review*, Vol. 35, No. 4, 797–816.

10 Carpenter et al. (2006), op. cit.; Aniruddha Das, Linda J. Waite, and Edward O. Laumann (2012), "Sexual expression over the life course: Results from three landmark surveys," in Laura M. Carpenter and John DeLamater (eds.), *Sex for Life: From Virginity to Viagra, How Sexuality Changes throughout Our Lives* (New York: NYU Press); Statistics Canada (2017), Data tables, 2016 Census, Marital Status (13), Age (16) and Sex (3) for the Population 15 Years and Over of Canada, Provinces and Territories and Census Metropolitan Areas, *2016 Census*, Product No. 98-400-X2016031 in the Statistics Canada Catalogue, <https://www12.statcan.gc.ca/census -recensement/2016/dp-pd/index-eng.cfm>.

11 Das et al. (2012), op. cit.; Julie Fraser, Eleanor Maticka-Tyndale, and Lisa Smylie (2004), "Sexuality of Canadian Women at Midlife," *Canadian Journal of Human Sexuality*, Vol. 13, No. 3–4, 171–87.

12 Bronwen Lichtenstein (2012), "Dating risks and sexual health among midlife women after relationship dissolution," in Laura M. Carpenter and John DeLamater (eds.), *Sex for Life: From Virginity to Viagra, How Sexuality Changes throughout Our Lives* (New York: NYU Press).

13 Monica Boyd and Anne Li (2003), "May–December: Canadians in age-discrepant relationships," *Canadian Social Trends*, Vol. 70, 29–33.

14 Vanier Institute of the Family (2010), *Families Count: Profiling Canada's Families IV* (Ottawa: Vanier Institute of the Family); Hernan Vera, Donna H. Berardo, and Felix M. Berardo (1985), "Age heterogamy in marriage," *Journal of Marriage and the Family*, Vol. 47, No. 3, 553–66.

15 United States Bureau of the Census (2015), *America's Families and Living Arrangements – Family Groups, Table FG3*, <https://www.census.gov/hhes/ families/data/ cps2015FG.html>, accessed February 21, 2017; United States Bureau of the Census

(2000), *America's Families and Living Arrangements, Table FG3*, <https://www.census.gov/hhes/families/data/cps2000.html>, accessed February 21, 2017.

16 Statistics Canada (2014), *Emerging Trends in Living Arrangements and Conjugal Unions for Current and Future Seniors*, Ottawa, Statistics Canada, Catalogue No.75-006-X, <https://www150.statcan.gc.ca/n1/pub/75-006-x/2014001/article/11904-eng.pdf>, accessed February 21, 2017.

17 Milaine Alarie and Jason T. Carmichael (2015), "The 'Cougar' phenomenon: An examination of the factors that influence age-hypogamous sexual relationships among middle-aged women," *Journal of Marriage and Family*, Vol. 77, No. 5, 1250–65.

18 Jacqueline E. Darroch, David J. Landry, and Selene Oslak (1999), "Age differences between sexual partners in the United States," *Family Planning Perspectives*, Vol. 31, No. 4, 160–67; Louis Duchesne (2004), "Quatre ans d'écart d'âge en moyenne entre les conjoints," *Données sociodémographiques en bref*, Quebec City, Institut de la statistique du Québec, Vol. 8, No. 3, 1–8, <http://www.stat.gouv.qc.ca/statistiques/conditions-viesociete/bulletins/sociodemo-vol08-no3.pdf>, accessed February 21, 2017.

19 Alarie and Carmichael (2015), op. cit.

20 Milaine Alarie (2019), "'They're the ones chasing the Cougar': Relationship formation in the context of age-hypogamous intimate relationships," *Gender & Society*, Vol. 33, No. 3, 463–85.

21 Alarie and Carmichael (2015), op. cit.

15

Sexual Assault of Older Women
An Unthinkable Reality

Mélanie Couture, Milaine Alarie, Sarita Israel, and Marie-Pier Petit

I'd like you to think of your mother, your grandmother, or perhaps an elderly aunt you love. Imagine that this is their story. As we get older, we always think about what could happen to us - falling in the bathtub and breaking an arm or a leg, or our heart stopping because we loved too much or have given too much - but we never, ever, imagine a night of terror with a man, an animal on the prowl seeking his prey, who for many long minutes tries to rape you as he beats you black and blue.

——————— Juliette, 75, sexual assault victim[1]

According to the Government of Quebec, sexual assault is

an act that is sexual in nature, with or without physical contact, committed by an individual without the consent of the victim or in some cases through emotional manipulation or blackmail, especially when children are involved. It is an act that subjects another person to the perpetrator's desires through an abuse of power and/or the use of force or coercion, accompanied by implied or explicit threats.[2]

In recent years, with the advent of the #BeenRapedNeverReported, #WeBelieveYou, and #MeToo movements, which have lit up social media, there has been renewed media and political interest in the issue of sexual assault. Although this collective conversation, combined with the recent political efforts to increase awareness of the issue and provide assistance to victims, may be viewed as cause for celebration, it must be recognized that several myths surrounding sexual assault persist. These misconceptions, shared by both assailants and the public at large, trivialize actual assaults or suggest that they never really happened.[3] In this chapter, we debunk one of the leading myths about sexual assault: that older women, because of their age, cannot be sexually assaulted.[4]

Beauty, Attraction, and Sexual Violence: Origins of the Myth

In many instances, the main cause of sexual assault against women is wrongly viewed as resulting from the physical attraction that an assailant feels for his victim. The victim is often portrayed as being a young woman whose appearance meets conventional beauty standards, and the assailant is seen as a man incapable of controlling his sexual desire for such an attractive woman.

Although this misconception may apply to all women, regardless of age, it particularly affects older women, given the ageist nature of the dominant cultural representation of female beauty. The idea that sexual assault against older women is unlikely or does not occur arises in part from this discourse, which presents beauty (especially that of women) as a quality that fades with age.

The inability to imagine an older woman as a victim of sexual assault also stems from the cultural opposition between aging and sexuality. The media perpetuate the stereotype of the asexual mature woman; the sexuality of older women, if discussed at all, is often depicted as undermining the stability of the nuclear family, as deviant or inappropriate, or it is presented in a humorous way.[5] Studies show that young adults tend to imagine that seniors, particularly women, do not have active sex lives.[6] Ultimately, the inability to imagine older women as sexual beings is one of the reasons that sexual assault goes unnoticed in that population.

Many feminist scholars argue that the cultural representation of older women as unattractive is a factor in maintaining the ongoing oppression of women in general.[7] The cultural devaluation of aging in women helps to discredit the grievances of older women who dare to criticize gender inequalities. This cultural discourse also hampers collective efforts of feminist resistance by creating divisions among women; it encourages competition for male attention and concomitant female jealousy. This devaluation of aging can also have a negative impact on older women's self-esteem, thus rendering them more docile and less inclined to rebel. In short, the connection between a woman's physical appearance and her worth as a person undermines gender equality in all areas of life; it may not only cast doubt on the testimony of sexual assault victims but also influence people to question women's ability to hold positions of power, such as those of president or prime minister.

Genesis of Sexual Assault

Sexual assault is a highly complex phenomenon, and any attempt to understand perpetrators' motives must consider many factors.[8] However, it is important to understand that human sexuality develops through a complex psychosocial process that is influenced by the social norms to which the individual is exposed.[9] Human beings learn what is "normal" from their interactions with others and the information that they receive from society; this socialization process shapes their sexuality to a great extent. Consequently, the many cultural messages encouraging the objectification of women and the sexualization of violence against women that are regularly conveyed in the media and in certain social environments reserved for men (fraternities, sports locker rooms, and others) may appropriately be viewed as factors that promote the development of attitudes conducive to sexual violence against women.[10]

In fact, a consideration of gender power dynamics and how society views masculinity is important to an understanding of what sexual assault is. Although alternative models of masculinity do exist, the dominant North American cultural representation still holds that a man should be physically strong and dominant in his interactions, repress feelings that might be interpreted as emotional weakness, and demonstrate a capacity for repeated sexual conquest.[11] Perpetrators' desire to reaffirm their masculinity by sexually dominating women is one of the main drivers of their actions in many sexual assault cases.[12]

Some attackers specifically target older adults. This type of perpetrator views residents of long-term care facilities as ideal victims because they are vulnerable and therefore offer little resistance.[13] Most older victims are women who are very elderly and in a state of physical and functional frailty; many suffer from cognitive problems and are dependent on others for care.[14] In addition, the testimony of older adults is often perceived as not credible due to their state of health, a factor that works in the perpetrator's favour.[15]

The fact that sexual violence sometimes occurs in romantic relationships and may be part of a dynamic of domestic violence should not be overlooked. Furthermore, although the victim's age is not necessarily a factor in the assault, it could have an impact on the way the assault is perceived. Older adults are less inclined than younger adults to identify a domestic rape scenario as a genuine sexual assault.[16] Spousal rape has been recognized as an indictable offence in Canada only since 1983, a fact that may influence older adults' perceptions of what actually constitutes sexual assault, as opposed to something related to what used to be called "conjugal duty."[17] It is therefore important to consider the impact of Canada's socio-historical legacy on older adults' conception of sexual assault.

Lastly, in the case of sexual assaults between residents of long-term care facilities, perpetrators usually suffer from cognitive impairments that may cause them to lose their inhibitions and thus exhibit sexually inappropriate behaviours.[18] Resident perpetrators may also fail to distinguish between public and private premises, mistake the victim for their spouse, or misconstrue the victim's actions as a sexual advance. This type of situation requires the institution to take charge of the matter to ensure the safety of the victim and other residents and to reduce the risk of repeat assaults.

Sexual Assault against Older Adults: Statistical Profile

An estimated one in three Quebec women and one in six Quebec men will be sexually assaulted during their lifetime.[19] The deviant behaviour may involve physical contact (e.g., touching) or non-physical behaviour (e.g., exhibitionism).[20] According to the Statistics Canada 2009 General Social Survey, in the population aged 15 and older, 472,000 sexual assaults were reported by women and 204,000 by men during the 12 months preceding the survey.[21] It is important to emphasize that, in 2014, only 5 percent of Canadians who claimed they had been sexually assaulted actually reported the matter to police.[22]

Although most victims are minors or young adults, many are older adults. It is hard to form a clear picture of the scope of this problem among the population of older adults because sexual assaults are sometimes included in mistreatment or physical assault statistics, and many victims fail to report their attackers. Nevertheless, it is estimated that older adults represent 3 percent to 4 percent of sexual assault victims.[23] The number of sexual assaults reported to police by Quebecers aged 55 and over rose from

54 in 2001 to 109 in 2008.[24] It is, however, impossible to determine whether the number of sexual assaults against older adults is increasing or whether older victims are now more inclined than in the past to report assaults to the authorities.

With regard to the sexual assault of older adults, there are generally five types of perpetrators: 1) a stranger or acquaintance; 2) a professional care provider; 3) a family member; 4) a spouse; and 5) a long-term care facility resident. Attackers are mostly male and may be of any age: this type of crime may be committed by adolescents or persons of very advanced age.[25] Most sexual assaults, regardless of the victim's age, take place in private homes.[26] Strangers represent only 20 percent of perpetrators.[27] In private homes, most sexual assaults of older adults are committed by family members.[28] Older victims, in many instances, are vulnerable: one third present physical or cognitive disabilities and approximately half are diagnosed with a psychiatric disorder at the time of the assault.[29] Some assaults are committed in the context of caregiving. Some individuals receiving genital or rectal care may suffer intrusive, painful, or unwarranted acts. Older adults requiring assistance with intimate personal care (e.g., bathing) are at risk of experiencing this type of sexual assault.[30]

Sexual assaults against older adults also occur in healthcare institutions, mostly in long-term care facilities. Healthcare facility staff and family members are responsible for some of the sexual assaults committed in this type of facility.[31] However, it is important to note that 67 percent to 90 percent of assaults in long-term care facilities are committed by residents suffering, in many cases, from cognitive impairments resulting in confusion or loss of inhibitions.[32]

Conclusion

The aging factor needs to be considered in society's efforts to counter sexual assault and provide assistance to older victims. First, to establish a clear picture of sexual violence against older adults, physical and sexual mistreatment must be distinguished in the terminology and statistics. Second, the context in which intimate personal care is provided seems to be conducive to sexual assault due to the vulnerability of some older adults. This problem must be acknowledged in the policies and procedures of healthcare and social services institutions, and monitoring should be increased for individuals who exhibit high risk factors for becoming either victims or perpetrators. Third, cognitive losses may cause some older adults to lose their inhibitions, thus increasing the risk of inappropriate sexual behaviour. This type of assault must be addressed differently from intentional sexual mistreatment cases.

The inclusion of sexuality-related themes in mistreatment awareness activities organized for professionals and the general public would help to make older adults' sexuality less of a taboo and encourage victims and their family and friends to report sexual assaults. Sexual assaults against older adults are very real and severely impact those who experience them. If an older woman or man tells you that she or he has been sexually assaulted, it is important to believe her or him and to intervene as quickly as possible.

Notes

1   R. c. G.R. (Cour du Québec, 2005-04-08), SOQUIJ AZ-50312666, J.E. 2005-1459, <http://citoyens.soquij.qc.ca/php/decision.php?ID=121CC57CB6F5467BDE243 A47A035Fl2C>, accessed February 23, 2017 (our translation).
2   Gouvernement du Québec (2001), *Orientations gouvernementales en matière d'agression sexuelle* (Quebec City: Gouvernement du Québec), 22, <http://publications. msss.gouv.qc.ca/msss/fichiers/2000/00-807-1.pdf>, accessed February 23, 2017.
3   Allison C. Aosved and Patricia J. Long (2006), "Co-occurrence of rape myth acceptance, sexism, racism, homophobia, ageism, classism, and religious intolerance," *Sex Roles*, Vol. 55, No. 7–8, 481–92; Renae Franiuk, Jennifer L. Seefelt, Sandy L. Cepress, and Joseph A. Vandello (2008), "Prevalence and effects of rape myths in print journalism," *Violence against Women*, Vol. 14, No. 3, 287–309.
4   Government of Quebec (2010), *Sexual Assault of the Elderly Happens and Is Damaging – Let's Be Vigilant*, <http://www.scf.gouv.qc.ca/fileadmin/Documents/ Violences/AS-ainees-EN.pdf>, accessed May 10, 2019 .
5   Shyon Baumann and Kim de Laat (2012), "Socially defunct: A comparative analysis of the underrepresentation of older women in advertising," *Poetics*, Vol. 40, No. 6, 514–41; Margaret Tally (2006), "'She doesn't let age define her': Sexuality and motherhood in recent 'middle-aged chick flicks,'" *Sexuality and Culture*, Vol. 10, No. 2, 33–55; Rose Weitz (2010), "Changing the Scripts: Midlife Women's Sexuality in Contemporary U.S. Film," *Sexuality and Culture*, Vol. 14, No. 1, 17–32.
6   Yvonne Lai and Michaela Hynie (2011), "A tale of two standards: An examination of young adults' endorsement of gendered and ageist sexual double standards," *Sex Roles*, Vol. 64, No. 5–6, 360–71.
7   Cheryl Brown Travis, Kayce L. Meginnis, and Kristin M. Bardari (2000), "Beauty, sexuality, and identity: The social control of women," in Cheryl Brown Travis and Jacquelyn W. White (eds.), *Sexuality, Society, and Feminism* (Washington: American Psychological Association); Naomi Wolf (1991), *The Beauty Myth: How Images of Beauty Are Used against Women* (New York: W. Morrow).
8   Cheryl Brown Travis (2003), *Evolution, Gender, and Rape* (Cambridge: MIT Press).
9   John H. Gagnon and William Simon (1973), *Sexual Conduct: The Social Sources of Human Sexuality* (Chicago: Aldine); William Simon and John H. Gagnon (1986),

"Sexual scripts: Permanence and change," *Archives of Sexual Behavior*, Vol. 15, No. 2, 97–120.

10   Richard Poulin (1993), *La violence pornographique* (Morges: Éditions Cabédita); Michael S. Kimmel (2008), *Guyland: The Perilous World Where Boys Become Men* (New York: Harper).

11   Raewyn Connell and James W. Messerschmidt (2005), "Hegemonic masculinity," *Gender and Society*, Vol. 19, No. 6, 829–59; James W. Messerschmidt (2012), *Gender, Heterosexuality, and Youth Violence: The Struggle for Recognition* (Lanham, MD: Rowman and Littlefield). On alternative models of masculinity, see Eric Anderson (2009), *Inclusive Masculinity: The Changing Nature of Masculinities* (New York: Routledge).

12   Travis (2003), op. cit.

13   Christine Poulos and Daniel Sheridan (2008), "Genital injuries in postmenopausal women after sexual assault," *Journal of Elder Abuse and Neglect*, Vol. 20, No. 4, 323–35.

14   Pamela B. Teaster and Karen A. Roberto (2004), "Sexual abuse of older adults: APS cases and outcomes," *Gerontologist*, Vol. 44, No. 6, 788–96; Wenche Malmedal, Maria Helen Iversen, and Astrid Kilvik (2015), "Sexual abuse of older nursing home residents," *Nursing Research and Practice*, Vol. 2015, No. 10, 1–7; Karla Vierthaler (2008), "Best practices for working with rape crisis centers to address elder sexual abuse," *Journal of Elder Abuse and Neglect*, Vol. 20, No. 4, 306–22; Teaster and Roberto (2004), op. cit.

15   Malmedal et al. (2015), op. cit.

16   Kathleen C. Basile (2002), "Attitudes toward wife rape: Effects of social background and victim status," *Violence and Victims*, Vol. 17, No. 3, 341–54.

17   Regroupement québécois des Centres d'aide et de lutte contre les agressions à caractère sexuel (RQCALACS) (2007), *Les femmes âgées victimes d'agressions sexuelles: briser le tabou*, <http://www.rqcalacs.qc.ca/publicfiles/pdf_archive/Memoire_MFA_SEPT_07.pdf>, accessed February 23, 2017.

18   Tony Rosen, Mark S. Lachs, and Karl Pillemer (2010), "Sexual aggression between residents in nursing homes," *Journal of the American Geriatrics Society*, Vol. 58, No. 10, 1970–79.

19   Table de concertation sur les agressions à caractère sexuel de Montréal (2012), *Guide d'information à l'intention des victimes d'agression sexuelle*, <http://www.scf.gouv.qc.ca/fileadmin/Documents/Violences/Guide_info_agr_sex.pdf>, accessed May 10, 2019.

20   Holly Ramsey-Klawsnik (2004), "Elder sexual abuse within the family," *Journal of Elder Abuse and Neglect*, Vol. 15, No. 1, 43–58.

21   Statistics Canada (2015), *Section 1: Prevalence and Severity of Violence against Women*, Ottawa, Statistics Canada, Catalogue No. 85-002-X, <https://www150.statcan.gc.ca/n1/pub/85-002-x/2013001/article/11766/11766-1-eng.htm>, accessed February 23, 2017.

22   Statistics Canada (2015), *Criminal Victimization in Canada, 2014*, Ottawa, Statistics Canada, Catalogue No. 85-002-X, <https://www150.statcan.gc.ca/n1/pub/85-002-x/2015001/article/14241-eng.htm>, accessed February 23, 2017.

23 Jeffrey S. Jones, Linda Rossman, Renae Diegel, Phyllis Van Order, and Barbara N. Wynn (2009), "Sexual assault in postmenopausal women," *American Journal of Emergency Medicine*, Vol. 27, No. 8, 922–29.

24 Gouvernement du Québec (2001), op. cit.

25 Holly Ramsey-Klawsnik, Pamela B. Teaster, Marta S. Mediondo, Jennifer L. Marcum, and Erin L. Abner (2008), "Sexual predators who target elders," *Journal of Elder Abuse and Neglect*, Vol. 20, No. 4, 353–76.

26 Table de concertation sur les agressions à caractère sexuel de Montréal (2012), op. cit.

27 Linda O. Eckert and Naomi F. Sugar (2008), "Older victims of sexual assault: An underrecognized population," *YMOB American Journal of Obstetrics and Gynecology*, Vol. 198, No. 6, 688.e1–688.e7.

28 Ramsey-Klawsnik (2004), op. cit.

29 Eckert and Sugar (2008), op. cit.

30 K. Chihowski and S. Hughes (2008), "Clinical issues in responding to alleged elder sexual abuse," *Journal of Elder Abuse and Neglect*, Vol. 20, No. 4, 377–400.

31 Malmedal et al. (2015), op. cit.

32 Ramsey-Klawsnik et al. (2008), op. cit.; Pamela B. Teaster and Karen A. Roberto (2003), "Sexual abuse of older women living in nursing homes," *Journal of Gerontological Social Work*, Vol. 40, No. 4, 105–19.

16

Are Older Adults Safe from Conjugal Violence?

Sarita Israel, Mélanie Couture, and Marie-Pier Petit

"She was beautiful; she was so kind. This Aunt Julia whom everyone cherished. No one had the slightest idea about the conjugal violence that she had been suffering for more than 20 years. How could she have kept all this from us, while always giving us the brightest smiles? At 62 years of age, on January 7, 1994, she was murdered by her husband because, that night, she refused to have sexual relations with him."

——— Annie, practitioner, Abitibi-Témiscamingue[1]

According to Quebec's 2012–17 Government Action Plan on Domestic Violence, domestic violence "includes psychological, verbal, physical and sexual abuse as well as acts of financial domination." The Plan notes that domestic violence and, in particular, conjugal violence "can be experienced in a marital, extra-marital, or dating relationship, and at any age."[2] And yet, conjugal violence at an advanced age receives very little attention from the public, practitioners, decision makers, or researchers, to the point that it is considered invisible. In this chapter, we aim to dispel the myth that conjugal violence does not occur among older adults by focusing specifically on elements contributing to its invisibility. We also address factors associated with conjugal violence and specific aspects of the phenomenon among older adults in comparison with younger populations.

Myth and Invisibility

Conjugal violence among older adults is difficult to detect for various reasons, thus perpetuating the myth that it does not occur among older couples. A number of factors explain this. The World Health Organization now recognizes, among others, the role of social norms and cultural traditions.[3] Older adults are also victims of the messages that society conveys. They are influenced by the negative stereotypes that they have internalized, or they blame themselves for the treatment they endure and, at the same time, refuse the interventions offered to them. Women's stereotypical roles are still present in social discourse and are accepted by many: a woman's role in the couple is to maintain order and peace in the family home, and to be obedient. It is important to remember that historically, in Quebec, women had little power in a marriage. It was only in 1964 that women obtained the right to dispose of their property without their husbands' explicit consent.[4] Furthermore, it was not until the early 1980s that the article in the Civil Code stating that a woman must obey her husband was abolished and that spousal rape was legally recognized. So, it is not surprising that the new conception of male-female equality within couples has not been fully integrated among older generations. The myths and erroneous conceptions have the effect not only of lessening victims' disclosure of conjugal violence and limiting its detection but also of contributing to its perpetuation.

Another reason for the invisibility of conjugal violence is an idyllic conception of older couples in long-standing relationships. Conjugal and romantic relationships display distinct characteristics and dynamics. The couple is an entity in which people have "chosen" each other, as opposed to a parent-child relationship, for example. This belief could give the impression that older adults living as a couple for decades must be experiencing a healthy and happy relationship, since they have remained together. One might think, in the event of dissatisfaction or violence within the relationship, that one of the partners would necessarily end it. Nevertheless, this is not always the case. In situations of conjugal violence, ending the relationship may prove to be difficult for a number of reasons, including fear of reprisals, financial or care-related dependency, lack of self-esteem, and fear of being alone or of being criticized for having left a partner experiencing a loss of autonomy.

Finally, invisibility is also partly attributable to the different terminologies used to identify violence against and, particularly, mistreatment of older adults. The definition of mistreatment is as follows: there is mistreatment when a single or repeated gesture, or a lack of appropriate action, intentional or otherwise, occurs in a relationship in which there should be trust, and this causes an older adult harm or distress.[5] This definition places violence in the context of a relationship of trust, which includes conjugal relations. Nonetheless, focusing on violence against older adults solely from the angle of mistreatment does not make it possible to highlight the particular context of conjugal relations and to introduce measures to counter this type of violence. The data on conjugal violence are "hidden" within the data on mistreatment in general and are therefore difficult to pinpoint.

What Is the Reality Regarding Conjugal Violence at an Advanced Age?

Conjugal violence certainly exists among older adults. Compared with younger populations, however, people aged 65 and over are more often victims of violence at the hands of a current partner than of an ex-partner.[6] Indeed, approximately 28 percent of situations of family violence against older adults are committed within a couple. In Canada, over a five-year period, 6.8 percent of individuals aged 60 and over stated that they had experienced conjugal violence.[7] Psychological violence is the most common form (6.3 percent), followed by financial exploitation (1.2 percent) and physical violence (0.9 percent). In psychological terms, conjugal violence can be expressed in 14 different ways, according to the testimony of older women who have experienced it, including control, denigration, deprivation, threats, manipulation, blame, indifference, and infantilization.[8]

Nevertheless, it is important to note that almost one third of victims of conjugal violence experience numerous forms of violence concurrently. Even though few studies examine conjugal violence against male victims, men, like women, may be victims. The risk of experiencing physical or psychological violence is the same for older men and women. However, older women report more financial exploitation than do older men.

The reported rate of conjugal violence nonetheless appears to decrease with age. Canadian research and international studies have demonstrated that it is less prevalent among those aged 60 and older than among the 45–59 age group.[9] This difference in reporting rates could be partly attributable to a cohort effect. Indeed, some results suggest that conjugal violence is more downplayed and less frequently identified for and by older adults.

Often, for older adults experiencing conjugal violence, violence is an integral part of their life story. Exposure to a form of family violence at a young age increases the risks of experiencing violence throughout one's life, including conjugal violence in old age.[10] In addition, women are often victims of violence committed by multiple partners during their lives.[11] These previous experiences of violence alter their perception of conjugal violence. They may feel that they have no (or very little) power over their lives, after being controlled first by a parent and now by a partner.[12]

Conjugal violence in later life may occur in the context of two distinct conjugal trajectories. In the first, it can be explained by the fact that it pre-existed within the relationship. For some older women, conjugal violence was perpetrated by the same partner over a number of decades and may increase when the partner retires.[13] Nevertheless, the types of violence perpetrated can evolve over time, with physical violence often giving way over the years to psychological violence. Some women's history of conjugal violence begins only at an advanced age in the context of a new relationship. One Canadian study showed that the risks of physical violence are greater for older couples who have been living together for less than 10 years.[14] The study also indicated that the length of the relationship seems to be associated with distinct forms of conjugal violence. Thus, psychological violence and financial exploitation seem more common among couples who have been living together for 10 to 29 years. However, among couples who have been together for 30 years or more, there is a relatively low probability of experiencing emotional or physical violence or financial exploitation.

The Particular Situation of the Caregiver-Care Receiver Relationship

To understand conjugal violence among older adults, one must also look at the state of health of the individuals and their partners in order to understand the influence of physical and cognitive disabilities on the life of the couple. Adults over 65 are at greater risk than younger people of presenting a number of simultaneous health problems, although aging-related functional incapacities more often appear at around age 75.[15] Stressful events associated with aging, such as illness and severe incapacities, may lead to an escalation of violence within a couple already experiencing conjugal violence or may even engender violence in a previously harmonious couple.[16]

Two particular situations may surface at an advanced age: the caregiver who mistreats the care receiver and the care receiver who mistreats the caregiver. Indeed, incapacitated older adults who take medication are at greater risk of experiencing conjugal violence.[17] The end of the conjugal relationship may signify not only the breakup of the couple, but also placement in an institution if the individuals lack the necessary resources to meet their health-care needs at home. Often, even faced with a crisis situation in which separation is necessary for safety reasons, there are no specialized resources for older women (or men) who are faced with a loss of autonomy and are victims of conjugal violence. Shelters welcome women of all ages, but, currently, they can accommodate only women who are autonomous.

However, one should not conclude that all caregivers who experience stress will mistreat their partners. The "caregiver stress model" has long perpetuated the idea that family caregivers lacking sufficient support or resources experience such tremendous stress that it can lead to violence against the older care receiver.[18] This perception of the situation absolves the partner of responsibility by attributing the situation to stress, and it thus blames the victim who needs the care. Many family caregivers experience stress, but only a minority are violent. Violence perpetrated by partners is often due to a combination of factors, such as difficulty with managing stress, substance abuse problems, and lower levels of education and income.[19]

When there is a pre-existing history of violence, female caregivers do not necessarily know how to assert themselves or are unable to set limits to ensure their own psychological or physical well-being.[20] Indeed, the dynamics of toxic power (for example, manipulation, shaming, and denigration) within violent relationships are maintained with advancing age, even if the violent partner is ill and needs care from his or her partner. Some older women still perceive their partner as being physically imposing and threatening even when this is no longer the case.[21] For some individuals, controlling behaviours intensify as health problems arise.[22] Women thus find themselves in difficult situations, since they are at the same time family caregivers and victims. Practitioners need to recognize this duality in order to help these women.

Conclusion

Conjugal violence does not disappear with age. It exists among older couples and is expressed mainly in psychological violence, which is no less harmful than other forms of violence. There may also be financial exploitation and physical violence, but to a lesser degree. The context of care (caregiver-care receiver) also fosters the deterioration of relationships that were already conflictual or the emergence of a new, unhealthy dynamic within the couple. The fact that psychological violence is more difficult to recognize than physical violence makes identification more challenging. Even the victims themselves are not always aware that their life history has been characterized by violence.

The objective of interventions with older victims of conjugal violence is to help them identify the violence in the couple's relationship and its consequences, and to promote respect for their fundamental right to live in safety and without violence. These interventions are also intended to maximize the victims' knowledge about the opportunities and resources available for them to obtain some respite if they are caregivers for their partner and about the legal recourses available for them to report the violence they are experiencing and initiate separation procedures. Acts of violence, whether intentional or not, must be taken seriously. Silence sometimes hides tremendous suffering.

Notes

1   Website of the awareness-raising campaign "Vivre la violence conjugale 2014," <http://vivrelaviolenceconjugale.ca/# !/?id=9>, accessed February 24, 2017.

2   Gouvernement du Québec (2012), *2012–2017 Government Action Plan on Domestic Violence* (Quebec City: Gouvernement du Québec), 1, <http://www.scf.gouv.qc.ca/fileadmin/Documents/Violences/Plan_d_action_2012-2017_version_anglaise.pdf>, accessed March 1, 2019.

3   World Health Organization (2002), "Chapter 5. Abuse of the elderly," in Étienne G. Krug, Linda L. Dahlberg, James A. Mercy, Anthony Zwi, and Rafael Lozano-Ascencio (eds.), *World Report on Violence and Health* (Geneva: World Health Organization), 123–46.

4   Jocelyne Légaré (1983), "La condition juridique des femmes ou l'historique d'une 'affaire de famille,'" *Criminologie*, Vol. 16, No. 2, 7–26.

5   Ministère de la Famille et des Aînés (2017), *Plan d'action gouvernemental pour contrer la maltraitance envers les personnes ainées 2017–2022* (Quebec City: Gouvernement du Québec), 15.

6   Statistics Canada (2016), *Family Violence in Canada: A Statistical Profile, 2014*, Ottawa, Statistics Canada, Catalogue No. 85-002-X, <http://www.statcan.gc.ca/pub/85-002-x/2016001/article/14303-eng.pdf>, accessed February 24, 2017.

7   Christopher Poole and John Rietschlin (2012), "Intimate partner victimization among adults aged 60 and older: An analysis of the 1999 and 2004 General Social Survey," *Journal of Elder Abuse and Neglect*, Vol. 24, No. 2, 120–137.

8   Lyse Montminy (2005), "Older women's experiences of psychological violence in their marital relationships," *Journal of Gerontological Social Work*, Vol. 46, No. 2, 3–22.

9   Yon Yongjie, Andrew V. Wister, Barbara Mitchell, and Gloria Gutman (2014), "A national comparison of spousal abuse in mid- and old age," *Journal of Elder Abuse and Neglect*, Vol. 26, No. 1, 80–105.

10   Christine A. Walsh, Jenny Ploeg, Lynne Lohfeld, Jaclyn Horne, Harriet MacMillan, and Daniel Lai (2007), "Violence across the lifespan: Interconnections among forms of abuse as described by marginalized Canadian elders and their care-givers," *British Journal of Social Work*, Vol. 37, No. 3, 491–514.

11   Jill Hightower, M. J. Greta Smith, and Henry Hightower (2006), "Hearing the voices of abused older women," *Journal of Gerontological Social Work*, Vol. 46, No. 3–4, 205–27.

12   Lori E. Weeks and Kristal LeBlanc (2011), "An ecological synthesis of research on older women's experiences of intimate partner violence," *Journal of Women and Aging*, Vol. 23, No. 4, 283–304.

13   Hightower et al. (2006), op. cit.

14   Poole and Rietschlin (2012), op. cit.

15   Susan E. Bronskill, Jacqueline E. Stevenson, John P. Hirdes, and A. Henry David (2011), "Aging in Ontario: Using population-based data in the evaluation of trends in health system use," *Health Quarterly*, Vol. 14, No. 2, 21–25; Neena L. Chappell (2011), *Population Aging and the Evolving Care Needs of Older Canadians* (Montreal: Institute for Research on Public Policy), <http://irpp.org/wp-content/uploads/assets/research/faces-of-aging/population-aging-and-the-evolving-care-needs-of-older-canadians/IRPP-Study-no21.pdf>, accessed February 24, 2017.

16   Walsh et al. (2007), op. cit.

17   Poole and Rietschlin (2012), op. cit.

18   Bonnie Brandl and Jane A. Raymond (2012), "Policy implications of recognizing that caregiver stress is not the primary cause of elder abuse," *Generations – Journal of the American Society on Aging*, Vol. 36, No. 3, 32–39.

19   Poole and Rietschlin (2012), op. cit.

20   Tova Band-Winterstein (2015), "A phenomenological conceptual framework for understanding elderly women who experienced lifelong IPV," *Journal of Elder Abuse and Neglect*, Vol. 27, No. 4–5, 303–27.

21   Rachel Lev-Wiesel and Bruria Kleinberg (2002), "Elderly battered wives' perceptions of the spousal relationship as reflected in the drawings of the couple," *Arts in Psychotherapy*, Vol. 29, No. 1, 13–17.

22   Montminy (2005), op. cit.

Part 4
SOCIAL ROLES

———————

17

Living Longer

Years of Retirement or Years of Work?

Yves Carrière, Patrik Marier, Jonathan Purenne,
and Diane Galarneau

The Myth

It's hard to forget all those "Freedom 55" ads that suggested that retirement at age 55 was the ultimate and appropriate outcome of a successful life. Those ads portrayed this highly sought-after "freedom" by showing workers in their forties imagining themselves on an idyllic beach when they reached 55. These images from the late 1980s were long held to be the ideal form of retirement: taking it as early as possible and enjoying life! When these ads were most popular, the labour force participation rate for adults aged 55 to 69, particularly men, was dropping dramatically. The trend continued into the mid-1990s, showing no sign of running out of steam. The dream of retiring at 55 years of age also seemed perfectly achievable with the imminent arrival of the leisure society. According to the myth, new retirees would inevitably spend more and more time in retirement, perhaps even longer than they spent in the workforce. The concept is still around, used by people promoting financial products designed for older workers. It can also be found in the relatively recent (2011) comprehensive report by a Quebec commission of inquiry onto the labour force participation of older workers, which notes that "Quebecers retire early and there is no indication that they intend to change this behaviour."[1] Are people really retiring increasingly early? Is the retirement period still growing apace? Is it a reality or simply a myth that tends to amplify the negative image of population aging and its consequences?

Description and Origins of the Myth

The myth persists because it is grounded in official statistics. Let's begin with life expectancy. Although it is true that life expectancy for Quebecers has been increasing steadily, this is nothing new; it occurred throughout the twentieth century. What is relatively recent, however, particularly for men, is the rapid increase in life expectancy at age 65. According to the Canadian Human Mortality Database, a 65-year old Quebec man in 1921 could expect to live for another 13.1 years.[2] By 1975, this life expectancy had increased by only 0.2 years, to 13.3 years; however, from 1975 to 2011, it jumped to 18.7 years, an increase of more than five years. Among women, life expectancy after 65 grew even more rapidly, from 13.6 to 17.0 years between 1921 and 1975, and then to 21.8 years in 2011.

Alongside this increase in life expectancy was an apparent decrease in the labour force participation rate for people aged 55 years and over, particularly men. In 1976, two thirds of Quebecers in the 60- to 64-year age group were in the workforce, and this figure dropped to just over one third (37 percent) in 1996. Over this same period, the percentage for 65- to 69-year-olds fell from one out of five (21.1 percent) to one out of 10 (10.7 percent). For women, the participation rate for those 55 years and older remained relatively stable, at below 20 percent for 60- to 64-year-olds and only around 5 percent for 65- to 69-year-olds.

These two trends observed between 1976 and 1996, combined with population aging, led to criticism of an unprecedented increase in the number of years of retirement, leading to a growing class of dependent retirees at risk of becoming an unbearable burden on future generations of workers.

Where Do Things Really Stand?

To better understand these trends, we will begin by analyzing the link between retirement age trends and life expectancy. Is it true that the number of years in retirement is still increasing steadily? We will then answer a second question that is a corollary of the first: Is it fair to consider those aged 65 years and older to be "dependent?" Will the growing size of this population within the overall population of Quebec become a growing burden on younger generations?

For the time spent in retirement to increase, either the retirement age needs to decrease or life expectancy needs to increase. Clearly, if both trends occur at the same time, the number of years spent in retirement will increase even faster. As we saw above, life expectancy has indeed increased over time. Let us now examine how the effective retirement age has changed.[3] The effective retirement age is the age at which workers exit the workforce to retire, and it should not be confused with the normal retirement age, which refers to the age at which people are usually entitled to their full pension under the Canada Pension Plan or the Quebec Pension Plan, which is 65 years of age.

Increasing the Effective Retirement Age

What does the estimated effective retirement age of Canadians tell us? The first finding is that there was indeed a period during which the effective retirement age decreased. For example, both men and women in the cohort born in 1932 took retirement slightly earlier than members of earlier cohorts. This result is not very surprising given that people born in 1932 were entering their sixties in the 1990s, a period during which there was an unprecedented rise in early retirement to offset federal and provincial deficits. The private sector had also adopted labour management policies that promoted the early retirement of aging workers. However, subsequent cohorts, both men and women, reversed this trend and began to retire later and later: the effective age of retirement reached 64.2 years and 63.0 years, respectively,[4] for men and women born in 1945,[5] an increase of at least a year compared to the men and women born in 1932 (for whom the effective retirement age was 62.3 years for men and 61.6 years for women).

The second finding is that we are heading toward a slow but steady increase in the effective retirement age. As can be seen in Figure 17.1, this age could well exceed 65 years for men born in 1966 and 64 years for women in the same birth cohort, the last of the baby-boom generation.

The increase in the effective retirement age can be explained by several trends that successively influenced people's retirement decisions, including later transition to adulthood (later entry into the labour force, marriage, starting a family, and so on). These delays have an impact on later stages in life, and stem to a great extent from more years of education. Other trends, such as steep declines in the coverage rate of pension plans and the increasingly frequent replacement of existing plans by less generous ones, as well as household debt, a decline in financial market performance, and an increase in life expectancy, had the effect, to some degree, of delaying the decision to retire. Nor should we discount the impact of the public retirement income system, which is not particularly generous for middle- and high-income workers.

FIGURE 17.1

Effective retirement age by sex and birth cohort, Canada, 1927–66

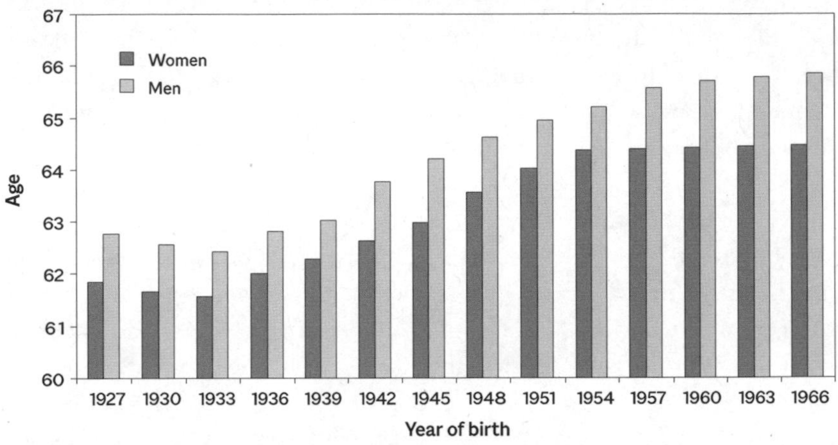

Note: For cohorts born after 1945, the effective retirement age is calculated partly from projections.

Source: Special tabulations from Statistics Canada based on Labour Force Survey data.

Is the Length of the Retirement Period Increasing?

As mentioned above, life expectancy at age 65 has increased significantly over the past four decades. This trend, combined with the general idea that people could retire at age 55, would lead us to believe that the retirement period has increased steadily over the years. That was the vision of the leisure society. Were we really going to spend more years in retirement than we spent in the workforce?

Retirement and mortality rates by age and sex for cohorts born in or after 1927 can be used to measure average lifespan before and after retirement for employed individuals aged 50. As Figure 17.2 shows, the expected retirement period increased by more than two years between men born in 1927 and those born in 1944. Also, based on our projections, this retirement period could gain another year and a half up to the cohort born in 1966. For women, the increase is more modest, at approximately two years over the whole period.

When the effective retirement period is expressed as a percentage of life expectancy at 50 years of age, the trend is very different: the proportion of years of retirement initially increased (rising from 54.9 percent for men born in 1927 to 58.4 percent for those born in 1938 and from 64.7 percent for women born in 1927 to 66.3 percent for those born in 1934), and then decreased for the following cohorts; according to our projections, it should

FIGURE 17.2

Expected length of retirement by sex and birth cohort, Canada, 1927–66

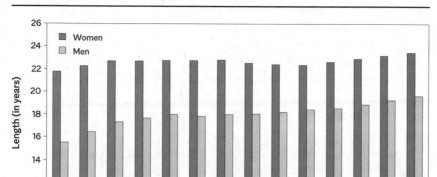

Note: For cohorts born after 1945, the effective retirement age is calculated partly from projections.

Source: Special tabulations from Statistics Canada based on Labour Force Survey data.

remain at approximately 55 percent and 61 percent for men and women, respectively, born in or after 1950 (Figure 17.3). The fact that people have been living longer in recent decades thus does not necessarily mean that these added years are years of retirement. It is nevertheless not impossible that this proportion could begin to rise again, but for that to happen, cohorts born after the 1950s would have to slow or reverse the trend toward postponing retirement.

Seniors, Retirees, and Dependency

As we saw above, the retirement period initially became longer as a proportion of life expectancy at age 50, while life expectancy at age 50 increased and people were retiring increasingly early. This trend toward a lengthening of the retirement period did not last, however, and for approximately 20 years now, the increase in the effective retirement age has been outpacing gains in life expectancy. Also noteworthy is that the proportion of members of a given cohort who are in the labour force has increased substantially over the past few decades with an unprecedented rise in labour force participation by women. Combined with this rise, the postponement of retirement has had an impact on what is generally called the elderly potential support ratio.

FIGURE 17.3

Expected length of retirement as a percentage of life expectancy at age 50, by sex and birth cohort, Canada, 1927–66

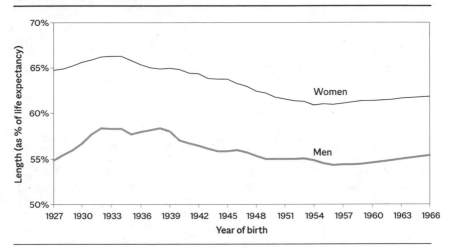

Note: For cohorts born after 1945, the effective retirement age is calculated partly from projections.
Source: Special tabulations from Statistics Canada based on Labour Force Survey data.

In spite of the positive impact of retirement deferral and the increase in labour force participation by women, this ratio, which is the number of 15- to 64-year-olds for each person aged 65 or over, dropped from around 10 in the 1970s to below five today, thus doubling the "burden" in 40 years! As defined, this ratio is, to say the least, misleading, but it is unfortunately still widely used in public policy analyses in industrialized countries. Its use was even strongly encouraged in the past by major international organizations, such the Organization for Economic Co-operation and Development and the World Bank, despite the many criticisms of its relevance and usefulness.[6]

The main drawback of the ratio is the assumption that people aged 15 to 64 are all in the labour force and that those 65 and over are not, thus assuming that the latter are "supported" by the former. This is far from an accurate picture. An alternative version of the ratio could use people's labour force status – that is, whether or not they are employed – rather than their age group. Thus defined, the trend line for the potential support ratio would look very different: far from having decreased by almost half, the potential support ratio based on labour force status would show an increase from 1.1 in 1976 to 1.4 in 2015. This increase is the result of the fact that we now have proportionately more employed people in the 15-and-over age group than 40 years ago, even though the population was much younger then! Why? Simply because more and more women and people aged 65 and over are now in the workforce. Being "supported" is linked not so much to age but to individual behaviour and characteristics. This alternative definition of the ratio still has some weaknesses, because we certainly cannot describe parents who remain at home to raise their children, or retired people who perform an active role in society by volunteering their services or financially or otherwise helping their children, friends, and relatives, as being supported by others.

Conclusion

These findings illustrate a reality that is much more complex than the long-standing myth perpetuated in the media and firmly fixed in the public mind. On the one hand, people are not retiring earlier. On the contrary, for at least two decades now, the effective retirement age has been increasing. This increase is of particular importance given that it would also be false to assume that the years added to life expectancy have all been years of retirement. We are not on the cusp of the leisure society. Even though it is difficult to predict the future, the trend in the length of retirement as a proportion of life expectancy at age 50 does not support the idea of a reversal of this trend over the short term.

More importantly perhaps, although it is true that population aging presents challenges with respect to economic growth, it is ridiculous to simply treat people aged 65 and over as a burden on the rest of the population. More than ever, they have been contributing to economic growth by remaining in the labour force longer, and this trend does not show signs of reversing for the time being. And when they do retire, these people are not, strictly speaking, supported or being "dependent" on the rest of society. The concept of dependency based solely on age marginalizes the contribution of retired people and seniors by creating a dichotomy between those who are being "supported" and those who are "active," as if their age group were a reflection of their status in the labour force. Lastly, although it may be true that seniors receive financial resources and services paid for by the employed population, it is also true that they contribute to social well-being – and hence to those who are active in the labour force – through contributions such as volunteer work, financial aid to children, and caring for grandchildren.

Acknowledgments

The authors would like to thank the Social Sciences and Humanities Research Council of Canada and Finances Montréal for their financial support, which made it possible to prepare the findings in this chapter.

Notes

1   Commission nationale sur la participation au marché du travail des travailleuses et travailleurs expérimentés de 55 ans et plus (2011), *Le vieillissement de la main-d'œuvre et l'avenir de la retraite: des enjeux pour tous, un effort de chacun*, Quebec City (our translation).

2   Canadian Human Mortality Database: <http://www.bdlc.umontreal.ca/CHMD>, accessed March 27, 2017.

3   For a detailed explanation of the method used to estimate effective retirement age, see Yves Carrière and Diane Galarneau (2011), "Delayed retirement: A new trend?," in *Perspectives on Labour and Income*, Ottawa: Statistics Canada, Catalogue No. 75-001-X, 3–18. The calculations used also take into account "involuntary" retirements for economic and health reasons and due to family responsibilities. For a definition of involuntary retirements, see Yves Carrière and Diane Galarneau (2012), "How many years to retirement?," *Insights on Canadian Society*, Ottawa, Statistics Canada, Catalogue No. 75-006-X. The retirement rates used to calculate the effective retirement age were extracted from the Labour Force Survey data. The effective retirement age was estimated by cohort – that is, everyone born in a given year. One advantage of this approach is that it makes it easier to identify changes in behaviour and to estimate not only the effective retirement age but also how long this retirement will last, based on life expectancy for each cohort. In principle, however, one needs to wait until every member of a cohort has retired or died to make these estimates. For example, the observed data cannot be used to estimate the rate of retirement by people over the age of 70 for those born after 1945, because they were only 70 years old in 2015. This means using projection methods to estimate retirement rates that have not been observed. For the purpose of this article, we have assumed that non-observed retirement rates remain constant over time at their observed 2012 level. For example, the retirement rates for 72-year old men in 2022 is assumed to be equal to the rate of retirement for men aged 72 years in 2012. To complete the estimate for the effective retirement age and length of retirement, we must also use mortality rates. Here again, we need projections to estimate future mortality rates by age and sex. In this chapter, we use the mortality assumptions developed by Statistics Canada (2015) to establish the mean assumptions for their most recent projections. See Statistics Canada (2015), *Population Projections for Canada (2013 to 2063), Provinces and Territories (2013 to 2038)*, Ottawa, Statistics Canada, Catalogue No. 91-520-X.

4   Many people will have retired before this age and many later. The logic is the same as that for the interpretation of life expectancy, which should be understood to be the mean age at death for an entire cohort.

5   The cohort born in 1945 was 70 years of age in 2015, and the history of their shift from working life to retirement is incomplete. We therefore assumed that the risk of

retirement after 70 years of age would be identical to that observed in 2012, even though there has been a downward trend in retirement rates over the past two decades. Nevertheless, the assumptions made for the retirement risk projections will have little effect on cohorts born prior to 1945 because their working life was largely over in 2012.

6   Rune Ervik (2005), "The battle of future pensions: global accounting tools, international organizations and pension reforms," *Global Social Policy*, Vol. 5, No. 1, 29–54.

18

Older Workers

A Societal Problem?

Marie-Michèle Lord and Pierre-Yves Therriault

Gaëtan, 59 years old, arrives at work after a forty-minute journey by car that he knows like the back of his hand. For almost sixteen years now, Gaëtan has left his suburban home every day to go to the office. He works as an assistant accountant in a private firm. This morning, the room that his cubicle is in is quieter than usual. He then remembers that most of his colleagues are at a training session to which he was not invited. With a sigh, he pulls out his chair and turns on his computer. From his bag, he takes out the Ignès Cagnati novel in which, last night, he read a sentence that still resonates with him: "The old people with the old people in nursing homes, the young people with the young people at work, and the children with the other children at school."[1] Gaëtan has the impression that this sentence accurately reflects his employer's thinking: older people are less productive and useful at work, and they should retire to leave room for young people!

The Myth: Older Workers No Longer Have a Place in the Work Environment

Gaëtan suffers from prejudices against older workers that are still very prevalent; within the labour market, negative beliefs about this group are deeply rooted. For example, social representations of aging as signifying reduced performance at work, a lack of flexibility and versatility, difficulty in adapting to technology, and resistance to change remain widespread.[2]

These prejudices have led to various situations of exclusion of older workers over the years: limited opportunities for advancement, strategies to push them to retire, and less access to training.[3] Furthermore, it is still more difficult today for people over 50 to find a job than it is for their younger colleagues.[4]

Negative beliefs about aging workers are connected to three common types of discourse: that the aging of the population is a catastrophe, that seniors are a burden to society, and that aging makes people less productive.[5] Unfortunately, the phenomenon of aging at work is often analyzed in the public arena, generally from the angle of social problems that might lead to a crisis in the funding of pension plans and a labour force shortage. Aside from concerns about people leaving the labour force to retire, employers pay little attention to aging workers, and the potential of experienced workers is often greatly underestimated.[6]

The myth analyzed in this chapter is that aging workers are usually a burden to employers and are no longer efficient.

Variable Losses Offset by Multiple Factors and Strategies

On the Level of Cognitive and Physical Capacities

The body generally begins to show the initial signs of aging around the age of 45. There are many possible results of this process, which may vary with each individual. The "normal" aging process is inevitably accompanied by more or less major changes to the body.[7]

First, aging has been shown to affect the brain. For example, to different degrees, depending on the individual, aging may impact divided attention (the capacity to do several things at once) and certain memory functions (see Chapter 5, "Grey-Haired Neurons: Does an Accurate Memory Have to Become a Memento of Younger Days?"), including working memory, which allows for the short-term retention of information in the brain and increases the speed at which information is processed.[8] One might conclude from this that aging workers underperform in tasks requiring retention of information or rapid processing of data. In fact, it is not that simple, as employees' expertise can make a significant difference. Indeed, for many people, performing the same tasks for a certain number of years allows the brain to benefit from the experience acquired, which lessens the changes in cognitive capacities. This is referred to as cognitive expertise.[9]

What about the capacity to learn new things? Procedural memory, associated with knowing how to do something, is generally not affected during normal aging and may even be enhanced.[10] Furthermore, although age has an effect on learning new subjects, and although older workers are likely to learn less quickly than their younger counterparts, their previous knowledge may compensate for the decline in working memory, which is called upon in the learning phase.[11] It is therefore wrong to believe that an employee who is growing older will not be able to integrate new learning. Rather, the conditions under which the learning takes place make a real difference.

Providing older workers with access to training could, on the contrary, have a positive effect on their health and retention at work. Indeed, research demonstrates that most older employees prefer a stimulating environment in which they can progress in terms of skills, knowledge, and involvement.[12]

Second, normal aging has an impact on strength and muscular endurance, which tends to diminish between 50 and 60 years of age. This phenomenon is known as dynapenia.[13] This reduced strength is accompanied by a loss of muscle mass of approximately 1 percent to 2 percent per year. This is called sarcopenia, and is characterized by the atrophy of muscle fibres and a reduction in their number.[14] Does this lessening of strength and endurance inevitably produce negative effects at work? Not necessarily. First, the reduction in functional capacities varies greatly from one individual to another. Second, for the majority, most functional impairment remains limited until the age of 65 or 70. Third, there is no generalized decline of overall capacity with age. Finally, a number of approaches could alleviate the potential problem of older workers' declining physical capacities. Adjustments could be made, for example, by assigning older workers to less physically demanding tasks.[15] In such a context, the physical effects related to aging will have little or no negative impact on the work accomplished.

On the Level of Work Performance

Are workers efficient at every age? A number of studies have examined the link between age and work performance. They show that the evolution of performance with age varies tremendously according to the working conditions and the worker's capacities to adopt appropriate strategies and draw upon his or her work expertise.[16] Thus, the possibility of aging workers performing satisfactorily without damaging their health depends on the experience acquired over the course of their career and their working conditions.[17]

Declines associated with age are usually counterbalanced by individuals' experience and the strategies that they employ, when the employer allows them to use such strategies. More flexible schedules, a reduction in the stress associated with work tasks, and more time to integrate new working methods are examples of factors that could have a positive effect on older workers' performance and their job retention.[18] Moreover, "All the surveys and studies agree that the primary condition that enables older workers to envisage prolonging their workforce participation beyond their age of eligibility for retirement is a lightening of their tasks."[19] The possibility of adapting tasks to take older workers' expectations and capacities into account seems essential for the optimal participation of these workers. Older workers' performance can thus be comparable to that of their younger colleagues if the conditions for carrying out the work are favourable.

On the Level of Flexibility and the Capacity to Adapt

Is it true that older workers are reluctant to adapt to changes at work? Various studies of the baby-boomer generation, currently between 50 and 69 years of age, instead show that a strong capacity to adapt, among other factors, is considered key by this group for adjusting to work demands.[20] Baby boomers do not wish to be identified with the image of the older person as unproductive, passive, and dependent. Instead, they want to have a say in the overall functioning of the work organization in order to be able to adapt. Furthermore, it is important for them to be able to use their work experience and knowledge to actively participate in the life of their work environment and find job satisfaction.[21] As well, ongoing research on the effect of changes at work on the mental health of older workers in the health sector tends to show that older workers do not feel particularly threatened by changes at work and that they manage to adjust effectively if given the opportunity.[22] Even more importantly, a strong need for recognition arises during the process of aging at work, and this need is even more intense in a context of innovation.

This does not mean that, at times, some older workers are not reluctant to confront change.[23] Resistance to change can sometimes constitute a defence strategy – for example, when older workers are faced with demands that they consider unacceptable – rather than being the result of an inability to adapt.[24] It may then be a conscious gesture of rejection by the worker, in order to protect his or her own mental and physical health.

Toward Healthy Aging at Work

Is healthy aging at work possible? For the most part, the manner in which people age depends on their environment, including their working conditions. "When these are difficult, the individual's work may prematurely reveal deficiencies that were not noticeable until that point, and it may also accelerate or amplify aging mechanisms, thus creating mechanisms of premature or accelerated fatigue."[25] Healthy aging at work is possible when working conditions do not lead to premature wear and tear or place the aging worker in a difficult situation.[26]

The question here is not whether the worker is aging but rather at what point he or she becomes unable to meet the requirements of a job.[27] On-the-job demands play a determining role in the equation.[28] If workers have at their disposal a margin of manoeuvre to develop adaptive strategies and if working conditions are adjusted so as to lessen the possible negative effects on health, aging healthily within an organization is possible.

For this to occur, employers must adopt different working methods within their organizations: for example, they need to improve working conditions, develop and draw upon older workers' skills, and encourage their recognition.[29] The last factor "is, moreover, a major failing of both public organizations and private enterprises. Employers must give their employees feedback" and value the involvement of older workers.[30] For their part, under the appropriate conditions, older workers can implement certain strategies, such as anticipating a problem based on their experience, choosing less demanding working techniques, and establishing priorities according to what is asked of them at on the job.[31]

Conclusion

A number of widely held perceptions tend to support the idea that older workers gradually become useless and cannot adapt and contribute to the working environment. However, it is possible to age healthily at work and remain useful to the employer. Older workers, moreover, represent major human, social, and technical assets to enterprises.[32] Although normal aging does indeed involve changes, both physical and cognitive, workers can successfully adapt to the effects of growing older. A work environment that provides the means for such an adjustment and that offers workers recognition for the efforts made in the process of adaptation is crucial. Consequently, the responsibility of employers in this context is to adjust to the aging labour force by adopting appropriate measures.

Notes

1   Ignès Cagnati (1979), *Mosé ou le Lézard qui pleurait* (Paris: Denoël) (our translation).

2   Kelly Harris, Sarah Krygsman, Jessica Waschenko, and Debbie Laliberte Rudman (2016), "Ageism and the older worker: A scoping review," *Congrès de l'Association canadienne d'ergothérapie (ACE): S'inspirer pour viser les plus hauts sommets,* Banff, April 22; Isabelle Faurie, Franco Fraccaroli, and Alexis Le Blanc (2008), "Âge et travail: des études sur le vieillissement au travail à une approche psychosociale de la fin de la carrière professionnelle," *Le travail humain,* Vol. 71, No. 2, 137–72; Michael G. Morris and Viswanath Venkatesh (2000), "Age differences in technology adoption decisions: Implications for a changing workforce," *Personnel Psychology,* Vol. 53, No. 3, 375–404.

3   Statistics Canada (2012), "Job-related training of older workers," *Perspectives on Labour and Income,* Ottawa, Statistics Canada, Catalogue No. 75-001-X, Summer.

4   Connie R. Wanberg, Ruth Kanfer, Darla J. Hamann, and Zhen Zhang (2016), "Age and reemployment success after job loss: An integrative model and meta-analysis," *Psychological Bulletin,* Vol. 142, No. 4, 400–26.

5   Martine Lagacé (2010), *L'âgisme: comprendre et changer le regard social sur le vieillissement* (Quebec City: Presses de l'Université Laval).

6   Commission nationale sur la participation au marché du travail des travailleuses et travailleurs expérimentés de 55 ans et plus (2011), *Le vieillissement de la main-d'œuvre et l'avenir de la retraite: des enjeux pour tous, un effort de chacun* (Montreal: Bibliothèque et Archives nationales du Québec), 31.

7   Catherine Hellemans (2006), "Les travailleurs âgés et la fin de carrière: stéréotypes et réalités," in Olivier Klein and Sabine Pohl (eds.), *Psychologies des stéréotypes et des préjugés* (Loverval: Éditions Labor).

8   Elizabeth L. Glisky (2007), "Changes in cognitive function in human aging," in David R. Riddle (ed.), *Brain Aging: Models, Methods, and Mechanisms* (Salem: CRC Press).

9   Naftali Raz (2000), "Aging of the brain and its impact on cognitive performance: Integration of structural and functional findings," in Fergus Craik (ed.), *The Handbook of Aging and Cognition* (New Jersey: Lawrence Erlbaum Associates).

10 Bénédicte Giffard, Béatrice Desgranges, and Francis Eustache (2001), "Le vieillissement de la mémoire: vieillissement normal et pathologique," *Gérontologie et société,* Vol. 2, No. 97, 33–47.

11 Jeanette N. Cleveland and Lynn M. Shore (2007), "Work and employment: Individual," in James E. Birren (ed.), *Encyclopedia of Gerontology* (Boston: Elsevier); Andreas Kruse and Eric Schmitt (2007), "Adult education," in James E. Birren (ed.), *Encyclopedia of Gerontology* (Boston: Elsevier).

12 Andrew Sharpe (2011), "Is ageing a drag on productivity growth? A review article on ageing, health and productivity: The economics of increased life expectancy," *International Productivity Monitor,* No. 21, Spring, 82–94.

13 Jacques Duchateau, Caroline Nicol, and Stéphane Baudry (2014), "Le vieillissement du système neuromusculaire: de la sarcopénie à la dynapénie," *Kinésithérapie, la Revue,* Vol. 14, No. 145, 45–51.

14 Ibid.

15 Jean-François Guilloteau (2011), "Vieillissement et pratiques des entreprises," *Regards sur le travail,* Vol. 7, No. 3, 1–13.

16 Stephan J. Motowidlo (2003), "Job performance," in Walter C. Borman (ed.), *Handbook of Psychology, Industrial and Organizational Psychology* (New Jersey: Wiley).

17 Jean Damasse and Brigitte Doyon (2000), *Travailler en vieillissant, vieillir en travaillant: une recension des écrits sur le vieillissement prématuré des travailleurs* (Quebec City: Équipe de recherche RIPOST).

18 Commission nationale sur la participation au marché du travail des travailleuses et travailleurs expérimentés de 55 ans et plus (2011), op. cit.

19 Ibid., 49 (our translation).

20 Antoine Laville, Corinne Gaudart, and Valérie Pueyo (2004), "Vieillissement et travail," in Éric Brangier, Alain Lancry, and Claude Louche (eds.), *Les dimensions humaines du travail: théories et pratiques de la psychologie du travail et des organisations* (Nancy: Hal); Laure Blein, Jean-Pierre Lavoie, Nancy Guberman, and Ignace Olazabal (2009), "Vieilliront-ils un jour? Les baby-boomers aidants face à leur vieillissement," *Lien social et Politiques*, No. 62, Fall, 123–24.

21 Julie Christin and Jean-Marie Peretti (2006), "Perception du travail chez les cadres du secteur privé français à l'approche de la retraite," *Actes du XVIIe Congrès de l'AGRH*, Reims, November.

22 Marie-Michèle Lord, Pierre-Yves Therriault, Ginette Aubin, and Hélène Carbonneau (2016), "Les risques à la santé mentale des travailleurs vieillissants de l'intime; prévention collective et pouvoir d'agir," *5e Colloque REIACTIS: Vieillissement et pouvoirs d'agir: entre ressources et vulnérabilités*, Lausanne, February 11.

23 Faurie et al. (2008), op. cit.

24 Antoine Laville, Corinne Gaudart, and Valérie Pueyo (2004), "Vieillissement et travail," in Éric Brangier, Alain Lancry, and Claude Louche (eds.), *Les dimensions humaines du travail: théories et pratiques de la psychologie du travail et des organisations* (Nancy: Hal).

25 Institut national de recherche et de sécurité (2011), *Bien vieillir au travail* (Paris: INRS), 6 (our translation).

26 Antoine Laville (1989), "Vieillissement et travail," *Le travail humain*, Vol. 52, No. 1, 3–20.

27 Catherine Teiger (1995), "Penser les relations âge/travail au cours du temps," in Jean-Claude Marquié, Dominique Paumès, and Serge Volkoff (eds.), *Le travail au fil de l'âge* (Toulouse: Octares).

28 World Health Organization (2015), *Ageing and Health*, FactSheet No. 404, September.

29 Institut national de recherche et de sécurité (2011), op. cit., p. 30.

30 Commission nationale sur la participation au marché du travail des travailleuses et travailleurs expérimentés de 55 ans et plus (2011), op. cit (our translation).

31 World Health Organization (2015), op. cit.

32 Ibid.

19

Do Older Adults Have All the Time in the World?

Isabel Wiebe, Anne-Marie Séguin, Philippe Apparicio, and Véronique Billette

The Myth: Free Time ... to Enjoy Life

Don't older adults have time to spare? Out of the labour force and released from family responsibilities that used to monopolize their time, isn't their sole concern to find a way to fill these hours, free from any constraints? This perception is widespread, for example, in advertising for senior housing. One such advertised residential complex proclaims that it "was designed to satisfy the needs of the most demanding customers. Here, all of the residents' skills and abilities – intellectual, athletic, artistic, and social – can be given free rein."[1] Older adults are said to have considerable time to devote to their choice of recreational and social pursuits (painting courses, organized outings, fitness activities, volunteer work, and so on). In political science, grey power is in part attributed to the time that seniors have available to put pressure on their representatives.[2]

According to Statistics Canada data, Canadian seniors do have more free time at their disposal than younger adults: 7 hours and 24 minutes a day for those aged 65 to 74, and 7 hours and 41 minutes for those 75 and older, compared with 4 hours and 22 minutes a day for people aged 35 to 44.[3] Yet the time devoted to active leisure pursuits, social or community activities, and volunteer work increases little with age, especially for those aged 75 and older. Older adults also have to spend more time on sleep, meals, and other personal care activities.

Beyond the Myth: Fragmented Time and an Imposed Pace in Aspects of Daily Life

It seems, instead, that older adults' time is fragmented and regimented according to a number of daily life activities. Social science research indicates that seniors take more time to accomplish certain everyday tasks.[4] Their daily pace slows down, especially due to health problems, lack of energy, or increased fatigue. Regular medication use may require that particular times be set for eating meals, getting up, and going to bed.[5] The scheduling of healthcare appointments may pose a constraint, particularly when these appointments involve examinations or the taking of samples (fasting, for example), and it is difficult for older adults to predict their duration. A senior's free time is also reduced if he or she is caring for a friend or relative.[6]

Daily activities (shopping, leisure pursuits, medical appointments) usually require seniors to travel from one place to another. Yet, with age, the ability to get around is affected by physical or functional difficulties, and older adults are sometimes confronted with urban obstacles (such as the problematic condition or maintenance of sidewalks or the presence of stairs) that can increase the time required for the trip. Seniors walk more slowly than younger adults, which poses problems when they must, for example, cross wide intersections in the time allotted by the traffic lights.[7]

Finally, older adults' daily routines often include periods of waiting. Seniors are more likely to wait for weather conditions to improve and for pedestrian paths to be cleared of snow before they go out because they are afraid of falling. They also tend to avoid leaving home in the evening, during rush hours, and when businesses and services are likely to be crowded. When they need help for various activities (such as grocery shopping and going to the bank), some must wait for family members to be free to drive them or help them. Consequently, the windows of time available for activities become narrower. The time "freed" from occupational and family responsibilities is not really that free, due to such new constraints.

The Reality: Daily Mobility Practices of Older Adults in Rosemont–La Petite-Patrie

For an overview of seniors' time use, we turned to data from a study of the daily mobility practices of older adults in the Montreal district of Rosemont–La Petite-Patrie. Interviews were conducted with 21 participants aged 70 and older who were living alone, in order to learn about their mobility experiences, the reasons that they use specific services or amenities in a particular place, and their strategies for getting around, despite certain incapacities.[8] We report their remarks here (all of which are translated from the French) in order to illustrate their experiences and mobility strategies.

Adopting a Slower Pace

Analysis of the interviews reveals that, for these seniors, dividing trips into several stages and moving more slowly is a common practice. They stop and rest along the way, which allows them to conserve their energy. Here is the example of Ms. Paquin, who divides her trip into precise stages:[9]

> *Ms. Paquin (70 years old, using a cane)*
> I leave here. I get to the bus stop. There, I sit down. Then I continue as far as the college ... And, there, there are big cement blocks in front of the college. So, I sit down on a block there ... I look at the squirrels, or whatever. Then, I'm rested, and then I get up again ... Then, a bit further on, there's a picnic table ... So, I stop at the picnic table ... Then, afterwards, I come here [home] ... If you do all that, all at once, that would be more difficult. I would arrive home too exhausted.

Walking more slowly alleviates certain difficulties, including problems with balance and visual acuity, and allows for anticipation of obstacles (sidewalks that are uneven or have holes, and the height of steps). Letting the crowd go ahead before following in their footsteps is a way to avoid being jostled. Taking their time also allows seniors to prepare for the complex tasks required to cross a street, such as choosing the best spot to cross, assessing the traffic, and selecting the ideal moment.[10]

In the following quotations, seniors refer to their carefulness, deliberately slow pace, and greater attention to detail as strategies that they use to avoid falling or to conserve their energy.

> *Mr. Pham (84 years old, using a cane)*
> Right now, I still feel capable. Though I have difficulty walking, I'm still able to manage. With my cane, I still walk carefully. Still carefully and a bit slowly, but I manage to do those things.

> *Ms. Saint-Amour (81 years old)*
> Going up ... then down [stairs]. Because sometimes your vision isn't right. So you could miss a step. I pay attention. Now, I have to look ... When there's

jostling, I wait until after [the crowd], then I go up with the others. The subway trains come about every 8–10 minutes ... Rather than fall! ... I go slowly and I take my time.

Ms. Deschênes (90 years old, using a cane)
The knees, the cane ... I'm not saying that it's painful, but I get short of breath as I go up [the hill], even if I go up slowly ... It used to take me 10 minutes to get there [to the community centre], but today it takes me 20 minutes ... I walk more slowly.

(De)synchronization of Schedules and Activities

The interviews conducted for this research enabled us to make a second observation about time: despite older adults' free time, the synchronizing and organizing of activities and transport may be problematic, as some schedules are not very flexible. Synchronization is especially challenging for those using paratransit for medical appointments. Before reserving their transport, they must estimate the duration of the journey, including a possible 30-minute delay that the transit commission builds in for logistical reasons. They must then find out approximately how long the appointment will take, in order to arrange a time for the return trip with the transit commission. On the day of the appointment, they have to be sure to be ready on time. Often, they are ready well in advance since, due to health problems, some actions may require more time than expected. When appointments take longer than expected, adjusting the return time for paratransit creates major delays and leads to considerable frustration.

Ms. Bernier (74 years old, using a motorized wheelchair)
You always have to be ready an hour in advance because sometimes they come for me here. Say I'm going to the General Hospital ... for 9 a.m. ... But, I darn well have to be ready ahead of time! When I have to leave at 9, I have to be ready by 8 ... So, that means that I must get up at 6 in the morning to be all set, to be able to keep things on track. To be ready at 8. If it takes longer there [at the hospital], well, I have to call the STM [the transit commission] to say "Cancel my ride; I'll call you back because I'm not ready."

Due to problems with coordinating activities and transportation, waiting is part of older adults' daily experience. It is even more difficult when the place is not set up properly (for example, when there are no benches or shelter from intemperate weather):

Ms. Côté (86 years old, using a motorized wheelchair)
Here [in the residence], you can wait between the two doors. In winter you freeze between the two doors because it's not heated. So, you stay there; you're going to freeze, unless you're bloody well dressed. Sometimes you can wait 5 minutes, but you can wait for 30 minutes between the two doors. If your transport is at 1 p.m., they have 30 minutes leeway to come and get you.

Poor urban planning and seniors' reduced capacities greatly complicate street crossing. At intersections, traffic lights are normally set for people to walk quickly. It is often difficult for older adults to get across in the allotted time, especially without a proper set-up (such as a traffic island) that would allow them to cross in two stages. This task is even more arduous for people using a wheelchair. For example, when Ms. Côté crosses a major boulevard at a traffic light in a motorized wheelchair, she waits for the audible signal and the countdown to cross at the start of the cycle. She then stops at the traffic island in the centre of the roadway. At the next light, she must manoeuvre her wheelchair to position it to descend from the sidewalk and wait for the other pedestrians to be out of her way. Then, she has to lift herself up to see better, since, otherwise, her field of vision would be too low, and then speed up to cross before the light turns red.

Meticulous Planning of Trips in Time and Space

The data from the interviews yield a third observation: meticulous planning in time and space is essential to making trips feasible. Given their mobility issues, many seniors try to limit the risks. They avoid certain times (when there is bad weather, when it's dark, and during rush hour) so as not to fall or have to navigate through crowds.

Planning outings requires considerable effort. To evaluate the feasibility of a trip, people with reduced mobility often ask questions to learn more about their destination. For example, they will call a restaurant to see whether there is an access ramp, to find out the location of the washrooms and the width of the aisles to make sure they can get around, or to ask whether there is a parking lot. Older adults who use public transport often ask the public transit commission about the duration of the journey, possible alternative routes, and whether there are escalators (and whether they're working!) at the entrance to the subway. Here are a few examples:

Ms. Bernier (74 years old, using a motorized wheelchair)
Having to get around means being limited. It's worse in winter, you know, I

mean to say ... You have to just ... not go out often. You need a lot of time ... ordering groceries and all that is annoying ... Last winter was long. It gets longer every year.

Ms. Thibault (83 years old, using a walker)
"[The aisles at Dollarama] are wide enough, but there are a lot of things, and then the people: there are a lot of people ... You have to not go at rush hour or when there are lots of people. You go there in the morning. And there's no one there, you know."

To make it easier to synchronize transportation with activities, many people adopt routine strategies. When Ms. Marois goes to the hairdresser, she arranges to take the last morning bus (less crowded), given that this line only operates during rush hour. When Mr. Pham makes an appointment with his barber, he inquires about the current parking regulations (no-parking signs and times) so he can more easily find a place to park.

Even during the trip, people must remain alert and ensure that conditions are good, for example, for parking nearby, finding and using the elevator, and knowing where they can sit and rest. The windows of opportunity for activities outside the home are therefore limited and, in the long run, the burden of planning and stress may induce people to forgo certain outings. Ms. Champagne explains the series of steps she takes when helping her partner, who uses a walker:

Ms. Champagne (73 years old)
Sometimes it works out all right [going out with my partner], but when I'm tired, I can't do it any more. I brought him to the Jazz Festival. I brought him ... to Place des Arts. But even there, you have to think of everything. Where am I going to park? ... I have to be able to find the elevator. In the concert hall, I have to locate a seat for the disabled ... Everything is planned. All the time.

The organization of trips calls on a variety of skills, aptitudes, and abilities, and it can generate considerable stress for some older adults, as the following quotation illustrates:

Mr. Pham (84 years old, using a cane)
Every time I go to the hospital for an appointment for a routine examination, the night before the examination, I can't sleep. I plan. I have to find a way to get to the hospital.

Conclusion: Much Narrower Windows of Time for Activities

The testimony of older adults enables us to rethink the common view of seniors as being freed of all time constraints. First, older people must often devote more time to their daily routine because of health problems. Second, it takes them longer to get around. They encounter numerous obstacles on their way that slow them down or that they must circumvent, and public transport does not always meet their needs. Paratransit, in particular, involves many periods of waiting, extending the time that they must spend on getting from one place to another. Finally, planning to ensure the feasibility of trips requires a great deal of time and energy. Thus, the free time that older adults gain in comparison with younger people does not necessarily translate into leisure time.

Moreover, the windows of time to accomplish activities outside the home are reduced because seniors choose the most propitious times and situations for going out. The burden of planning, stress, and fatigue may cause them to give up certain types of outings. Our research has allowed us to assess the complexity surrounding seniors' trips, and to appreciate and value their ability to adapt and their determination to continue their activities despite the many obstacles that they encounter.

Considering older adults' needs in terms of getting around is essential in a context in which one would hope that they retain their autonomy for as long as possible. Urban planning (places to sit and rest, the quality and maintenance of sidewalks, and other factors), road infrastructure management (traffic lights), paratransit, and public transport in general are among the areas of intervention that should be prioritized in order to meet these needs. The design of many locations should also be re-examined (elevators or escalators, places to sit and rest, washrooms, and so on). These improvements will also benefit other types of users, such as younger disabled people, those with debilitating illnesses, and parents with very young children.

Notes

1 La Presse (2010), "Chez soi 55+," *Mon toit*, September 18 (our translation).
2 Andrea Louise Campbell (2003), *How Policies Make Citizens: Senior Political Activism and the American Welfare State* (Princeton: Princeton University Press).
3 Statistics Canada (2011), *General Social Survey – 2010: Overview of the Time Use of Canadians*, Ottawa, Statistics Canada, Catalogue No. 89-647-X, 15, 18–19.
4 Monique Membrado (2010), "Les expériences temporelles des personnes aînées: des temps différents?," *Enfances, Familles, Générations*, No. 13, Autumn, i–xx.

5   Debbie Lager, Bettina van Hoven, and Paulus Huigen (2016), "Rhythms, ageing and neighbourhoods," *Environment and Planning A*, Vol. 48, No. 8, 1565–80.

6   Vanessa Stjernborg, Anders Wretstranda, and Mekonnen Tesfahuneya (2015), "Everyday life mobilities of older persons – A case study of ageing in a suburban landscape in Sweden," *Mobilities*, Vol. 10, No. 3, 383–401.

7   Laura Asher, Maria Aresu, Emanuela Falaschetti, and Jennifer Mindell (2012), "Most older pedestrians are unable to cross the road in time: A cross-sectional study," *Age and Ageing*, Vol. 41, No. 5, 690–94.

8   The interviews were conducted in the context of Isabel Wiebe's PhD dissertation, "Les pratiques et expériences de mobilité des aînés à Rosemont – La Petite-Patrie," Montreal, Institut national de la recherche scientifique, Centre Urbanisation Culture Société.

9   Pseudonyms are used to identify participants.

10 Florence Huguenin-Richard, Marie-Soleil Cloutier, Marie-Axelle Granié, Aurélie Dommes, and Cécile Coquelet (2014), "La marche à pied chez les personnes âgées – le rôle de l'aménagement urbain," *Forum régional habiter, vivre et vieillir dans la région de la Capitale-Nationale*, Quebec City, October 8.

20

Can One Enjoy a Happy Retirement without Volunteering?

Julie Castonguay, Julie Fortier, Andrée Sévigny,
Hélène Carbonneau, and Marie Beaulieu

Nowadays, with the promotion of "active," "productive," and "successful" aging, the shift toward a perception of volunteering as an obligation is a worrisome trend.[1] The following excerpt from an article in *Bel Âge* magazine titled "Le secret d'une retraite heureuse" (The secret to a happy retirement) makes this quite clear:

> Paul and Lise may be retired, but they have packed schedules. That's because these two retirees ... operate in high gear. They each have an office, and sometimes they're so busy they don't even have time to talk to one another.

> At age 63, Paul, a former professor, devotes a day or two a week to serving on the board of a cultural non-profit organization and leading a book club ...

> Lise, 62, is a former manager in the healthcare system. She is involved with an organization that encourages school children to read. She makes regular visits to an elementary school ... to read to and speak with a small group of students ... But it doesn't stop there. When she's relaxing, she knits socks, hats, and mitts for homeless people.

> These baby boomers are clearly very active in retirement, but are they workaholics? Of course not! ... They simply feel that retirement should not

mean withdrawing from the world. "Retirement has no meaning if you're only having fun. You need to continue learning, growing as a person, and being useful to society," says Paul.[2]

The assumption that retirement goes hand in hand with volunteerism is so well entrenched that when a person is nearing retirement, the inevitable question arises: "Will you get involved in volunteering?" This pressure to contribute to society comes not only from peers but also from non-profit and recreational organizations, which depend largely on volunteers to operate.[3] But it is also very evident in social policies relating to aging, the scientific literature, and the media (see Chapter 21, "The Social Participation of Older People: Get on Board, as They Used to Say!").

In recent years, a number of guides have been published, aimed at urging baby boomers to volunteer as a way of continuing to be active and useful members of society.[4] Accounting for 29 percent of Canada's population, or roughly 9.6 million people, baby boomers are seen as a large pool of potential volunteers.[5] People aged 55 and up devote more time to volunteerism than do members of younger age groups.[6] The older members of the baby-boom generation turned 65 in 2011, and therefore many of them have already taken full or partial retirement or will be doing so in the near future. As the baby boomers retire, there could be a positive impact on the number of volunteers and the number of hours of volunteerism performed. But is volunteering an essential part of a happy and fruitful retirement?

Although volunteering is to be encouraged as a form of social participation, in this chapter we call into question the myth that it is vital to a successful retirement. To shed some light on the issues that underlie the purported obligation to take up this form of engagement, it is important to begin by clarifying the nature of volunteerism today. We then demonstrate that volunteers need to act freely and willingly and that any effort to constrain, normalize, or exploit volunteerism will distort its nature. This analysis is based on the findings from our work on volunteerism. The interview excerpts that we present here (all of which are translated from the French) have been taken from the results from the principal author's PhD dissertation[7] – which deals with the factors that tend to encourage or prevent early baby boomers from volunteering for non-profit organizations that offer home support to older adults – and from the evaluation report for the Trouver sa voie à la retraite (Finding one's way in retirement) program.[8]

Giving Freely and Willingly Makes All the Difference

It may seem simple to define, but volunteering quickly proves to be a paradoxical notion that is difficult to pin down, particularly because of the way it converges with other types of activities.[9] For example, in the area of home support, a number of the activities performed by volunteers (transportation, meals-on-wheels deliveries, accompaniment, and friendly visits, for example) could just as well be done by paid workers or loved ones. What is it, then, that distinguishes volunteering from paid employment or other forms of solidarity (family, neighbourhood, and other)?

According to Andrée Sévigny and Annie Frappier's definition, volunteerism is a gift based on principles of freedom and willingness: "An unpaid act carried out within a structured organization by people with whom there are no contractual, family, or friendly obligations."[10] Volunteering is neither an entitlement nor a service that can be demanded, and no one should be obliged to perform it.[11] As the next section shows, the principles of freedom and willingness – the focus being more on the absence of constraint than on the lack of pay alone – are conducive to individuals taking up volunteering and then continuing to act as volunteers.

When Freedom Gives Way to a Sense of Obligation

Anyone is free to volunteer and to choose the area and the type of activity. However, the perceived connection between volunteering and obligation persists, for early baby boomers in particular. For many of them, retirement is idealized as a way of regaining a degree of freedom.[12] Volunteering can then be perceived as a constraint that interferes with this freedom.

> I retired in 2002. I was so burnt out that I said to myself, "I'm not ready to get back on a schedule again." I really wanted to take it easy, to not have anything specific I had to do ... I guess I'm so happy to be able to do what I want, when I want, that I'd really rather not. (Micheline, non-volunteer)

Other people who are ready to try new things give themselves the right to explore before volunteering: "Giving yourself a chance to explore, to see what's out there, to try things out: for me, anyway, this was so important that I wouldn't have wanted it any other way" (Madeleine, participant).[13]

Because it is not an obligation, volunteering can end at any time.[14] "You're not a prisoner here, and you haven't signed a contract. You're free to leave whenever you like" (Yves, volunteer). Because of this, volunteering needs to be in line with a person's interests, availability, capacities, and resources. Through the support and guidance that they provide to volunteers in particular, organizations have an important role to play in ensuring that this is the case and for making the volunteer experience a positive one.

Conversely, someone who does not feel competent in the volunteer activity that he or she is doing will feel less useful and will be less motivated to continue. For example, one volunteer said that she sometimes felt overwhelmed by the problems of the older adult she had been matched with for friendly visits.

> There were certain times that were particularly depressing. I found this tough ... I really felt I couldn't handle it ... If at some point ... I can see that I'm no longer the right person for him, then I'll have to be able to talk about it, to see how ... to make a change. It's not a job you're tied down to. (Pauline, volunteer)

The most important thing is for volunteers to enjoy their involvement. That being said, some older adults feel guilty about having fun – an indication that enjoyment is still taboo in contemporary society, which stresses continuous productivity or self-improvement.[15] The following comments speak volumes in this regard: "You can't withdraw from the world and spend the rest of your days having fun. Humans can't be childish like that. They need to feel useful and they need to continue growing and developing."[16]

As long as it does not become a chore, and as long as the disadvantages or annoyances that go with it do not become overwhelming, volunteering remains possible. However, freedom does not mean an absence of responsibilities. Even though volunteers do not sign a contract, they nonetheless make a moral or symbolic commitment to the organization and, where applicable, to the person receiving their support. "[The person] was told we would be there for as long as he lived. That's a commitment, but it has to be honoured" (Johanne, volunteer).

Yet if a volunteer is not aware of or does not respect his or her own limits, a sense of obligation can set in, and freedom falls by the wayside. The person no longer feels like a volunteer, and the situation becomes akin to paid employment, leading to burnout and abandonment of the activity.[17]

I walked away from my first experience as a volunteer, because I was working as much as when I was working, except that I wasn't being paid. I was tired, I was bringing my work home with me, I wasn't sleeping, I was under a lot of stress. After that, I learned to balance things, so that it was still a part of my life, but not my whole life. (Johanne, volunteer)

After an episode of burnout, individuals may turn away from volunteering altogether. If they try to go back to it, they will probably have some concerns or hesitation, at least at the beginning. Either way, it is quite likely that they will tell others about their experience, thereby strengthening negative preconceptions about volunteerism. Word of mouth is, in fact, the most common way that people hear either good or bad things about volunteering.[18]

Normalizing and Exploiting Volunteering Ultimately Distorts Its Spirit

The connection between the individual and the community is a central concern of volunteerism. The fact that people volunteer freely and willingly testifies to their recognition of the inestimable value of the other person.[19] For older adults, for example, feeling that they are valued by another person (a stranger not related to them) boosts or maintains morale, self-esteem, and social ties. In order to preserve the unique nature of volunteerism and its positive impacts, for both the person receiving support and the volunteer, group, or community, it is important not to constrain volunteering.

However, the fervour surrounding volunteerism may do more than just instil a sense of obligation in some people; it may also contribute to establishing a certain standard regarding what it means to be a "good" older woman or man – one who becomes socially engaged for the sake of the community's well-being.[20] A distinction then emerges between those who live up to this normative vision of volunteering and those who do not. People are seen no longer in terms of who they are, but of what they do.

Yet not everyone wishes, or is able, to become a volunteer.[21] Volunteering is a complex and multidimensional process that results from a combination of various factors: personal (availability, knowledge, motivation, capacities, and others), organizational (the organization's mission, proposed activities, support provided, and so on), interrelational (relationships between the volunteer and other members of the organization), and social (preconceived notions about volunteering, and so on). People with conditions or disabilities that may affect their social participation, as well as those who simply do not wish to volunteer, run the risk of being further marginalized if they are not able to live up to this standard.

What is more, with the aging of the population, it is important to remain vigilant to ensure that promotion of volunteering does not go hand in hand with state disengagement. Volunteers may appear to offer a low-cost way of patching the holes in the social safety net. "The greater the reliance on volunteers ... donations ... and generosity aside, the more there seems to be sort of a disengagement from more formal measures in society" (Sylvie, non-volunteer).

Volunteerism is a gift that is offered freely and willingly, and it must remain so to preserve what makes volunteering unique. If it were to be forced, normalized, or exploited, volunteerism would lose its very essence. It would then become a form of conscription with the objective of carrying out tasks essential to the well-being of members of society and thereby compensating for the state's abdication of responsibility in the social arena.

Conclusion

Is volunteering the one and only path to a happy and successful retirement? It is clearly a form of social participation that deserves to be recognized and encouraged. Its positive impacts are undeniable, both for volunteers and for the people receiving their support, for non-profit organizations, and for society as a whole.[22]

However, vigilance is needed to ensure that the appeal to older adults to contribute to society is not exploited and turned into a moralizing or prescriptive discourse that masks the state's disengagement.[23] In short, volunteerism is and must remain just one of the options that retired people can choose in order to live in a way that is in harmony with their needs and aspirations.[24] It is important that their freedom to decide whether or not they take this path be recognized and respected.

Notes

1   Marty Martinson and Jodi Halpern (2011), "Ethical implications of the promotion of elder volunteerism: A critical perspective," *Journal of Aging Studies*, Vol. 25, No. 4, 427–35.
2   Simon Diotte (2016), "Le secret d'une retraite heureuse," *Bel Âge*, January 20, <https://www.lebelage.ca/santeet-mieux-etre/mieux-etre/le-secret-duneretraite-heureuse?page=all>, accessed July 27, 2016 (our translation).

3   Centre d'action bénévole de Montréal-Nord (2012), "Les baby-boomers: une res-
    source vitale à l'avenir de l'action bénévole," *Portail Internet Arrondissement.com*,
    September 6, <http://www.arrondissement.com/tout-get-document/u4609-baby
    -boomers-ressource-vitaleavenir-action-benevole>, accessed August 7, 2016.

4   Melanie Hientz and Paula Speevak Sladowski (2011), *Composantes fondamentales
    de l'engagement bénévole des baby-boomers* (Ottawa: Bénévoles Canada/Volunteer
    Canada and Financière Manuvie/Manulife Financial); Centre catholique pour immi-
    grants d'Ottawa/Catholic Centre for Immigrants – Ottawa (n.d.), *Attention les
    babyboomers! Changez le monde ... Encore! Un guide d'outils pour du bénévolat
    significatif* (Ottawa: Centre catholique pour immigrants d'Ottawa/Catholic Centre
    for Immigrants – Ottawa); The term "baby boomers" refers here to people born in
    Canada between 1946 and 1965. The upper and lower limits of the birth years that
    define this generation may vary somewhat from one author to the next. See, for ex-
    ample, L. Martel and F.-P. Ménard (2012), *Generations in Canada*, Ottawa, Statistics
    Canada, Catalogue No. 98-311-X2011003.

5   Martel and Ménard (2012), op. cit.

6   Martin Turcotte (2015), *Spotlight on Canadians: Results from the General Social Sur-
    vey – Volunteering and Charitable Giving in Canada* (Ottawa: Statistics Canada).

7   Julie Castonguay (2019), "Bénévolat dans les organismes à but non lucratif de sout-
    ien à domicile des aînés: freins et leviers à l'engagement des premiers-nés du bébé-
    boum, " unpublished thesis, Université de Sherbrooke, Sherbrooke.

8   Hélène Carbonneau, Julie Fortier, and Marie-Laurence Audet (2014), *Rapport d'éva-
    luation du programme Trouver sa voie à la retraite* (Trois-Rivières: Laboratoire en
    loisir et vie communautaire de l'Université du Québec à Trois-Rivières).

9   Éric Gagnon, Andrée Fortin, AmélieElsa Ferland-Raymond, and Annick Mercier
    (2013), *L'invention du bénévolat: genèse et institution de l'action bénévole au Québec*
    (Quebec City: Presses de l'Université Laval); Andrée Sévigny and Julie Castonguay
    (2013), "Le bénévolat auprès des aînés québécois qui reçoivent des soins palliatifs à
    domicile: un survol de la situation québécoise," in Andrée Sévigny, Manal Guirguis-
    Younger, and Manon Champagne (eds.), *Le bénévolat en soins palliatifs ou l'art
    d'accompagner* (Quebec City: Les Presses de l'Université Laval); Andrée Sévigny and
    Annie Frappier (2010), "Le bénévolat 'par' et 'pour' les aînés," in Michèle Charpentier,
    Nancy Guberman, Véronique Billette, Jean-Pierre Lavoie, Amanda Grenier, and
    Ignace Olazabal (eds.), *Vieillir au pluriel: perspectives sociales* (Quebec City: Presses
    de l'Université du Québec).

10 Sévigny and Frappier (2010), op. cit., p. 435 (our translation).

11 Éric Gagnon and Andrée Sévigny (2000), "Permanence et mutations du monde bé-
    névole: note critique," *Recherches sociographiques*, Vol. 41, No. 3, 529–44.

12 Dominique Thierry (2010), *L'engagement bénévole des seniors: une implication ré-
    fléchie!* (Paris: France Bénévolat).

13 Carbonneau et al. (2014), op. cit., p. 30.

14 Sévigny and Frappier (2010), op. cit.

15 Carbonneau et al. (2014), op. cit.

16 Diotte (2016), op. cit. (our translation).

17 Robert A. Stebbins (2000), "Antinomies in volunteering – choice/obligation, leisure/
    work," *Society and Leisure*, Vol. 23, No. 2, 313–24.

18   Maire Sinha (2015), *Spotlight on Canadians: Results from the General Social Survey – Volunteering in Canada, 2004 to 2013* (Ottawa: Statistics Canada).

19   Gagnon et al. (2013), op. cit.; Sévigny and Castonguay (2013), op. cit.; Sévigny and Frappier (2010), op. cit.

20   Martinson and Halpern (2011), op. cit.

21   Julie Castonguay, Marie Beaulieu, and Andrée Sévigny (2016), "Bébé-boumeurs bénévoles? Les freins et les leviers de leur engagement," *Retraite et Société*, No. 71, 127–46.

22   Sheila Novek, Verena Menec, Tanya Tran, and Sheri Bell (2013), *Exploring the Impacts of Senior Centres on Older Adults* (Winnipeg: Centre on Aging); Virginie Galdemar, Léopold Gilles, Anne Loones, and Mélissa Petit (2013), *Étude qualitative des effets de l'intervention bénévole sur l'isolement et la perte d'autonomie des personnes âgées* (Paris: Centre de recherche pour l'étude et l'observation des conditions de vie – Département Évaluation des politiques sociales); Sévigny and Frappier (2010), op. cit.; Mark W. Skinner and Neil Hanlon (2015), *Ageing Resource Communities: New Frontiers of Rural Population Change, Community Development and Voluntarism* (London: Routledge).

23   Martinson and Halpern (2011), op. cit.; Julie Castonguay, Marie Beaulieu, and Andrée Sévigny (2015), "Implantation des politiques sociales québécoises de soutien à domicile des aînés: une analyse ctitique pour mieux comprendre les enjeux liés au bénévolat," *Revue canadienne de politique sociale*, Vol. 72-73, 169–91; Skinner and Hanlon (2015), op. cit.

24   Carbonneau et al. (2014), op. cit.

21

The Social Participation of Older People

Get on Board, as They Used to Say![1]

Émilie Raymond, Julie Castonguay, Mireille Fortier, and Andrée Sévigny

Social Participation: The Focus for a New Discourse about Older People

The view that older people can make a meaningful contribution to society through their social participation now seems generally accepted. Until as recently as the late 1990s, however, the Western world tended to treat old age as a problem to be solved.[2] Being old meant being inactive or even "socially dead," and social policies tended to frame older people as a vulnerable and dependent population.[3] Attitudes began to shift markedly in the early twenty-first century, as the social role of older people became more apparent and valued. Since then, social participation has emerged in most policies and models as a central element in an ideal aging trajectory. Social participation is now seen as an across-the-board remedy for the individual and collective problems associated with demographic changes.

In this chapter, we revisit the dominant consensus about the social participation of older people. Although such participation clearly deserves to be recognized and encouraged, should we not also be questioning whether the prevailing discourses differentiate between older people who participate "appropriately" and those who do not? In other words, does the accepted definition of social participation prioritize certain types of older people or certain forms of social participation, while essentially downplaying other groups or participatory choices?[4] In order to better understand how the concept of social participation is central to current discourses about aging, we begin by exploring what social policy, scientific research, and the media have to say about the social participation of older people. We then present arguments that help to clarify the risks involved in adopting a simplistic and universal vision of participation, based on individual free will. We conclude by sharing a number of reflections that underscore the need for more inclusive practices with respect to the social participation of older people.

Social Policies

The primary thrust of the Quebec government's policy, *Vieillir et vivre ensemble* (Aging and living together), concerns the social participation of older people in the community and takes the World Health Organization's active aging model as its basis.[5] The active aging model is one of a range of aging models that emerged in the early 2000s, along with the "successful aging" and "productive aging" approaches.[6] All share the common characteristic of seeing social participation as an ideal means not only of personal fulfilment but also of being socially useful. Indeed, contrary to the view that older people constitute an economic burden, in these models this age group is considered "a precious, often-ignored resource that makes an important contribution to the fabric of our societies."[7]

Accordingly, when many national governments began to wonder how to address the decrease in the number of people available to support so-called economically dependent populations, the social participation of older people appeared to be an effective solution. Because such participation, whether in a volunteer or paid capacity, contributes to collective wealth and wellness, the thinking went, it needs to be supported and encouraged.[8] The potential payoff seemed to be attractive: rely on the social participation of older people to transform the burden of an aging population into a source of enrichment for society. As a result, many countries have adopted policies that target this goal.[9]

Research

The findings of numerous scientific studies fuelled governments' interest in the social participation of older people as a source of countless health benefits, such as better quality of life, higher life expectancy, slower cognitive decline, and fewer symptoms of depression.[10] Older people themselves confirmed the positive effects of social participation on their well-being.[11] This demonstration of consistent connections between the social participation of older people and improved health outcomes helped to make such participation a central theme in discourses about aging in a context in which the costs of healthcare services related to aging were seen as alarming, even though they turned out to be overestimated.[12]

Media

Several studies carried out since the early 2000s on how aging is depicted in Canadian print media have identified ambivalent attitudes.[13] Although the economic impact of aging causes concern, appreciation of the participatory role of older people has mitigated fears about the potentially catastrophic consequences of an aging population. The media portray the social participation of older people as stemming from an individual choice to age "well," which implies a determination to take care of oneself and others and to become involved in various activities, such as volunteering. In this way, older people can achieve optimal health and contribute to economic prosperity, while largely avoiding recourse to expensive public services. However, this reassuring media image of "young," "active" older people is offset by another media image of "vulnerable" and "powerless" seniors requiring medical care.

Revisiting the Current Consensus

This overview of the political, scientific, and media discourses concerning the social participation of older people confirms that it is universally seen in a positive light – as a desirable, naturally occurring behaviour that produces both individual and collective benefits essential to society. Yet, in our view, this reasoning is problematic, as it ushers in a kind of moral obligation or imperative that defines the scope of "appropriate" participation in a way that is likely to marginalize people who are not engaged in social participation in expected ways. It therefore seems wise to question an overly positive view of the social participation of older people. In fact, we will show that social participation is not value-neutral, not necessarily beneficial, and not always accessible. Our purpose is to elucidate a conception of participation that is less elitist and more inclusive.

The Current Discourse about Social Participation Is Not Value-Neutral

The social participation of older people is portrayed as something positive and vibrant that gives seniors a role in society, and thereby social legitimacy. Michel Foucault's concept of biopower can help us see beyond the obvious evidence concerning the social participation of older people.[14]

According to the concept of biopower, although public policies intended to prolong or improve human existence are generally seen in a positive light, they can exert a constraining effect on people. Since the eighteenth century, public health strategies have been a central component of Western societies, with vaccination, public hygiene, and birth control programs all designed to improve living conditions. This goal is achieved by encouraging individuals to make sound decisions that, for example, correspond today to healthy life-style choices. In other words, the state exercises its power via messages that encourage the population to adopt values deemed important, such as not smoking, eating well, and being physically active.[15] This type of authority, subtler than the raw power exercised by medieval rulers, nevertheless makes it possible to control the population by monitoring bodies and individual choices. In a context in which governments are seeking to reduce public services and their related costs, these messages, based on individual accountability, can be seen as profitable.[16] Many people will also accept these options in the belief that they are exercising free will and doing what needs to be done.

For older people, this rationale can underscore the importance of adopting healthy behaviours to prevent or slow down the onset of health problems. Social participation would appear to be an optimal behaviour for achieving this goal. The biopower concept, then, raises the question of whether the call for social participation, as promoted in policies on aging, can be used by the state to discipline aging bodies. The belief is that, thanks to social participation, older people will maintain their capacities and use healthcare services either later in life or less intensively, while continuing to be useful to society.

Older people who cannot or do not want to meet this expectation – dubbed "inactives" – are clearly subject to being accused of not playing ball and thereby being found guilty, directly or indirectly, of not assuming their responsibilities and becoming a burden on the system. In fact, an analysis of how the concept of social participation evolved in policies on aging in Quebec between 2005 and 2012 shows that a distinction was made between older people in a state of health seen as conducive to optimal, participatory aging, and those on the margins due to their disabilities.[17] The situation of the latter is perceived as the consequence of personal irresponsibility, a rationale that is explicitly articulated in the policy document *Vieillir et vivre ensemble*: "Most of the chronic health problems affecting older people stem from the long-term cumulative effect of relatively poor lifestyle habits, such as poor nutrition and physical inactivity, which highlights the importance of adopting healthy habits early in life."[18] This statement implies that if older people are ill, it is because they have not made the right choices and have not followed the rules of aging well, which has undermined their capacity for social participation. Deemed not to have made a useful contribution, they are placed in a separate category and are seen as different from older people who meet the expected standards of "good" health and an active lifestyle.

The Social Participation of Older People Is Not Necessarily Beneficial

Without discounting the benefits of social participation for older people's health, it is helpful to weigh these benefits against the findings of qualitative studies in which older people describe and comment on their social participation. Their accounts are, in fact, less celebratory. For example, in a study involving seven focus groups of older people, many participants spoke of challenges and difficulties associated with their social participation activities, such as:[19]

- Lack of time to do everything they wanted to do
- Feeling pressured by relatives to perform certain tasks, such as looking after grandchildren
- Difficulty in turning down requests
- Feeling tired and wanting to slow down.

A review of studies evaluating the impact of programs that encourage the social participation of older people has shown that some programs produce mixed results.[20] In one study of older people serving as volunteers in a hospital, it was found that they developed new friendships as a result of their involvement. However, these relationships were not associated with improvements in psychological health due to the stress connected with certain interactions, especially with medical staff.[21] On balance, although social participation may appear to be good for the health of older people, we should not overlook certain pitfalls, such as activity overload or stressful participatory contexts.

Older People Do Not Always Have Access to Opportunities for Social Participation

Portraying the social participation of older people as a form of responsible individual behaviour encourages us to see participatory trajectories as being different for each person. Although in theory people can participate as they wish, the spaces for potential participation are not universally welcoming. This can be the case for older people living with disabilities.

Our research has shown that these people either feel or are excluded from many social participation spaces, especially organizations and associations for older people.[22] Barriers to the inclusion of older people with disabilities in these spaces can be physical (environmental obstacles or inadequate technical aids) or symbolic (stereotypes or prejudices).[23] Participants aging with disabilities explained that when they wanted to join these types of organizations, their requests for accommodation were often rejected or underestimated, thereby depriving them of the conditions necessary for their participation. They also felt judged by their "disability-free" counterparts, as if their limitations were not only the result of a lack of personal discipline but also, and especially, the embodiment of the greatest fears of healthy older people: decline, decrepitude, and dependency.[24]

This scenario explains how older people with disabilities' access to social participation spaces can be more problematic than is generally believed. In addition to the reality experienced by this group, researchers and practitioners working with older people from minority or excluded communities will easily identify other structural factors that can impede or prevent full social participation.

Conclusion: The Possibilities for a New Ethos to Frame the Social Participation of Older People

Our critique of the current universally held consensus about the social participation of older people argues in favour of an approach that is more nuanced and more representative of the diversity of older people's realities and choices. For older people, social participation is not a panacea but one vector among several that lead to full citizenship in old age. What we mean by citizenship is opportunity to help to shape and feel part of society.[25]

In order for all older people to access spaces for social participation, it seems crucial to revisit 1) the idealized vision of active, healthy, and participatory older people; 2) the perception that social participation automatically equates with health; and 3) the willingness of the various participatory settings to welcome every older person. With a view to developing participatory discourses that embrace full citizenship for older people, it is important to consider their experiences and aspirations insofar as they represent diverse realities. In this way, the appeal to older people to become more involved would become more inclusive.

Notes

1   René Goscinny (1967), *Le tour de Gaule d'Astérix* (Paris: Dargaud).

2   Christine Fry (2010), "Social anthropology and ageing," in Dale Dannefer and Chris Phillipson (eds.), *The SAGE Handbook of Social Gerontology* (London: SAGE Publications).

3   Anne-Marie Guillemard (1972), *La retraite, une mort sociale* (Paris: Mouton); Peter Townsend (1981), "The structured dependency of the elderly: A creation of social policy in the twentieth century," *Ageing and Society*, Vol. 1, No. 1, 5–28.

4   The active aging model promoted by the World Health Organization in 2002 defines the social participation of older people as active participation in social, economic, cultural, spiritual, or civic affairs.

5   Ministère de la Famille et des Aînés (MFA) and Ministère de la Santé et des Services sociaux (MSSS) (2012), *Politique Vieillir et vivre ensemble – Chez soi, dans sa communauté, au Québec* (Quebec City: Gouvernement du Québec); World Health Organization (2002), *Vieillir en restant actif: Cadre d'orientation* (Madrid: World Health Organization).

6   James Hinterlong, Nancy Morrow-Howell, and Michael Sherraden (2001), "Productive aging: Principles and perspectives," in Nancy Morrow-Howell, James Hinterlong, and Michael Sherraden (eds.), *Productive Aging: Concepts and Challenges* (Baltimore: John Hopkins University Press).

7   World Health Organization (2002), *Active Ageing: A Policy Framework* (Madrid: World Health Organization), 6.

8   MFA and MSSS (2012), op. cit., 70.

9   Donna Marie Wilson, Jane Osei-Waree, Jessica Anne Hewitt, and Andrew Broad (2012), "Canadian provincial, territorial, and federal government aging policies: A systematic review," *Advances in Aging Research*, Vol. 1, No. 2, 38–46.

10 Sheila Novek, Verena Menec, Tanya Tran, and Sheri Bell (2013), *Exploring the Impacts of Senior Centres on Older Adults* (Winnipeg: Centre on Aging).

11 Émilie Raymond, Andrée Sévigny, and André Tourigny (2012), *Participation sociale des aînés: La parole aux aînés et aux intervenants* (Quebec City: Institut national de santé publique du Québec, Institut sur le vieillissement et la participation sociale des aînés de l'Université Laval, Direction de santé publique de l'Agence de la santé et des services sociaux de la Capitale-Nationale, and Centre d'excellence sur le vieillissement de Québec).

12 Heather Gilmour (2012), "Social participation and the health and well-being of Canadian seniors," *Statistics Canada Catalogue – Health Reports*, Vol. 23, No. 4; Francis Fortier and Guillaume Hébert (2015), *Quels seront les impacts du vieillissement de la population? Note socio-économique* (Montreal: Institut de recherche et d'informations socioéconomiques).

13 Julia Rozanova (2010), "Discourse of successful aging in *The Globe & Mail*: Insights from critical gerontology," *Journal of Aging Studies*, Vol. 24, No. 4, 213–22; Martine Lagacé, Joëlle Laplante, and André Davignon (2011), "Construction sociale du vieillir dans les médias écrits canadiens: de la lourdeur de la vulnérabilité à l'insoutenable légèreté de l'être," *Communication et organisation*, Vol. 40, 87–102.

14 Michel Foucault (1980), *Power/Knowledge: Selected Interviews and Other Writing, 1972–1977*, trans. Colin Gordon, Leo Marshall, John Mepham, and Kate Soper (London: Harvester).

15 Michel Foucault (1976), *Histoire de la sexualité* (Paris: Gallimard).

16 Stephen Katz (2000), "Busy bodies: Activity, aging, and the management of everyday life," *Journal of Aging Studies*, Vol. 14, No. 2, 135–52.

17 Émilie Raymond, Amanda Grenier, and Nadine Lacroix (in press), "La participation dans les politiques du vieillissement au Québec: discours de mise à l'écart pour les aînés ayant des incapacités?," *Développement humain, handicap et changement social*.

18 MFA and MSSS (2012), op. cit., p. 23 (our translation).

19 Raymond et al. (2012), op. cit.

20 Émilie Raymond, Andrée Sévigny, André Tourigny, Aline Vézina, René Verreault, and Alexis C. Guilbert (2013), "On the track of evaluated programmes targeting the social participation of seniors: A typology proposal," *Ageing and Society*, Vol. 33, No. 2, 267–96.

21 Karen S. Rook and Dara H. Sorkin (2003), "Fostering social ties through a volunteer role: Implications for older-adults' psychological health," *International Journal of Aging and Human Development*, Vol. 57, No. 4, 313–37.

22 Émilie Raymond and Amanda Grenier (2015), "Social participation at the intersection of old age and lifelong disability: Illustrations from a Photo-Novel Project," *Journal of Aging Studies*, No. 35, 190–200; Émilie Raymond, Amanda Grenier, and Jill Hanley (2014), "Community participation of older people with disabilities," *Journal of Community and Applied Social Psychology*, Vol. 24, No. 1, 50–62.

23 Nadine Lacroix and Émilie Raymond (2014), *La participation des aînés ayant des incapacités dans les milieux associatifs et communautaires: des balises pour la réflexion et l'action* (Quebec City: Marcelle-Mallet Research Chair on Philanthropic Culture).

24 Meredith Minkler and Pamela Fadem (2002), "'Successful aging': A disability perspective," *Journal of Disability Policy Studies*, Vol. 12, No. 4, 229–35.

25 Daniel Weinstock (2000), "Vivre la citoyenneté," in Yves Boisvert, Jacques Hamel, and Marc Molgat (eds.), *Vivre la citoyenneté. Identité, appartenance et participation* (Montreal: Éditions Liber).

Part 5

DEATH AND BEREAVEMENT

22

How Older Adults Experience Bereavement

Does Greater Frequency Make Death Easier to Bear?

*Valérie Bourgeois-Guérin, Isabelle Van Pevenage,
Jeanne Lachance, Rock-André Blondin, and
Antonin Marquis*

As this book clearly shows, pervasive myths based on prejudices and stereotypes may shape the way we look at older adults and their experiences. When it comes to bereavement or grieving, we may feel that as people age, they become accustomed to the deaths of others and to the idea of their own death. As we have often heard in clinical settings, and as found by one research project, people who come into contact with bereaved seniors tend to imagine, "This is something that's been developing in them for some time ... I think they experience loss differently than younger patients. In a way, I think they're more used to experiencing loss."[1]

Marie Frédérique Bacqué, an academic and clinician who has written several articles on bereavement, confirms that older people are often considered "particularly well adapted to putting up with loss" because they have become inured to it in the course of their lives.[2] However, she adds, "this trivializing view" of death and aging provides no support for bereaved seniors dealing with their distress. In this chapter, we clarify a number of aspects of bereavement in older adults in order to familiarize the reader with the complex nature of this experience and the various trajectories it may follow.

Origins of the Myth

The impression that older people deal more easily with bereavement because they experience it more frequently derives in part from certain views of aging that are widespread today. We live in a society in which old age and aging are often seen in reductive and black-and-white terms.

In certain geriatrics-based theoretical models focusing mainly on the medical aspects of aging, old age is viewed solely in terms of loss, degeneration, and pathology. However, this narrow vision of advancing age may also bolster the simplistic notion that aging is merely a succession of losses and bereavements. It also embraces the view that the "normal" and "natural" character of these losses diminishes their more painful aspects. However, aging is not restricted to these experiences of loss, and, although they are more numerous, they are not necessarily easier to endure.

At the other end of the spectrum, many new publications have emerged in recent years and widespread efforts have been made touting the concept of "aging well," the aim of which is to encourage "successful aging" by promoting positive experiences associated with the aging process. Despite their initial good intentions, the excessive nature of some of these models has promoted a kind of aging so "successful" that it leaves little room for the difficulties and suffering of the aging experience, such as bereavement. Focusing solely on the more "positive" aspects of aging may contribute to the silence that often surrounds the more problematic aspects of the bereavement and losses that older adults experience. Given this reductive framework, it is not surprising that many of the losses and bereavements that seniors face may cause discomfort among their families and friends.

A certain ageism may also underlie the silence about – and downplaying of – the significance of bereavement in the older population. As noted above, we often imagine that these people have already experienced so many losses that they know how to manage them and even no longer suffer from them.[3] However, although it is true that some people, as they age, may be resilient in the face of bereavement and other kinds of losses, these experiences remain difficult for many others.

Some Guidelines for Understanding Bereavement in Seniors

We now look at the nature, sources, and effects of bereavement by considering the complex and diverse nature of the factors involved in that experience.

Bereavement: Factors and Types

There are many definitions, models, and conceptions of bereavement, each rooted in various theoretical perspectives. As a general rule, however, the bereavement process is viewed as a series of reactions and emotions experienced following the loss of a loved one. The bereaved frequently experience reactions and feelings that may range from shock to incredulity, and include sadness, anger, ambivalence, guilt, and relief. Although they may appear contradictory in some instances, it is not unusual for these emotions to coexist and to peak in the months following the loss. Furthermore, although the experience of bereavement is universal, the ways in which people undergo and react to it are highly diversified and are influenced by several factors, including culture and personality. Although there are many causes of bereavement (loss of employment, loss of autonomy, and so on), in this chapter, we focus more particularly on the feelings of grief that emerge following a death.

Although we know that death and bereavement are not experienced in the same way in different cultures and religions, research shows that other factors, such as the gender and socioeconomic situation of the bereaved, also influence the bereavement process. Loss of a spouse, for example, is experienced differently by men and women. First, given the differences in life expectancy, women are more likely to lose a spouse. Second, research has shown that older men experiencing the loss of a spouse tend to receive more support than do women in the same age group.[4] Socioeconomic status may affect the way that seniors experience bereavement, particularly because the stress associated with a poor financial situation may add to the sense of loss. It is therefore important to consider these factors in attempting to gain a clearer understanding of bereavement among older adults, which, like the individuals involved, is highly diverse.

Bereavement is also experienced differently depending on the nature of the relationship between the bereaved and the deceased and the cause and circumstances of the latter's death. Consequently, many specific bereavement situations may be less well recognized or even overlooked. For example, loved ones will generally acknowledge the death of family members to a greater degree than the loss of a friend or acquaintance. However, the loss of a friend or neighbour who had lived at the same seniors' residence or in the same building for years may be very meaningful to the bereaved. The death of a same-sex spouse may also be a taboo subject or be passed over in silence, as a result of which the bereaved may receive little or no support from loved ones or, more broadly, from the circle of friends and acquaintances. The death of a pet is another type of loss that may often not be acknowledged, even though it, too, can strongly affect the individuals who experience it. Lastly, death by suicide is a particularly trying experience around which there may frequently be a solid wall of silence. This type of loss is similar in nature to other types of bereavement, but certain emotions experienced, such as guilt, shame, and shock, are often felt more intensely.[5] It has also been shown that individuals who are bereaved as a result of a suicide are at greater risk of trying to take their own lives.

Suffering and Bereavement in Older Adults

As noted above, the incidence of bereavement is definitely higher among seniors. Despite this fact, however, the loss of loved ones continues to bring its share of suffering in old age.

Accumulated Bereavement: Isolation and Other Losses

> The old man's circle is thus gradually populated by as many of the deceased as of the living.
>
> ———— Michel Hanus, *Les deuils dans la vie*[6]

With advancing age, many people will experience various losses (such as their homes when they must leave them, their jobs when they have to retire, or their autonomy when they experience physical or cognitive health problems). In addition, most will mourn deaths, as the probability of losing loved ones increases in old age, and especially in extreme old age. These losses and bereavements may cause significant suffering, which is all the more difficult to experience and endure as the losses multiply and happen more frequently. Losses may also reawaken or rekindle other bereavements, which can make the experience more painful and complex. Lastly, some of seniors' accumulating losses may remain unknown to the people around them and be passed over in silence.

The accumulation of various losses also tends to reduce seniors' social circle, thus further isolating them. Mourning the loss of a spouse or of friends, family members, and other loved ones can accentuate older people's loneliness. Being more aware that life is fragile or because they fear other losses, for example, some older adults may be reluctant to forge new ties with the people around them, which may further exacerbate their isolation. Although the death of a member of one's circle may revive interactions with some family members in the short term, several studies have shown that older people's feelings of solitude tend to increase in the medium and long terms.[7] These feelings of loneliness following the deaths of loved ones are more readily understood in light of the fact that older adults' social networks already tend to shrink and consolidate around their most significant relationships. Having to make choices in order to "save their strength," they select the relationships, places, and activities most meaningful to them. It is easily understandable how the deaths of loved ones, and with them the disappearance of a referential framework, can have a major impact.

Secondary losses – those that stem from the death of a loved one – are another important aspect of bereavement in seniors. When the house or apartment becomes too big for one person, for example, the loss of a spouse may compel some individuals to move. It is also not unusual for the male spouse in an older couple to be the only one to have a driver's licence (see Chapter 8, "Seniors and Their Cars: Choice or Necessity?"). For the female spouse, her partner's death may therefore result in a significant loss of her own mobility. Some research has focused on the loss of identity caused by the death of a person whom one has taken care of for several years. With the death of that person, some caregivers lose a role in which they have invested very heavily.[8]

When Bereavement Becomes Complicated

In some instances, bereavement may become complicated and pathological. Without dwelling on the diagnostic criteria for pathological grief, it must be acknowledged that, in certain cases, the grief of some older adults does not resolve on its own, and they require professional help. Persistent grief, intense sadness that fails to diminish over time, and categorical and sustained denial of loss may all be indications that the individual's grief has become pathological. This is a further reminder that it is important to realize how painful bereavement can be, even at an advanced age. However, care must be taken to avoid too quickly characterizing grief as "pathological" (associated with a disease) and to remember that most people – and this is even truer for older adults – experience bereavement without any complications or need for professional help.

Acknowledging the significance of bereavement in older adults is not merely a matter of identifying its most painful aspects. To gain a better understanding of the full complexity of this experience, it must also be recognized that bereavement may bring meaning and learning.

For many people, bereavement triggers thoughts of their own mortality. The loss of others tends to remind us of the finite nature of our lives. In addition, the prospect of death moves ever closer as we advance in age, and at times seniors' thoughts about it become more pronounced. Being confronted with the loss of a loved one may also spark fears or anxiety about our own death. As a result, the end-of-life experience, the rituals surrounding death, and how the deceased is treated by his or her circle (community, loved ones, and society) influence older adults' thinking about their own death. Although thinking about this is sometimes difficult, it can also be a meaningful exercise, especially when it encourages people to review their priorities or to redirect their lives in more meaningful and authentic ways. For example, some people may wish to reconsider their relationships, plans, or values after losing a loved one.

Although we live in an increasingly individualistic society, people still want to leave a legacy, and sometimes the act of *transmitting* something seems to make bereavement a more meaningful experience, as remembering the dead and passing something down to the living helps to link us to past and future generations.[9] Transmitting, cultivating the memory of oneself in others, and telling the story of one's loved ones and social circle appear to be life-enhancing acts for grieving older adults. Objects bequeathed or given before death – some of which have no monetary value but are of great sentimental or cultural value – may serve in playing this role of transmission.[10] Being part of a process in which something valuable is passed on may thus provide comfort and meaning for many bereaved seniors.

Conclusion

In a social context in which death is often a taboo subject or something that is denied or individualized, it is not surprising that increasingly limited time and space are accorded for bereavement and that the bereaved are encouraged to "move on *quickly* to something else."[11] When bereavement occurs in conjunction with aging, the prejudices and stereotypes associated with growing older and certain ageist attitudes can contribute to these views of death and to a tendency to downplay or overlook the bereavement of older adults, or simply to pass over it in silence. However, our reflections here on the bereavement of seniors show how important it is to acknowledge the range of bereavement experiences and the diverse paths they may take, as, even though bereavement clearly happens more frequently among older adults, those who go through the experience do not necessarily find it easy.

Notes

1 Quoted from the record of a focus group involving professionals working with aging men as part of a research project titled "How to better understand the psychological suffering of elderly men with incurable cancer in order to give them better support: The professionals' point of view" (our translation).

2 Marie-Frédérique Bacqué (2004), "Augmentation de la longévité, multiplication des deuils. Les nouveaux 'vieux' sont aussi de grands endeuillés," *Études sur la mort*, Vol. 126, No. 2, 149–58 (our translation).

3 Michel Hanus (2007), *Les deuils dans la vie* (Paris: Maloine).

4 Kate Mary Bennett (2009), "Gender difference in bereavement support for older widowed people," *Bereavement Care*, Vol. 28, No. 3, 5–9.

5 Hanus, (2007), op. cit.

6 Ibid.

7 Ibid.

8 Pam Orzeck (2016), "Identities in transition: Women caregivers in bereavement," *Journal of Social Work in End of Life and Palliative Care*, Vol. 12, Nos. 1–2, 145–61.

9 Jacques De Visscher (2010), *De la gratitude au-delà de la réciprocité* (Montreal: Conférences de Montréal).

10 Elsa Ramos (2010), "Voir partir ses aînés familiaux: les preuves du temps et la consistance de la réalité," *Enfances, Familles, Générations*, No. 13, Fall, 21–35.

11 Jean Hugues Déchaux (2000), "L'intimisation de la mort," *Ethnologie française*, Vol. 30, No. 1, 153–62.

23

Palliative Care for Those Dying of "Old Age"
Unmet Needs

Isabelle Van Pevenage, Patrick Durivage,
Véronique Billette, Patricia Friesen, and
Eleonora Bogdanova

Dying of Old Age: The Ideal Scenario?

> Old people don't die
> One day they fall asleep
> And sleep for too long ...

The words to the song "Les Vieux" by Jacques Brel (our translation) conjure up the common belief that most older adults pass away in their sleep, quietly and without suffering. This type of death is often perceived as peaceful, both physically and emotionally: dying is the final and entirely "natural" phase of life, and older adults are accustomed to the idea, having seen relatives and friends die. They are prepared to go, and they do so willingly. If this belief were accurate, older adults would not need any special support at the end of their lives. But is that how it really is?

In this chapter we show that, for older adults, death does not always come easily, peacefully, and without suffering. We also argue that end-of-life care adapted to their special needs is necessary and desirable not only for them and their relatives or friends, but also for society.

Facing Our Own Mortality

In our view, the belief that older adults die without suffering, in their sleep, without the need for any specific palliative or end-of-life care comes from our *desire* for it to be that way. Although death is inevitable, it is nonetheless inconceivable for many. It thus seems normal and healthy to hope for it to come as comfortably and as late in life as possible. No one wants to lose autonomy, fall ill, experience cognitive decline, or die slowly in physical and emotional pain. To think about the end of an older adult's life as difficult, protracted, and full of suffering is to project ourselves into this undesirable situation. The popular belief that most older adults die in their sleep is no doubt partly a reflection of our own wishful thinking.

Our conception of how older adults die cannot be separated from the society in which we live – a society marked by fear of death and old age that can lead us to distance ourselves from, or deliberately overlook, the suffering of older adults.[1] The comforting idea of their death as different, gentle, and accepted spares us from having to confront an unpleasant reality, but it also means ignoring what older adults go through and what they actually need. In reality, the death of an older adult is often accompanied by pain, impairment, discouragement, fear, worry, regret, confusion, and anger. Such sensations and emotions are normal and can be part of the end-of-life experience for anyone.

The End-Of-Life Period and Death for Older Adults: Beyond the Fiction

Palliative Care: What Does It Actually Mean?
In Quebec, approximately one in three people aged 65 and over dies of cancer. The other main causes of death for this age group are heart disease (18 percent), respiratory disease (5 percent), cerebrovascular disease (5 percent), and Alzheimer's disease (5 percent). Other causes include suicide, chronic liver disease, and influenza (36 percent).[2]

With the rising incidence of cancer among the general population over the past 50 years, researchers and doctors have learned much more about the disease, and there have been major medical advances. As we have just seen, one third of older adults die of cancer, but life expectancy has increased considerably, and there is better and better documentation of the various stages of the illness, including survival prognoses and how the terminal stages of cancer unfold.

To help meet the needs of people who will not recover from their illness, a body of knowledge around support for end-of-life patients has been amassed, leading to the development of palliative care. This type of care differs from that in the rest of the healthcare system in many respects, but two are particularly significant. First, the purpose of palliative care is not to cure the patient but to provide support up to the time of death. Second, in response to the tremendous suffering that such patients experience, experts came to realize that a global approach had to be developed to address a broad spectrum of needs, from relieving physical pain to assuaging psychosocial and spiritual suffering.[3] This type of care can be provided in a palliative care residence but also at home, in a residential long-term care facility, in hospital, or elsewhere.

For several decades (and still too often today), receiving palliative care generally meant that attending physicians who had tried everything to save their patient, only to see the symptoms worsen, had to face the fact that the patient was going to die. Doctors would not resign themselves to transferring a patient to palliative care until a few days or weeks before they were expected to die. Over time, the teams charged with providing palliative care came to realize that many patients were being referred too late in the end-of-life process. This meant that the care professionals did not have the time needed to assess the situation and manage the multiple needs. They therefore advocated to have such care made available when the attending physician determined that a patient was likely to die within three to six months. This assessment of how long a patient is expected to live is referred to as a "reserved prognosis." However, it must be noted that there is no consensus on how long a person's case should be managed by a palliative care team. It is therefore not surprising to see that this period can vary depending on the care setting, the teams involved, and the particular field of medicine.

While it is accurate to say that end-of-life care has greatly expanded around the world over the past 50 years, many people – including many older adults – still do not have access to it. In fact, as we will see, most older adults die of illnesses other than cancer, for which it is difficult, if not impossible, to determine life expectancy.

Palliative Care in Quebec

Since 2014, Quebec has had a legislative framework governing the administration of palliative care: the *Act respecting end-of-life care*. Under this legislation, palliative care is defined as "the total and active care delivered by an interdisciplinary team to patients suffering from a disease with reserved prognosis, in order to relieve their suffering, without delaying or hastening death, maintain the best quality of life possible and provide them and their close relations the support they need."[4] By this definition, it is in fact a reserved prognosis that triggers the offering of palliative care. However, no specific time frame is given for the end-of-life period.

The position held by many palliative care experts regarding the consideration that triggers palliative care is somewhat different from that in the legislation. Research has shown that it would be desirable to depart from the reserved prognosis paradigm and expand access to such care to include people who are suffering from chronic illnesses and whose life expectancy is difficult, if not impossible, to estimate, despite the incurable nature of their illness.[5] Many researchers also argue that palliative care professionals (doctors as well as interdisciplinary teams) should be involved not just during the terminal phase of an illness, but as soon as possible after an incurable illness has been diagnosed, in light of the many positive effects that this would have both for patients and for their relatives or friends.[6]

Palliative Phase, Terminal Phase, End of Life: A Few Definitions

The notions of "reserved prognosis," "end-of-life care," and "palliative care" lead us to question the meaning of the term "end of life." As French sociologist Bernard Ennuyer asks, when does the "end of life" start?[7] The end-of-life period can last for varying periods of time, but when the concept is referred to in the scientific literature it often designates a fairly short period (a few hours, days, or months before a person's death). Nevertheless, palliative care specialists in every field recognize that it is not easy to identify specific events or symptoms that would indicate whether a person is in the palliative, terminal, or end-of-life phase.

Many experts agree that the *palliative phase* should start not when a reserved prognosis has been established but when a doctor diagnoses an incurable illness. It is important to note that curative treatment may still be provided to a patient alongside palliative care. The aim of curative treatment is to address secondary pathologies or to slow the patient's decline. That being said, the more time passes, the more likely it is that curative treatment will give way to palliative treatment.

In most cases, the *terminal phase* of an illness begins when there is an unstable clinical condition leading to an accelerated loss of autonomy. During this period, which defines the final days and hours of a person's life, treatment needs tend to be more acute. This is the final stage of the palliative phase.

End of life is a notion that is difficult to pin down. The *Act respecting end-of-life care* does not provide a definition, but it does indicate that palliative care is care that is offered to "patients suffering from a disease with reserved prognosis." It can therefore be assumed that, as far as the legislation is concerned, end of life is the period between the time a reserved prognosis is assigned and the person's death. It must then be asked what is meant by "end of life" when a person is dying of an illness for which it is difficult, if not impossible, to estimate life expectancy and therefore to establish a reserved prognosis.

End of Life for Older Adults: A Few Scenarios

To better understand the development and evolution of incurable illnesses, doctors have analyzed and grouped the trajectories of patients suffering from various pathologies into different categories. Three major trajectories have been identified.[8]

Trajectory 1: characteristic of *cancer* patients. Following their diagnosis, such patients tend to maintain essentially the same level of autonomy as they had before. With the appropriate care and medication, their level of autonomy is similar to that of other people their age, up to the time when therapeutic treatment proves unsuccessful. This is followed by a progressive deterioration that leads, sooner or later, to the person's death. It is at this point that palliative care may be offered. The expertise developed by oncology services makes the terminal phase of the illness fairly predictable, so it is relatively easy to anticipate the needs of patients and their families.

Trajectory 2: characteristic of patients with *cardiac or pulmonary impairment*. Once a diagnosis has been made, the patient's autonomy deteriorates gradually, with acute periods that generally lead to hospitalization. These are followed by recovery, but without a full return to the level of autonomy that the patient previously enjoyed. There is thus a progressive loss of autonomy, and death may occur suddenly and unexpectedly depending on the acuteness of the patient's condition. This trajectory is marked by a progressive but uneven deterioration in the person's health, with each acute event being followed by only a partial resumption of capacity, until the patient's death.

Trajectory 3: characteristic of older adults who are fragile or suffering from dementia (such as Alzheimer's disease). There is a gradual decline over an extended period that can last as long as 15 years. Unlike trajectory 2, this one is more linear, with losses in autonomy being more gradual and subtler. In such situations, it is very difficult – if not impossible – to predict when the terminal phase will begin.

These three trajectories were developed in an effort to establish a streamlined classification of end-of-life experiences, and there are other scenarios. The reality is actually more complex, particularly for older adults, who are more likely to die as a result of pathologies that fall under the second and third trajectories (cardiac or pulmonary illnesses and fragility or dementia, respectively). Nor is it uncommon for people to suffer from multiple pathologies, including chronic illnesses, with coinciding end-of-life trajectories. This makes things more complicated for patients, their relatives and friends, and for the professionals caring for them.[9]

End of Life for Older Adults and Palliative Care

Our description, above, of the different phases experienced by patients with incurable illnesses and the three possible end-of-life trajectories for older adults shows that the appealing image of a person dying in his or her sleep without suffering may not necessarily be accurate. Providing end-of-life comfort by offering palliative care is just as important for older people as it would be for younger people, and it necessitates adjustments to handle their specific needs (for example, end-of-life trajectory other than that associated with cancer). But how could we revisit our ideas and practices in regard to palliative care for older adults with incurable illnesses? And what would the benefits be?

In Chapter 24, "Do Older Adults Wish to Die at Home (and Can They)?" we note that the medical conditions of older adults who are ill and nearing the end of their lives are complex and that their management requires more intense and personalized care. Palliative care programs organized specifically around treatment geared to end of life can address such needs.[10]

In addition to the positive effects on their physical and mental well-being, palliative care offers a number of benefits to patients and their relatives and friends. Research has shown that speaking openly with palliative care practitioners about the situation and about the illness can reduce stress and anxiety among patients and their relatives and friends. Palliative care teams offer people the opportunity to discuss plans for the type of care they would like, treatment possibilities, and the potential risks and benefits. When people are armed with information about their situation, they are also able to take an active role in their own care and to anticipate certain events. In some cases, this can prove to be a good coping strategy that may involve acquiring information, participating in decision making, and proposing alternatives.[11] In addition to increasing their level of comfort – physical, psychological, social, and spiritual – research has shown that this type of care can increase the length of a patient's life and reduce the burden on relatives or friends.[12]

It may initially seem that having an older adult's case managed by an inter-disciplinary team would be costlier than a "regular" treatment approach. However, many studies have shown that this is by no means accurate. On the contrary: when treatment objectives are communicated and made clear, the number of unwanted hospital admissions and readmissions (to intensive care in particular) is reduced, as is the number of inappropriate interventions (invasive diagnostic procedures and unnecessary therapeutic treatments, for example).[13] The information currently available to us thus suggests that making palliative care accessible to older adults is beneficial (including from a cost standpoint) both to them and their relatives or friends and to Quebec society as a whole.

Conclusion

At a time when society is engaging in a collective reflection on how to en-sure a dignified end of life, against a backdrop of cuts to publicly funded healthcare and other services, the question of palliative care offered to older adults must be examined. This segment of the population does not have much access to palliative care, not because they do not need it but because it is not being offered to them. Dying in dignity means not simply the oppor-tunity to receive medical assistance with dying to reduce suffering, but also – and more importantly – access to appropriate, high-quality care at the end of life.

The purpose of palliative care is to ensure that people nearing the end of their lives receive care designed to relieve all of their symptoms and their suffering, be it physical, psychological, social, or spiritual. Historically, such care was initiated during the terminal phase of a person's illness, when every form of treatment had been tried and the person could not be cured. Such care was offered primarily to cancer patients given that their end-of-life per-iod could reasonably be estimated. However, for many years now, research-ers have agreed on the need to expand access to palliative care to people who are suffering from incurable pathologies but whose life expectancy can-not be accurately estimated. This group consists mainly of older adults with incurable chronic illnesses or degenerative cognitive diseases. Researchers have in fact been able to show that, in contrast to the image portrayed in the Jacques Brel song, older adults do not always end their days in peace and tranquility. Quite the opposite: the end-of-life period for older adults can be a complex time, a time of suffering. For many who are ill, this period may stretch out for a number of years, during which time they, along with their relatives or friends, do not receive any kind of special support.

It is therefore obvious that older adults suffering from incurable chronic illnesses and dementia would benefit from receiving palliative care, given the many positive effects that have been shown for both the sick person and his or her relatives or friends. The merits of this idea become even clearer when two other points are taken into consideration. First, it would result in substantial savings for the health and social services system; second, it would address public concerns about the possibility of growing old and dying in dignity, whether it be at home, in a residential long-term care facility, in hospital, or in a palliative care residence.

Notes

1   David J. Roy (2010), "Mourir vieux au début du XXIᵉ siècle," *Pluriâges*, Vol. 2, No. 1, 17–18.
2   According to the 2012 data published by the Institut national de santé publique du Québec, *Santéscope – Principales causes de décès*, <https://www.inspq.qc.ca/santescope/syntheses/principales-causesde-deces>, accessed January 12, 2017.
3   The definition of palliative care that is most widely accepted by the research community is that proposed by the World Health Organization in 2002: "Palliative care is an approach that improves the quality of life of patients and their families facing the problems associated with life-threatening illness, through the prevention and relief of suffering by means of early identification and impeccable assessment and treatment of pain and other problems, physical, psychosocial and spiritual"; World Health Organization (2002), *National Cancer Control Programmes: Policies and Managerial Guidelines* (Geneva: WHO), xv–xvi, <https://www.who.int/cancer/media/en/408.pdf>.
4   *Act respecting end-of-life care*, updated May 1, 2019, 3, <http://legisquebec.gouv.qc.ca/en/pdf/cs/S-32.0001.pdf>, accessed June 11, 2019.
5   Elizabeth Davies and Irene J. Higginson (2004), *Better Palliative Care for Older People* (Copenhagen: World Health Organization, Europe).
6   Ibid.
7   Bernard Ennuyer (2013), "Une 'fin de vie', ça commence quand?," in Philippe Pitaud (ed.), *Vivre vieux, mourir vivant* (Paris: Érès), 103–11.
8   June R. Lunney, Joanne Lynn, Daniel J. Foley, Steven Lipson, and Jack M. Guralnik (2003), "Patterns of functional decline at the end of life," *JAMA*, Vol. 289, No. 18, 2387–92.
9   Institut de la statistique du Québec (2015), *Le bilan démographique du Québec* (Quebec City: Gouvernement du Québec).
10 Rory Fisher, Margaret M. Ross, and Michael J. MacLean (2000), *A Guide to End-of-Life Care for Seniors* (Ottawa and Toronto: University of Ottawa and University of Toronto).

11   Jean Bacon (2012), *Integrating a Palliative Approach into the Management of Chronic, Life-Threatening Diseases: Who, How and When?* (Ottawa, Association canadienne des soins palliatifs/Canadian Hospice Palliative Care Association), <http://www.hpcintegration.ca/media/36315/TWF-integrating-palliative-approach -report-Eng_final3.pdf>.

12   Davies and Higginson (2004), op. cit.; Fisher et al. (2000), op. cit.

13   Corinne Hodgson (2012), *Cost-Effectiveness of Palliative Care: A Review of the Literature* (Ottawa: Association canadienne des soins palliatifs/Canadian Hospice Palliative Care Association), <http://hpcintegration.ca/media/24434/TWF-Economics -report-Final.pdf>.

24

Do Older Adults Wish to Die at Home (and Can They)?

Isabelle Van Pevenage, Patrick Durivage,
Anne-Marie Séguin, and Laurence Hamel-Roy

A Myth and Its Origins

> Everyone wants to die at home, which is convenient because it costs the
> healthcare system less to care for the sick at home than in hospital.
>
> ——— Monique Forget, "Mourir chez soi, c'est possible"[1]

Home – where we find privacy, memories, and safety – would seem to be the ideal place in which to spend our final days. That contention seems all the more accurate when contrasted with the negative images conjured up by hospital corridors and emergency rooms.

This apparently widely held view is also conveyed by the Quebec government in its 2010–15 palliative care development plan (*Plan de développement 2010–2015 des soins palliatifs*), in which it reiterates its desire to prioritize in-home palliative care. This approach reflects the fact that a significant proportion of the population, according to the Ministère de la Santé et des Services sociaux (Quebec Ministry of Health and Social Services), would prefer to die at home. It is nevertheless worth pointing out that the ministry's motivations are also economic, as in-home care yields substantial savings over the costs generated when people die in hospital or in a residential long-term care facility (centre d'hébergement de soins de longue durée, or CHSLD).

The question of where people prefer to die essentially involves older adults, as 80 percent of the people who died in Quebec in 2012 were 65 years of age or older, and 50 percent were 80 or older.[2] Does research on the subject support the assertion that older adults wish to die at home? Is dying at home possible and desirable not only in the current context of budget constraints and public service cutbacks, but also in terms of complex end-of-life circumstances? Can we say with certainty, as Forget and the Quebec government maintain, that everyone (including older adults) wishes to die at home? Furthermore, does that wish persist when older adults and their relatives and friends realize what is required to bring this about?

Dying at Home: From Wish to Reality

Living at home until death entails a number of challenges. Studies have highlighted the combination of conditions required, as well as factors that can have a considerable impact on the experience. However, it is important to note that most research in this regard deals with cancer patients, regardless of age. As a result, the information presented here is based on findings that do not necessarily factor in the specific characteristics of older adults. Whenever possible, we will complete the picture with data pertaining to older adults.

Place of Death: Wishes, Expectations, and Reality

To our knowledge, there is no scientific research in Quebec or Canada on people's preferences concerning their place of death. The only data we have come from a survey conducted for the Canadian Hospice Palliative Care Association in 2013, which showed that around 4 out of every 10 Canadians surveyed have no preference as to their place of death; of those expressing a preference, 75 percent hoped to die at home, 14 percent in hospital, and 12 percent in some other facility.[3] These results alone challenge the contention that everyone wants to die at home, since it seems that fewer than half of those questioned wished to do so.

The survey also shows that people's expectations differ from their wishes. Of those who expressed a preference as to place of death, only 50 percent expected to die at home, and the others expected to die in a hospital or some other care facility. If these data are compared with the responses from everyone surveyed, it emerges that only 3 people out of 10 expect to die at home. These mismatches between wishes and expectations suggest that many respondents realize that, whatever their current wishes, the conditions necessary for them to die at home will probably not be met.

Moreover, when we look at where people actually die, we find that the gaps between wishes and reality are even greater: in Quebec in 2010, only 11 percent of deaths occurred at home, whereas 19 percent in occurred in CHSLDs, 61 percent in hospitals, and 10 percent elsewhere.[4] The differences among myths, wishes, expectations, and reality are thus substantial. How do we account for them?

What Does "Dying" Mean When You Are Old?

If older adults supposedly wish to die at home, the question of what dying at home involves must first be addressed. Dying at home presents few challenges when one is not suffering from any disease or serious disability. Even though this is what sometimes happens, many older adults will experience a different end-of-life scenario. We therefore find it difficult to support the contention that the end-of-life process takes the same form and has the same meaning for everyone.

Advances in medicine have significantly raised life expectancy. In Quebec, women currently live to 84 years of age on average, and men to 80. Yet increases in life expectancy also have consequences in terms of health condition, as the incidence of heart disease and other chronic illnesses increases significantly with age. As explained in Chapter 23, "Palliative Care for Those Dying of 'Old Age,'" the trajectory of a disease characterized by slow decline can be relatively long.

Apart from the duration of the disease, which may be considerable, disease symptoms and treatment side effects can be severe in terms of pain, dehydration, extreme fatigue, respiratory ailments, digestive disorders, mental confusion, and so on, particularly in the final months and days. These physical symptoms may be accompanied by suffering related to anxiety and existential issues, and pathologies that worsen symptoms and pain may also proliferate. The picture is a sombre one, but it helps us to better understand that it is necessary to manage symptoms and pain and to deal with psychological, spiritual, and social needs if people are to be able to end their lives at home.[5]

Since we are talking about older adults, we must also consider the end-of-life issues specific to those with cognitive disorders because their situation presents additional challenges. For example, communication problems may complicate symptom or pain assessment, and decision-making impairments due to cognitive disorders raises ethical issues surrounding the level of care.[6]

Accommodation Arrangements for Dying at Home

In Chapter 6, "Do Most Very Old Quebecers Live in Residential Long-Term Care Centres?," we saw that older adults live in different forms of housing, ranging from rented apartments to condos or houses. We also noted that although the term "home" means different things to different people in different situations, home is, in many cases, synonymous with a place that reflects one's identity – a safe, familiar place where one controls one's own life and privacy. We also noted that not all older adults wish to grow old at home: some prefer to move to a place that is better suited to their circumstances for various reasons, such as a need for more comfort, more continuous support, or a more appropriate environment.

Moreover, as people gradually lose their autonomy, it is not unusual to see their "home" change into a care facility, as medical equipment or supported independent-living arrangements gradually take over their living space. This is even truer when health deteriorates at the end of life. As older adults' living space is disrupted and transformed, it may no longer feel like the home it once was, and therefore it is no longer the secure, familiar place in which they hoped to die. These factors may combine to make in-home care impossible if the location no longer meets the conditions required. All these challenges can interfere with the wish to live out one's final days at home.

The Essential Presence of Family and Friends

As we will see, although it is indispensable for professionals to be present and available if people are to be able to die at home, the presence of caregivers willing and able to care for a sick person is also a key requirement.[7] Depending on their resources, personality, shared history with the sick person, family atmosphere, and the particular illness, relatives or friends will react differently to the challenges of caring for a person dying at home. Generally, however, research has shown that the experience takes a significant physical, emotional, social, and financial toll on caregivers, who have essential needs in terms of both information and psychological support or respite.[8] It is therefore fair to say that it is not enough for caregivers to be willing to accompany someone close to them who is dying at home: they themselves also need to have the support required to perform the duties expected of them.

The presence of family or friends and the meeting of needs are essential when an older adult is dying at home, because the older seniors become, the more likely they are to be living alone, and this makes dying at home complicated, if not impossible.[9] We also know that the primary caregivers for sick persons who are losing their autonomy are spouses – and, more specifically, wives. As they are also older adults, providing care can be extremely difficult.

The findings of a number of studies on the wishes of older adults with respect to their care also show that for many, the fear of being a burden is a key factor in their choice of where to live; some prefer to move into a seniors' residence or long-term care facility to avoid becoming dependent on their family or friends.[10] The same fear is manifested in the context of dying at home. Aware as they are of the numerous implications of their choice, older adults characteristically do not wish to become a serious burden on those around them, and this desire may be especially keen in older adults facing the end of their lives.[11]

Formal Services Geared to Needs

The presence of professionals who can meet all the needs of both patients and their family or friends is obviously another essential factor in end-of-life care at home, given the complex and changing situations that can arise. Dealing with upheaval, insecurities, and unforeseen developments increases the amount of time that must be devoted to patients and those tending to them. Care teams must therefore be able to respond quickly and be available on an almost constant basis. Furthermore, because physical, psychological, social, and spiritual needs can take many forms, teams must be interdisciplinary, including professionals such as respiratory therapists, social workers, occupational therapists, nutritionists, and home support workers, and they must have specific geriatric and end-of-life care skills.

In the current context, we feel that it is particularly relevant to emphasize the importance of proper professional follow-up in terms of both intensity of service and diversity of approach. The fact is that in-home care and services for older adults have been facing significant difficulties for many years. As the poor relative of the healthcare system, such services are still seriously underfunded, and users face numerous obstacles, such as long wait lists, significant staff turnover, reduced access to services in some geographical areas, increased incidental expenses billed to patients, and the privatization of some services.[12] There are reasons, therefore, to wonder about the ability of the system to meet the requirements of in-home end-of-life care when needs that are already not being met become more intense and diverse.[13]

Financial Costs

When a person wishes to die at home, consideration must also be given to the financial costs related to that decision. The already-high costs associated with staying at home can increase substantially as a person's state of health deteriorates. These costs are varied in nature, and include such things as heating or air conditioning for the patient's comfort, the cost of travel to medical appointments, the rental of equipment such as hospital beds and wheelchairs, and the cost of medication and other medical supplies. Given the inadequacy of public in-home services, it is quite common for private end-of-life services to be used. However, as such costs accumulate, they become a major obstacle to high-quality end-of-life care at home.

Conclusion

According to both popular belief and government claims, "everyone wants to die at home." But is that really true, regardless of circumstances? Even though there are no statistics on older adults' preferences concerning place of death, the relevant research does raise many questions and provide some findings that, at the very least, add nuance to such a statement.

Dying at home without suffering in a familiar, private, and secure place, surrounded by family and friends, clearly remains an ideal for many people, whether they are elderly or not. However, such a scenario is more the exception than the rule, since most people will actually have a complicated and difficult end-of-life experience. Given those difficulties, they may come to question their wish to die at home.

There is therefore room to wonder whether older adults still wish to die at home when their pain and other symptoms become too invasive and distressing. Do they still want to die at home when their housing does not lend itself to optimal care, or when they cannot afford the equipment they need in order to be comfortable? Do they still want to die at home when they realize that the burden of their care is becoming too heavy for family or friends?

The current public healthcare system is not able to meet the needs of older adults who wish to stay in their homes. These shortcomings become all the more acute in end-of-life situations, when needs become more intense and wide-ranging. Older adults who have sufficient financial resources – thus, a minority – can make use of private services to meet the needs that public services cannot provide. This situation is all the more egregious in that it costs the government more when people die in hospital: in other words, as long as in-home care is underfunded, hospitalization costs will remain high.

Given their inability to pull together all the requirements for an acceptable end-of-life experience at home, many older adults may prefer to end their days in a place better suited to their circumstances. The wish to die at home can change as the situation evolves to the point that the idea of staying at home until death may become unsustainable. These observations provide a better understanding of the gaps between wishes, expectations, and reality with regard to where people die.

In light of the above description, we feel justified in refuting the idea – apparently well established in the public mind – that everyone wishes to die at home. In fact, it seems that the question of choice is more one of possibility and accessibility. Instead of claiming that everyone *wants* to die at home, we should be asking ourselves who *can* die at home.

Notes

1 Monique Forget (2013), "Mourir chez soi, c'est possible," *L'actualité*, May 20, <http://www.lactualite.com/santeet-science/sante/mourir-chez-soi-cestpossible>, accessed March 3, 2017 (our translation).

2 Institut de la statistique du Québec (2016), *Tableau des décès selon le groupe d'âge et le sexe, Québec, 2011 à 2015*, <http://www.stat.gouv.qc.ca/statistiques/population -demographie/decesmortalite/302.htm>, accessed August 31, 2016.

3 A survey was conducted of 2,976 Canadians, including 301 Quebecers, concerning their perceptions and attitudes toward palliative care. Because the survey was based on an exclusive online panel, no margin of error can be supplied. Canadian Hospice Palliative Care Association (2015), *What Canadians Say:* The Way Forward *Survey Report* (Ottawa: Canadian Public Health Association).

4 Ministère de la Santé et des Services sociaux (2015), *Pour une meilleure qualité de vie. Soins palliatifs et fin de vie. Plan de développement 2015–2020* (Quebec City: Gouvernement du Québec).

5 Marie Beaulieu and Julie Lamontagne (2004), "Être âgé et mourir chez soi: les éléments du possible," *Les cahiers de soins palliatifs*, Vol. 5, No. 2, 29–50.

6 Christian Swine, Didier Schoevaerdts, and Bernadette Choteau (2009), "Fin de vie du patient atteint de démence," *Gérontologie et Société*, Nos. 128–29, 243–55.

7 Beaulieu and Lamontagne (2004), op. cit.

8 Penny E. Bee, Pamela Barnes, and Karen A. Luker (2008), "A systematic review of informal caregivers' needs in providing home-based end-of-life care to people with cancer," *Journal of Clinical Nursing*, Vol. 18, No. 3, 1379–93.

9 Ministère de la Famille et des Aînés (2011), *Un portrait statistique des familles au Québec* (Quebec City: Gouvernement du Québec).

10 Nancy Guberman, Jean-Pierre Lavoie, Laure Blein, and Ignace Olazabal (2012), "Baby Boom Caregivers: Care in the Age of Individualization," *The Gerontologist*, Vol. 52, No. 2, 210–18.

11   Merryn Gott, Jane Seymour, Gary Bellamy, David Clark, and Sam Ahmedzai (2004), "Older people's views about home as a place of care at the end of life," *Palliative Medicine*, Vol. 18, No. 5, 460–67.

12   Jean-Pierre Lavoie, Nancy Guberman, and Patrik Marier (2014), *La responsabilité des soins aux aînés au Québec. Du secteur public au secteur privé* (Montreal: Institut de recherche en politiques publiques/Institute for Research on Public Policy), No. 48, September.

13   Kareen Nour, Marie-Jo Hébert, Patrick Durivage, Véronique Billette, and Zelda Freitas (2012), "Portrait des soins palliatifs à domicile au Québec," *Cahiers francophones de soins palliatifs*, Vol. 12, No. 1, 1–37.

Part 6
CAREGIVER SUPPORT

25

Are Families Abandoning Older Relatives?

Isabelle Van Pevenage, Zelda Freitas,
Patrik Marier, and Pam Orzeck

In the Media ...

In June 2016, CBC News reported that in Halifax, Nova Scotia, an older woman in good health, who was being looked after by her grandchildren, was left by them in the hospital emergency room. When contacted by the hospital, the woman's children, who were in Florida at the time, refused to come and get her. She stayed at the hospital for nine days. The ER doctor said that "elder 'abandonment'" was "a growing issue."[1] In May 2016, CTV reported that the police in Calgary, Alberta, were looking for a family that had abandoned a 68 year old woman, who was left alone for several days In a "trash-filled rental" without food or water.[2]

The media regularly report that families have abandoned their aging parents. People are struck by this news because it is so appalling, and they end up thinking that such practices are widespread – that many families are abandoning older relatives. Beyond cases like these that are given heavy media coverage, what is the actual situation?

Less Respect for Older People and the Disappearance of Solidarity

The belief that there is widespread abandonment of older family members may stem from the association between two treasured idealizations of the past: that of the role played by older adults in families and that of solidarity among family members and, more broadly, in the community at large. The role once played by older adults is often romanticized as an idyllic and nostalgic image of old age as a glorious time experienced in an intergenerational world. This is the image found in children's books, in which older people are almost systematically depicted as wise and experienced "old folks" who share their knowledge and are surrounded by a family interested in what they have to convey.

To complete the picture, there is the belief that in the past, families, and society more broadly speaking, looked after their old people. It was a moral and religious obligation. There was a spirit of community, with people taking care of the more vulnerable among them. According to this idealized vision, it was the introduction of the welfare state that paved the way for families to desert their role of supporting older family members. With the state taking the place of solidarity among family members and in the community at large, families were said to no longer have a sense of responsibility for their older members.

Since the mid-twentieth century, families have undergone many changes that have had a major impact both on individuals' lives and on how family solidarity is organized. Such changes include:

- Smaller families, which has an effect on the number of people available when the need for care arises
- The massive entry of women into the labour force, which makes them less available to support other family members
- Increased marital instability and the diversification of family structures, which complicates the task of identifying who a family member is
- An increase in the number of years young people are in the education system, during which time they require extended family support
- Increased life expectancy leading to more free time for seniors (to provide support and participate in civil society), but also generating new assistance requirements for them.

These many upheavals make it easier to understand why, in the context of an aging population, the question of family solidarity with older family members raises concerns. With all of the demands placed on them, families might be tempted to abandon their support role, including care for older family members.

But What Are Families Doing for Their Older Relatives?

In order to obtain a clearer picture, we begin by summarizing the kinds of assistance provided to older adults. We then examine what seniors themselves would like in terms of where the help for them comes from, and we end with a description of some of the consequences that can arise as a result of the assistance provided to older relatives.

Assistance for Older Adults: A Few Facts

Caregivers may well be family members, but they may also be friends or neighbours. Statistics Canada surveys can be used to build a profile of caregivers. In 2012, the General Social Survey on care provided and received showed that 8 million Canadians aged 15 and over provided care to family members or friends with a disability or chronic health condition.[3] In Quebec, relatives provided more than 80 percent of the care required by older adults.[4] By converting the assistance provided by caregivers aged 45 and over into hourly wages, researchers estimated that the monetary value of this type of assistance in Canada in 2002 ranged from $13 billion to $31 billion, and in Quebec in 2007, from $3.95 billion to $10 billion.[5]

It is important to note that caregivers are generally between 45 and 64 years old, which makes them susceptible to being "sandwiched" between the needs of their aging parents and the requirements of their children's education. Approximately 30 percent of caregivers have at least one child under 18 still living with them. Moreover, 60 percent of caregivers are still working and therefore need to juggle their caregiving and career responsibilities.

Various types of assistance are provided to older adults and cover a wide range of activities. There are, of course, the everyday household tasks such as meals, housework, laundry, finances, and house and garden maintenance. But there are many other kinds of assistance as well, including hygiene and health-related care and monitoring. Researchers have also demonstrated that there are all kinds of support that are not often mentioned because they are less concrete or visible.[6] For example, there are the needs associated with protection and monitoring and those more closely tied to relational and emotional support.

The issue of gender is also unavoidable because every study on caregiving shows that women are largely responsible for informal care.[7] In Quebec, 36 percent of women and 24 percent of men aged 45 to 64 are caregivers. Of these caregivers, 56 percent of women and 43 percent of men spend four hours or more a week on providing support to a relative or friend.[8] This well-documented finding may be explained by the fact that the caregiving role is directly related to the tasks traditionally performed by women, who are usually called upon when families are required to provide more support. Many authors have noted that the expression "family-based care" really means "care provided by women."[9]

Although men handle certain caregiving tasks, their commitments take a more episodic or remote form. This means that women are more responsible for repetitive tasks over the long term, such as household tasks, meal preparation, personal and medical care, and managing and coordinating care. Men tend more to perform tasks that can be done on a more flexible schedule, such as administrative tasks or outdoor work around the house. The kind of help provided by women is therefore more restrictive than the support provided by men.

What Do the Main Stakeholders Want?

Researchers at the Centre for Research and Expertise in Social Gerontology conducted a major study in 2005 on the sense of responsibility toward older adults. The findings show that the vast majority of people (75 percent) in Quebec feel that it is the duty of family members to care for their older relatives. However, according to the research participants, caregivers' responsibilities for their aging parents should not require them to be so caught up in their role as caregivers that it affects their family life and careers. Furthermore, many felt that families should focus more on the tasks involved in providing love and attention and being there for their aging parents. Only a minority believed that the family should handle healthcare and other, more technical tasks. In other words, it was felt that family responsibilities should be combined with services provided by the government.[10]

It is also important to investigate what older people themselves want in terms of who provides the care when the need arises. In Quebec, the findings of a number of different research projects concur that the vast majority of older adults, when they need care, do not want to move in with one of their children and would not want their children to be solely responsible for their needs. They are particularly reluctant about the idea of depending solely on family members to care for them. In addition to the fact that they cherish their own – and their children's – freedom, they explain this reluctance in terms of wanting to protect the relationship: they want relations with their families to be harmonious. They also mention their fear of becoming a burden to their family.[11]

Family Caregiving for Older Adults: Some Consequences

Needless to say, although caring for an older family member may be highly gratifying for caregivers, many different kinds of negative impacts can arise in a variety of areas when the care extends over a lengthy period of time and the burden becomes more difficult. As early as the 1980s, studies drew attention to the many repercussions on caregivers' physical and psychological health. More recently, in Canada, 60 percent of those caring for an aging relative felt worried or anxious, and more than 20 percent were depressed or said that they had health problems.[12]

In addition to these considerations is the fact that many caregivers are older adults themselves. Although those in the 65-and-over age group are the least common, they are more likely than younger people to spend more hours providing care. Specifically, nearly one quarter of caregivers aged 65 and over spend 20 hours or more per week providing care. This can undoubtedly be explained in part by the fact that these caregivers generally care for the spouse with whom they are living and their tasks are ongoing. Indeed, older adults caring for a spouse tend to ask for less respite and fewer services than do children caring for an aging parent.[13] That being the case, it is clear that older caregivers are particularly at risk of developing health problems or disabilities themselves.[14] When this happens, the needs of the caregiving spouse are added to the needs of the spouse receiving care.

Caregiving can affect social and family life in many different ways. In Quebec, 49 percent of caregivers aged 15 and over said that their caregiving responsibilities led to their spending less time with their spouse, 44 percent had less time to spend with friends, 35 percent had to change or cancel vacation plans, and 27 percent said that their caregiving role created tensions with family or friends.[15]

There are also career and financial impacts to consider. To begin with, 35 percent of people with a job provide assistance or informal care. In order to care for a relative or friend, these caregivers may have to be late for or take time off from work, or even work shorter hours, turn down a promotion, or take early retirement.[16] In addition to the direct effects on workers, these adjustments have implications for government finances (fewer taxes collected, possible recourse to social programs when financial difficulties arise, and so on) and employers (absenteeism, unpaid leave, replacements, and other effects).

In terms of direct costs, relatives and friends may also have to cover various kinds of expenses, including transportation, accommodation, professional services, and medication. It is therefore not surprising to find that many caregivers experience financial difficulties and are forced to borrow money, defer savings, or change their consumption habits.[17]

Conclusion

Caregivers face complex realities and often work in the shadows, with no real political or media attention: they are not recognized by the healthcare and social services system, and media coverage of what they do is very rare.[18] When there is media coverage, it usually focuses on a few unfortunate events, such as those mentioned in the opening paragraph of this chapter.

This media aspect is, to say the least, sensationalistic and leads people to ask, "Are families really abandoning their older relatives?" In light of what we have just reported, the answer is, obviously, no. A closer look shows not only that families are providing the vast majority of the care that older relatives need but that they are also covering many of the costs and burdens involved.

The expression "natural caregiver," used in many public policy documents, assumes that it is natural for family members to care for their aging relatives. But as we have seen, the situation is much more nuanced, not only for older adults but also for their families. Although families feel responsible for their aging relatives, this responsibility is specific and limited. The assistance that they provide should be focused on relational and emotional needs and on protecting their aging relatives. Indeed, they should not have to jeopardize their family life or careers.

As we have seen, however, the types of assistance provided by families cover a much wider range of needs, often including healthcare and personal care – tasks that should be performed by professionals. We also found that providing care can have many impacts on caregivers' physical and psychological health and, in fact, on their family life and careers.

Approximately 80 percent of the needs of older adults are handled by relatives or friends. Families therefore contribute enormously. But they can do only so much. It is clear that they cannot on their own assume full responsibility for helping and providing care to older adults. Governments should therefore provide them with more support for the tasks they perform. This is all the more important because if caregivers become discouraged, exhausted, or ill as a result of the burden of these duties, governments will have much higher expenditures to deal with.

Notes

1 Aly Thomson (2016), "Halifax ER doctor says elder 'abandonment' a growing issue," *CBC News,* June 9, <https://www.cbc.ca/news/canada/nova-scotia/elder-left-halifax-erfor-nine-days-1.3625531>, accessed March 10, 2017.

2 CTV News (2016), "Calgary police seek family who abandoned woman in trashfilled rental," broadcast on May 3, <http://calgary.ctvnews.ca/calgary-police-seek-family-who-abandoned-womanin-trash-filled-rental-1.2885024>, accessed March 10, 2017.

3 Martin Turcotte (2013), "Family caregiving: What are the consequences?," *Insights on Canadian Society* (Ottawa: Statistics Canada).

4 Jean-Pierre Lavoie, Nancy Guberman, and Patrik Marier (2014), *La responsabilité des soins aux aînés au Québec. Du secteur public au secteur privé* (Montreal: Institut de recherche en politiques publiques/Institute for Research on Public Policy), No. 48, September.

5 Marcus J. Hollander, Guiping Liu, and Neena L. Chappell (2009), "Who cares and how much? The imputed economic contribution to the Canadian healthcare system of middle-aged and older unpaid caregivers providing care to the elderly," *Healthcare Quarterly*, Vol. 12, No. 2, 42–49; Marianne Kempeneers, Alex Batagliani, and Isabelle Van Pevenage, with Adrienne Gagnon, Émilie Audy, and Jessica Gerlach (2015), *Chiffrer les solidarités familiales*, Carnet Synthèse du Centre de recherche et de partage des savoirs InterActions, CSSS Bordeaux-Cartierville – Saint-Laurent-CAU, No. 4, March.

6 Barbara Bowers (1987), "Intergenerational caregiving: Adult caregivers and their aging parents," *Advanced Nursing Science*, Vol. 9, No. 2, 20–31.

7 By "informal care," we mean all assistance provided by non-professionals. These may be family members, but also friends and neighbours.

8 Charles Fleury (2013), "Portrait des personnes proches aidantes âgées de 45 ans et plus," *Coup d'œil sociodémographique* (Quebec City: Institut de la statistique du Québec), No. 27, June.

9 Claude Martin (2002), "Les solidarités familiales: bon ou mauvais objet sociologique?," in Danielle Debordeaux and Pierre Strobel (eds.), *Les solidarités familiales en questions. Entraide et transmission* (Paris: Éditions LGDJ).

10 Nancy Guberman, Jean-Pierre Lavoie, and Éric Gagnon, with Valérie Bourgeois-Guérin, Michel Fournier, Lise Grenier, Anna Ghergel, Nicolas Rousseau, Hélène Belleau, and Aline Vézina (2005), *Valeurs et normes de la solidarité familiale: statu quo, évolution, mutation?*, a report submitted to the Fonds québécois de recherche sur la culture et la société as part of a project titled "Action concertée sur les impacts démographiques et socioéconomiques du vieillissement de la population."

11 Nancy Guberman, Jean-Pierre Lavoie, Laure Blein, and Ignace Olazabal (2012), "Baby boom caregivers: Care in the age of individualization," *The Gerontologist*, Vol. 52, No. 2, 210–18.

12 Turcotte (2013), op. cit.

13 Maire Sinha (2013), *Portrait of caregivers, 2012*, Ottawa, Statistics Canada, Catalogue No. 89-652-X.

14 Michael Raschick and Berit Ingersoll-Dayton (2004), "The costs and rewards of caregiving among aging spouses and adult children," *Family Relations*, Vol. 53, No. 3, 317–25.

15 Chantale Lecours (2015), "Portrait des proches aidants et les conséquences de leurs responsabilités d'aidant," *Coup d'œil sociodémographique* (Quebec City: Institut de la statistique du Québec), No. 43, November.

16 Sinha (2013), op. cit.

17 Ibid.

18 Patrik Marier and Isabelle Van Pevenage (2016), "The invisible women: Gender and caregiving in francophone newspapers," *Journal of Communication and Public Relations*, Vol. 18, No. 3, 77–88.

26

Multiple Autonomies

Navigating the World of Home Care Services

Norma Gilbert, Annette Leibing, and Patrik Marier

> Most seniors don't realize the inadequacies in the public system until
> they suffer a personal crisis, like a fall or a medical emergency. That's when
> they realize that the social safety net they helped build throughout their
> lives is broken when they need it most.
>
> ———— Editorial, *Montreal Gazette*[1]

Research on aging baby boomers indicates that older adults and those close
to them expect to maintain a satisfactory level of independence with the
help of government-provided health and social services when they begin to
experience loss of autonomy.[2] The quotation above reflects their unpleasant
discovery of a system of care and services for older adults that does not always meet their expectations. According to the 2016 report of the Quebec
Health and Welfare Commissioner, many people feel that services for older
adults have not been well adapted to today's healthcare and social service
needs.[3] The report also notes that finding their way through the health and
social services maze can be difficult for older adults, particularly at a time
when they need help. Moreover, their expectations with regard to services
may be based on previous experience or on word of mouth that may or may
not apply to their present situation. Once a request for help has been made,
older adults discover that home care services are assigned according to an
exhaustive and complex assessment of loss of functional autonomy, which,

although efficient, does not always take into account the needs that they consider important.

Below, we look at issues relating to what older adults would need to remain independent. Although many share the same goal of maintaining autonomy, individual expectations for achieving this may vary widely. In this context, we will be focusing on Quebec, but we believe that similar issues may arise in other jurisdictions.[4]

Are Home Care Services Adequate?

It is no surprise that many people expect the government to provide adequate and appropriate home care services to older adults so that they can stay in their own homes.[5] Since the early 2000s, this has been a well-defined and publicly stated objective of the government of Quebec, particularly in two policy documents: *Chez soi, le premier choix* (Home support: Always the option of choice) (2003) and *Vieillir et vivre ensemble. Chez soi, dans sa communauté, au Québec* (Aging and living together – At home, in your community, in Quebec) (2012).[6] These policies are based on abundant scientific literature that advocates keeping older adults as long as possible in the environment in which they feel that they have the most independence – in other words, in their own homes.[7] However, there are a number of indications that inadequate spending in recent years has led to a decrease in the level and duration of services provided to support aging individuals at home. In the mid-1990s, people experiencing loss of autonomy received 20 hours a week of home care services that included bathing, housekeeping, meal preparation, and a few errands.[8] Budget cuts and an attempt to harmonize services led to changes in how these services are provided, including, for example, a reduction in the hours allocated and the addition of criteria for exclusion from services. As noted in the Quebec Ombudsman's 2012 and 2016 reports, recent reforms have had a significant impact on many older adults; furthermore, the level of services provided is by no means uniform but varies from district to district. In other words, older adults who move to or enter a care facility in a different location may find that the services they once received are no longer available.[9] Despite a recent budget increase approved by the government of Quebec, the Health Ministry admitted that funding was still insufficient, in part because of the growing number of older adults requiring services.[10] At the individual service level, therefore, budget increases are not necessarily reflected in a more ample provision of existing services.

Home care services for older adults are not routinely provided; rather, they are usually allocated following an assessment. The purportedly object-ive process – based on profiles associated with support recommendations – involves an extensive questionnaire, the Multi-clientele Assessment Tool (MCAT). However, this process also raises a number of issues. Below, we review the ways in which loss of autonomy is assessed by examining the contradictions and tensions inherent in the process, as well as the associ-ated social and political context.

The Complex Task of Assessing Loss of Autonomy

Various issues can be identified related to assessing loss of autonomy: 1) differences of opinion between the older adult and his or her caregivers regarding his or her situation; 2) weaknesses inherent in the questionnaire; and 3) misunderstandings about the reason for the assessment because of the older adult's fear of moving to a care facility.

The meeting between an older adult and the home care services repre-sentative is often triggered by an acute health issue, but it can also be due to the process of a gradual loss of autonomy. Because a person's degree of func-tional autonomy is at the heart of the assessment, the notion of autonomy itself becomes central to matters of health and aging. Elsewhere in Canada, the Resident Assessment Instrument, Minimum Data Set (RAI-MDS) is the data-collection tool used to determine a person's needs in terms of care and support; the corresponding tool in Quebec, similar to the RAI-MDS, is the MCAT.[11] According to the MCAT, functional autonomy refers to an individ-ual's ability to pursue "activities of daily living" – bathing, dressing, running errands, keeping house, and preparing meals. The MCAT also assesses chal-lenges for older adults and their relatives or friends in managing health issues, such as a chronic illness. The importance of and need for an assess-ment tool is unquestionable, but some people feel that the results obtained with the MCAT do not reflect the complex and multifaceted nature of the situation that the assessed person is dealing with. The main criticisms in-volve its failure to take into account the social circumstances and points of view of both the assessed person and his or her family members.[12]

Differences of Opinion within the Family about Loss of Autonomy
A number of studies indicate that family and friends do not always concur with the aging person's perception of his or her autonomy. In many cases, older adults' opinions of their abilities are positive, whereas their caregivers

tend to assess them as weak.[13] This discrepancy in how the situation is perceived makes it difficult to achieve consensus on the older adult's need for care and support, even before the formal assessment procedure begins. Older adults often consider themselves self-sufficient, relatively well adapted to their situation, and able to cope.[14] Caregivers, on the other hand, perceive the loss of an older adult's autonomy and increased dependence in terms of the care and support that they deliver.[15] Families and practitioners sometimes find themselves in a paradoxical situation, caught between their respect for the older adult's desire for independence and the need to convince them to accept help to live safely at home.[16]

Some caregivers go to great lengths to support the older adult's independence and resort to subterfuge to maintain their illusion of self-sufficiency.[17] Others magnify the older adult's vulnerability or attempt to slant the assessment process in order to obtain more public assistance. For instance, a caregiver – parent, child, or spouse – may try to exaggerate the symptoms described by the patient.[18] The presence of a caregiver may also affect the assessment by the healthcare professional, as family caregivers are regarded as a resource that can offset an older adult's diminished capacity. Consequently, the assessment score may be higher or lower depending on the level of support provided by the family, sometimes without taking into account that support from caregivers may change and that it may not be consistent or adequate.

Fear of Institutionalization

As part of a recent aging-in-place study, 26 older adults living alone in Montreal were interviewed. Their declining health was making them more dependent on outside help.[19] We learned that the interviewees liked where they lived, even in cases where it clearly did not meet their needs. They also expressed their fear of ending up in a place where they could no longer live as they wished and would need to depend on strangers for care. One woman, aged 96, living alone on a government pension in low-income housing, expressed a fairly common feeling:

> Why don't I want to move? Because I feel good here ... [There] you have no control over your things ... And if you don't like the food, you have to eat it anyway. You have to sleep when they tell you to. You have to ... you have to!

To keep control over their lives and maintain their independence, the respondents expected – in vain, in many cases – to receive help from their local community service centre to stay in their homes. They also felt embarrassed about asking for help from their children or other relatives or from friends, but they would nevertheless accept it willingly to reduce the risk of having to leave their homes. For many older adults, being independent is a matter of pride, something they have to prove to the healthcare professional. Some may find the assessment process intimidating, associating it with the fear of being "placed," an eventuality that many of them dread.[20]

Difficulties Generated by the Assessment Tool

The MCAT has also been criticized for its lack of attention to psychological and social factors.[21] From talking to social workers as part of a research project, we learned that although some older adults may appear to be relatively functional, according to the MCAT, they may be seriously handicapped by alcoholism or substance abuse.[22] When there is a discrepancy between the score produced by the assessment tool and the assessment by the healthcare professional, the professional is forced to argue – unsuccessfully, in some cases – with his or her superiors to obtain the support services required. One social worker described the situation as follows: "We enter the data into the computer, and then we cross our fingers."[23]

Another caseworker stressed some incongruities in applying the score. In one district, a score may result in home care services, whereas in another, the services may be very different for the same profile due to different budget priorities.[24] Healthcare practitioners also pointed to other task-related issues caused by time constraints and performance measurements, as well as to resource cutbacks and reduced budgets that make it difficult to deliver services. According to the interviewees, the most disturbing – and absurd – aspect is the follow-up to the long and complicated assessment process. There is no guarantee that the older adult's needs as identified by the assessment will be addressed as, very often, tight budgets make it impossible to provide the services required. One of the interviewees observed, "As things stand, we prefer to tell them right away what we can give them – even before the assessment – rather than let them have expectations and then be cruelly disappointed."[25]

Conclusion

In this chapter, we underscore the importance of gaining a better understanding of the process of assessing loss of autonomy, which does not always yield the expected results. Given the reduction in some services, this aspect is all the more crucial in the context of scarce home-care resources and services that force families to make up the shortfalls themselves or pay for private services. In a nutshell, issues related to older adults' autonomy cannot be dealt with solely as a healthcare, psychological, or social matter. Issues related to policies and to the resources and tools used in their application (the concept of autonomy, resource deployment, assessment methods, and others) also come into play. In the context of an aging population, one of the challenges is how to enable older adults who are gradually losing autonomy to maintain their independence by responding appropriately to their needs.

Notes

1   Montreal Gazette Editorial Board (2015), "Editorial: Quebec and the Eldercare Challenge," *Montreal Gazette*, November 6, <http://montrealgazette.com/opinion/editorials/editorial-quebec-and-theeldercare-challenge>, accessed September 6, 2017.
2   Nancy Guberman, Jean-Pierre Lavoie, Laure Blein, and Ignace Olazabal (2012), "Baby boom caregivers: Care in the age of individualization," *The Gerontologist*, Vol. 52, No. 2, 210–18.
3   Quebec Health and Welfare Commissioner (2016), *Entendre la voix citoyenne pour améliorer l'offre de soins et services: rapport d'appréciation thématique de la performance du système de santé et de services sociaux 2016 – Un état des lieux* (Quebec City: Gouvernement du Québec).
4   Annette Leibing, Nancy Guberman, and Janine Wiles (2016), "Liminal homes: Older people, loss of capacities, and the present future of living spaces," *Journal of Aging Studies*, Vol. 37, 10–19; our comments are based on the professional experience of the first-named author and her recent interviews with healthcare professionals in the context of her doctoral studies.
5   Ibid.
6   Gouvernement du Québec (2003), *Chez soi: Le premier choix. La politique de soutien à domicile/Home Support: Always the Option of Choice. The Homecare Support Policy* (Quebec City: Santé et services sociaux Québec; Ministère de la Famille et des Aînés, and Ministère de la Santé et des Services sociaux); Gouvernement du Québec (2012), *Politique Vieillir et vivre ensemble – Chez soi, dans sa communauté, au Québec* (Quebec City: Gouvernement du Québec).
7   Janine Wiles, Annette Leibing, Nancy Guberman, Jeanne Reeve, and Ruth Allen (2012), "The meaning of 'Aging in Place' to older people," *The Gerontologist*, Vol. 52, No. 3, 357–66.
8   Jacques Roy (1994), "L'histoire du maintien à domicile ou les nouveaux apôtres de l'État," *Service social*, Vol. 431, No. 1, 7–32.
9   Quebec Ombudsman (2012), *Is Home Support Always the Option of Choice? Accessibility of Home Support Services for People with Significant and Persistent Disabilities* (Quebec City: Gouvernement du Québec); Quebec Ombudsman (2016), *2015–2016 Annual Report* (Quebec City: Gouvernement du Québec).

10 Régys Caron (2016), "Québec injecte 22 millions dans les soins à domicile," *Journal de Québec*, August 24, <http://www.journaldequebec.com/2016/08/24/quebec-injecte-22-millions-dans-lessoins-a-domicile>, accessed September 5, 2017.

11 Réjean Hébert, Johanne Desrosiers, Nicole Dubuc, Michel Tousignant, Joanne Guilbeault, and Eugénie Pinsonnault (2003), "Le système de mesure de l'autonomie fonctionnelle (SMAF)," *La Revue de gériatrie*, Vol. 28, No. 4, 323–36.

12 Marie Beaulieu and Francine Caron (2000), "La place de la personne aînée dans la définition de son autonomie," *Le Gérontophile*, Vol. 22, No. 3, 47–55.

13 Isabelle Van Pevenage (2015), "Les sens de l'autonomie: regards d'enfants du babyboom sur leur mère âgée," in Catherine Bonvalet, Ignace Olazabal, and Michel Oris (eds.), *Les baby-boomers, une histoire de familles. Une comparaison Québec-France* (Quebec City: Presses de l'Université du Québec); Janice E. Graham and Raewyn Bassett (2006), "Reciprocal relations: The recognition and co-construction of caring with Alzheimer's disease," *Journal of Aging Studies*, Vol. 20, 335–49; Amy Horowitz, Caryn R. Goodman, and Joann P. Reinhardt (2004), "Congruence between disabled elders and their primary caregivers," *The Gerontologist*, Vol. 44, No. 4, 532–42; Jeanne R. Snyder (2000), "Impact of caregiver-receiver relationship quality on burden and satisfaction," *Journal of Women and Aging*, Vol. 12, Nos. 1–2, 147–67.

14 Josée Grenier (2011), "Regards d'aînés: justice, autonomie et responsabilité partagée," PhD dissertation, Université de Montréal.

15 Van Pevenage (2015), op. cit.

16 Ibid.; Graham and Bassett (2006), op. cit.; Horowitz, Goodman, and Reinhardt (2004), op cit.

17 Van Pevenage (2015), op. cit.; Allison M. Reamy, Kim Kyungmin, Steven H. Zarit, and Carol J. Whitlach (2011), "Understanding discrepancy in perceptions of values: Individuals with mild to moderate dementia and their family caregivers," *The Gerontologist*, Vol. 51, No. 4, 473–83; Graham and Bassett (2006), op cit.; Horowitz, Goodman, and Reinhardt (2004), op. cit.

18 Sylvie Fainzang (2016), "From solidarity to autonomy: Towards a redefinition of the parameters of the notion of autonomy," *Theoretical Medicine and Bioethics*, Vol. 37, No 6, 463–72.

19 Leibing, Guberman, and Wiles (2016), op. cit.

20 Sarah Hillcoat-Nallétamby (2014), "The meaning of 'independence' for older people in different residential settings," *Journals of Gerontology, Series B: Psychological and Social Sciences*, Vol. 69, No. 3, 419–30; Grenier (2011), op. cit.; Debbie Plath (2008), "Independence in old age: The route to social exclusion?," *British Journal of Social Work*, Vol. 38, No. 7, 1353–69.

21 Nathalie Delli-Colli, Nicole Dubuc, Réjean Hébert, Catherine Lestage, and Marie-France Dubois (2013), "Identifying psychosocial variables for home care services and how to measure them," *Home Health Care Services Quarterly*, Vol. 32, No. 4, 197–217.

22 Norma Gilbert (2019), "The Social and Interpersonal Dimensions of Measuring Loss of Autonomy: Expectations among Family Caregivers and Home Care Social Workers in Quebec," PhD dissertation, Université de Montréal.

23 Ibid. (our translation).
24 Ibid.
25 Ibid. (our translation).

27

LGBT Older Adults

Who Is There to Support Them and Care for Them as They Age?

Julie Beauchamp, Shari Brotman, Line Chamberland,
and Ilyan Ferrer

Diane decides to retire early to look after her husband, who is in failing health. Marie takes a long period of leave to care for her elderly mother who broke her hip. Her brother Martin will help with the move to a more accessible place to live. These types of care situations are seen as natural and desirable. But what would happen if Roger, a former nurse, were to commit to accompanying Léonil, his gay friend of many years, to his chemotherapy treatments? And what if Lise, Magda, and Louise were to arrange to prepare meals and bring them to their friend Thérèse, who lives alone, while she recovers from heart surgery? Would this type of caregiving help be recognized? Would these caregivers receive the same level of support? Would they be accorded the same legitimacy, or would it be seen as a last resort? In this chapter, we question the myth that the only people who can provide care and support to older adults with a loss of autonomy are spouses (presumably heterosexual ones) and adult children or, alternatively, other family members.

A Closer Look at the Myth

This myth, which stems from the belief that only the traditional nuclear family is a natural source of assistance and care for older adults,[1] does not reflect the diversity of family configurations that exist in contemporary Quebec society. It also makes it harder to see or recognize the realities experienced by older adults who are lesbian, gay, bisexual, or trans (LGBT). This was exemplified in the comment that one practitioner made in the context of a Canadian research study: "I have been working with caregivers for the past 12 years and never, never have we stopped to think about gays and lesbians. No one has ever told us that their experiences could be different, or that they needed something ... never!"[2]

This myth acts as a filter that prevents other people who provide support from being granted recognition and legitimacy. It can lead to discrimination, as illustrated by the following comments from a caregiver that were made in connection with the same study: "When I asked to see her, they wouldn't let me in because I wasn't an immediate relative. So I sat in the waiting room until the shift changed and went back up to the desk and told them I was her sister so they let me go see her."[3]

Where the Myth Originated

Where does the assumption that family represents the best, if not the only, source of assistance and care for older adults come from? It is a preconception rooted in a normative model of the traditional nuclear family as the natural source of support and caregiving.[4] In this model, family relationships are structured around the couple and their offspring. Its prevalence leads to a type of hierarchy in relation to other types of families that deviate from the standard model.[5] Prior to 1999, same-sex couples did not receive legal recognition in Quebec and were therefore deprived of a series of benefits granted to heterosexual couples, such as permission to take care of a sick partner and the right to survivor benefits.[6]

This restrictive perception of the notion of family is largely influenced by heteronormative attitudes, among other things.[7] Heteronormativity refers to a dominant discourse that promotes a family framework based on differentiation and on the so-called natural complementarity between men and women within the family. In other words, this discourse "presupposes a binary relationship between the sexes (male/female), genders (man/woman), social roles (e.g., father/mother) and sexual orientations (heterosexual/homosexual), and the alignment of these dimensions (female sex/woman/mother/heterosexual; male sex/man/father/heterosexual)."[8] Heteronormativity thus entails a restrictive interpretation of the notion of family that can lead to a failure to recognize family configurations that differ from the dominant model. It can have serious repercussions on the support and care provided to LGBT older adults by disregarding their realities and failing to take into consideration and recognize the legitimacy of potential sources of help – whether as advocates in determining the type of care or as caregivers – when these older adults experience a loss of autonomy.

Deconstructing the Myth

Although it is true that most people receive support and care from their immediate family, the fact remains that some older adults benefit from various types of assistance offered by an informal network whose members are not considered family in the traditional sense.[9] The notion of family today encompasses a diversity of family situations and structures within society. The spousal relationship between same-sex partners and the relationship with same-sex parents have been recognized under the law and are increasingly receiving social recognition and acceptance.[10] To reflect this diversity, an expanded and inclusive conception of what is meant by family and, concretely, the people who can be considered as family members is being proposed.[11]

Support and Care Networks for LGBT Older Adults: Caregivers outside the Normative Model

Research has shown that, compared with heterosexual individuals, LGBT older adults are more likely to live alone and not to have children (or have fewer children) to support them as they grow older.[12] Moreover, because of the social discrimination that has marked a portion of their adult lives, some (although not all) LGBT older adults have been unable to maintain close ties with their family of origin and have instead created a "chosen family."[13] A chosen family can be composed of partners (legally recognized or not), former partners, and close friends who are considered family; it can also selectively include one or more members of the family of origin with whom there is a positive relationship.[14] The chosen family creates a sense of belonging and is akin to a family of origin in that there are shared values and the provision of support and care.[15] For LGBT older adults, the entire informal network of support and care, which includes the chosen family, communities of belonging, and community resources, is of central importance as they grow older.[16] That being said, heteronormative conceptions of family, discrimination (past, present, or anticipated), and issues around disclosure of sexual orientation or gender identity can have an impact on the visibility, recognition, and legitimacy of this network as far as services are concerned.[17]

What Does the Research Tell Us?

In a study on the healthcare and social services needs of gay and lesbian older adults and their families carried out in three Canadian cities, care-givers in particular highlighted the central role played by partners, friends, and the community in the support and care provided to this population.[18] In a context of invisibility and discrimination in health and social services, participants talked about how some gay and lesbian older adults avoid or delay seeking services, relying instead on the informal support provided by friends or family. Moreover, the role of caregiver was often perceived as more intense given the need to keep an eye on the system in order to anticipate, prevent, or respond to discrimination. One caregiver said the following about her partner: "She's going to have care from this person on the night shift ... she is more vulnerable ... I wouldn't want to leave her there on her own."[19] In addition to the support of a partner, when there is one, participants reaffirmed the important role of the chosen family in providing care to the person. Aside from personal relationships, the reasons that caregivers provide care stem from broader commitments related to their identity and solidarity with the community, which are often built up over decades. Unfortunately, the strong connection found in LGBT communities is not often recognized by the health and social services system. The same study revealed that healthcare providers do not know about social and community resources for LGBT people and are not aware of the specific needs and realities of these communities.

Among trans older adults, the diversity of family situations observed in a Quebec study that looked primarily at trans women should serve to counter any assumptions or generalizations regarding family support.[20] Like gays and lesbians, many trans people have no partners. If partners exist, they may be of the opposite sex – in most cases – or of the same sex. Many trans older adults had children (now adults) before their transition, and the quality of their relationships with their children varies greatly. Some older adults who transitioned decades earlier managed to maintain close ties with one or more members of their family of origin. However, acceptance of what is perceived as their "new" gender identity often means denying their transsexual past and observing a pact of silence on this topic. This erasure of the past creates a sense of isolation, as it excludes any possibility of sharing this aspect of their life. Trans people who start their transition at an older age often cause tension within their family (parents, former partners, children) and expose themselves to hostile reactions, including possibly even being cut off, from that family.

Friends can be part of a support network, but the size and the strength of this network may vary greatly, and the number of people with whom trans older adults have close ties seems rather limited. A large number of them express feelings of isolation and loneliness. As people grow older, certain needs become more acute. Some examples would be the need for welcoming resources within the healthcare system for health problems related to transition or aging, the need to receive emotional support and be able to speak openly, and the need to share similar experiences. These needs lead some trans older adults to maintain contact or to discreetly reconnect with peers from their age group or with associations representing trans people. For one trans older adult who took part in the study, these people ultimately became "another family."

Lastly, a study on LGBT older adults carried out in Quebec as part of a Canada-wide study on the needs, experiences, and constraints that they encounter in planning their future and their end of life confirmed the findings presented above.[21] The results attest to how important it is for LGBT older adults to have a support and care network and the difficulties encountered in maintaining this network. For many participants, the chosen family is in fact the primary source of support and care. This study showed two things. First, whether or not their identity is accepted by their family of origin has an impact on the relationship with that family and on the support that is offered. Second, the changes (geographic distance, loss of a partner or friends, and others) that may occur as a person grows older can make this network more fragile. The community workers also stressed the importance of creating and maintaining mutual support networks among LGBT older adults, including the development of a caregiver network.

Implications and Interventions

Over the course of their lives, many LGBT older adults establish strong and reliable support networks. In many cases, these networks become their primary family. Accordingly, a broader definition and understanding of the notion of "family" may help to deconstruct the myth that the traditional family is the only natural source of support and caregiving for older people experiencing a loss of autonomy. Recognition and inclusion of this network composed of partners, members of the chosen family, and community organization staff are therefore essential in facilitating the proper mobilization of formal services to meet the needs of LGBT older adults.

A number of avenues are available for promoting sexual and gender diversity within formal services: increasing the visibility of documentation on the realities and needs of LGBT older adults; creating awareness strategies to enhance understanding of the relationships and family situations of LGBT older adults and the acquisition of cultural competencies by staff through the use of available tools (including training programs, practical guides, and brochures); and developing policies and practices geared to the needs of LGBT older adults and their caregivers (specific support groups and other resources).[22] These approaches will serve to enhance services and reduce discrimination and stigma so as to ensure respect for the dignity and rights of LGBT older adults, their families – chosen or otherwise – and their caregivers.

Notes

1   Judith C. Barker (2002), "Neighbors, friends, and other nonkin caregivers of community-living dependent elders," *Journal of Gerontology: Social Sciences*, Vol. 57B, No. 3, p. S158–S167; Karen A. Roberto and Rosemary Blieszner (2015), "Diverse family structures and the care of older persons," *Canadian Journal on Aging/La Revue canadienne du vieillissement*, Vol. 34, No. 3, 305–20.

2   Shari Brotman, Bill Ryan, Elizabeth Meyer, Line Chamberland, Robert Cormier, Danielle Julien, Allen Peterkin, and Brenda Richard (2006), *The Health and Social Service Needs of Gay and Lesbian Seniors and Their Families in Canada* – Summary report, Montreal, McGill School of Social Work; Shari Brotman, Bill Ryan, Shannon Collins, Line Chamberland, Robert Cormier, Danielle Julien, Elizabeth Meyer, Allen Peterkin, and Brenda Richard (2007), "Coming out to care: Caregivers of gay and lesbian seniors in Canada," *The Gerontologist*, Vol. 47, No. 4, 490–503.

3   Brotman et al. (2006), op. cit.; Brotman et al. (2007), op. cit.

4   Barker (2002), op. cit.; Roberto and Blieszner (2015), op. cit.

5   Katherine R. Allen, Rosemary Blieszner, and Karen A. Roberto (2011), "Perspectives on extended family and fictive kin in the later years: Strategies and meanings of kin reinterpretation," *Journal of Family Issues*, Vol. 32, No. 9, 1156–77.

6   Manon Tremblay (2015), "Quebec and sexual diversity: From repression to citizenship?," in Manon Tremblay (ed.), *Queer Mobilizations. Social Movement Activism and Canadian Public Policy* (Vancouver, UBC Press), 106–24.

7   Sasha Roseneil and Shelley Budgeon (2004), "Cultures of intimacy and care beyond 'the family': Personal life and social change in the early 21st century," *Current Sociology*, Vol. 52, No. 2, 135–59.

8   Mona Greenbaum (ed.) (2015), *Familles LGBT au Québec: le guide* (Montreal: Les éditions du Remue-ménage), 12 (our translation).

9   Céline Le Bourdais, Magali Girard, Liam Swiss, and Évelyne Lapierre-Adamcyk (2013), "Entre famille et vieillissement: impact des transformations familiales aux âges avancés," *International Journal of Canadian Studies*, Vol. 47, 10, 35; Barker (2002), op. cit.

10   Lois Harder (2011), *La fin du modèle nucléaire? Nouvelles réalités touchant les familles et le droit de la famille au Canada* (Ottawa: Vanier Institute of the Family); Greenbaum (2015), op. cit.

11   Shari Brotman and Ilyan Ferrer (2015), "Diversity within family caregiving: Extending definitions of 'who counts' to include marginalized communities," *HealthcarePapers*, Vol. 15, No. 1, 47–53; Roberto and Blieszner (2015), op. cit.

12   Samia Addis, Myfanwy Davies, Giles Greene, Sara MacBride-Stewart, and Michael Shepherd (2009), "The health, social care and housing needs of lesbian, gay, bisexual and transgender older people: A review of the literature," *Health and Social Care in the Community*, Vol. 17, No. 6, 647–58; Steven P. Wallace, Susan D. Cochran, Eva M. Durazo, and Chandra L. Ford (2011), *The Health of Aging Lesbian, Gay and Bisexual Adults in California* (Los Angeles : UCLA Center for Health Policy Research).

13   Shari Brotman, Bill Ryan, and Robert Cormier (2003), "The health and social service needs of gay and lesbian elders and their families in Canada," *The Gerontologist*, Vol. 43, No. 2, 192–202; Judith C. Barker, Gilbert Herdt, and Brian de Vries (2006), "Social support in the lives of lesbians and gay men at midlife and later," *Sexuality Research and Social Policy*, Vol. 3, No. 2, 1–23; Kath Weston (1991), *Families we Choose: Lesbians, Gays, Kinship* (New York: Columbia University Press).

14   Katherine R. Allen and Karen A. Roberto (2016), "Family relationships of older LGBT adults," in Debra A. Harley and Pamela B. Teaster (eds.), *Handbook of LGBT Elders* (Springer International Publishing), 43–64.

15   Ibid.

16   Brotman and Ferrer (2015), op. cit.; Roberto and Blieszner (2015), op. cit.; Mark Brennan-Ing, Liz Seidel, Britta Larson, and Stephen E. Karpiak (2014), "Social care networks and older LGBT adults: Challenges for the future," *Journal of Homosexuality*, Vol. 61, No. 1, 21–52; Catherine F. Croghan, Rajean P. Moone, and Andrea M. Olson (2014), "Friends, family, and caregiving among midlife and older lesbian, gay, bisexual, and transgender adults," *Journal of Homosexuality*, Vol. 61, No. 1, 79–102.

17   Brotman et al. (2003), op. cit.; Brennan-Ing et al. (2014), op. cit.; Croghan et al. (2014), op. cit.; Catherine Barrett, Pauline Crameri, Sally Lambourne, J.R. Latham, and Carolyn Whyte (2015), "Understanding the experiences and needs of lesbian, gay, bisexual and trans Australians living with dementia, and their partners," *Australasian Journal on Ageing*, Vol. 34, Suppl. 2, 34–38; Paul Willis, Nicki Ward, and Julie Fish (2011), "Searching for LGBT carers: Mapping a research agenda in social work and social care," *British Journal of Social Work*, Vol. 41, 1304–20.

18   Brotman et al. (2006), op. cit.; Brotman et al. (2007), op. cit.; Brotman et al. (2003), op. cit.

19   Brotman et al. (2006), op. cit.; Brotman et al. (2007), op. cit.

20   Unpublished data collected for a qualitative study of trans seniors and health and social services practitioners. See Billy Hébert, Line Chamberland, and Mickaël Chacha Enriquez (2015), *Mieux intervenir auprès des aîné.e.s trans* (Montreal: Chaire de recherche sur l'homophobie, Université du Québec à Montréal), <https://chairehomophobie.uqam.ca/wp-content/uploads/2015/07/upload_files_Rapport_final_Aine-e-s_Trans_Septembre2015.pdf>, accessed August 5, 2016.

21   Line Chamberland, Julie Beauchamp, Jean Dumas, and Olivia Kamgain (2016), *Aîné.e.s LGBT: favoriser le dialogue sur la préparation de leur avenir et de leur fin de*

vie, et la prise en charge communautaire, Research report – Montreal component, Montreal, Chaire de recherche sur l'homophobie, Université du Québec à Montréal, <https://chairehomophobie.uqam.ca/publication/aine-e-s-lgbt-favoriser-le-dialogue -sur-la-preparation-de-leur-avenir-et-de-leur-fin-de-vie-et-la-prise-en-charge -communautaire/?hilite=%27TVN%27>, accessed August 5, 2016.

22   On the tools available, see Chamberland et al. (2016), op. cit., 74–75, and Chaire de recherche sur l'homophobie website, <https://chairehomophobie.uqam.ca/publication/ adaptation-des-services-sociaux-et-de-sante/>, accessed August 5, 2016. On policies and practices, see Brotman et al. (2006), op. cit.; Brotman et al. (2007), op. cit.; Brotman et al. (2003), op. cit.; Brennan-Ing et al. (2014), op. cit.; Barrett et al. (2015), op. cit.; Willis et al. (2011), op. cit.; Hébert et al. (2015), op. cit.; Chamberland et al. (2016), op. cit.; Croghan et al. (2014), op. cit.

28

Care Provision to Older Immigrants by Their Families
When Discrimination Creates Barriers to Services

Ilyan Ferrer and Shari Brotman

Older adults from ethnocultural-minority immigrant communities encounter many challenges when they seek access to health and social services in Quebec. These include problems communicating in French and a limited understanding of how the healthcare system works. Few health and social service organizations establish outreach or networking strategies with ethnocultural community groups to lower these barriers. Community organizations serving ethnocultural minority and immigrant communities also have little funding to invest in advocacy efforts to improve service-delivery options.[1] To make matters worse, many healthcare and social service professionals operate on the assumption that "the family," particularly adult children, generally provides whatever care may be required. The expression "people of different ethnicities take care of their own" reflects a long-standing belief that older adults from ethnocultural and immigrant communities do not ask for formal services because they prefer to receive care from family members at home. As a result, a commonly held myth is that older adults from ethnocultural-minority and immigrant communities do not require services. This myth can be attributed in part to the understanding of the role played by "culture" as presupposing that adult children are obliged to care for their aging parents.[2] In this chapter, we discuss, deconstruct, and dispel the widely held myth that ethnocultural-minority immigrant families prefer to take care of their own and are always available to do so. We present case examples from our research highlighting the alternative models of reciprocity that we have encountered in our research and practice.[3]

Mary's story: Local care recipient and transnational care provider
Mary is a widowed 81-year-old Filipina grandmother living on her own in an apartment in Montreal. Mary's isolation is due largely to the fact that members of her immediate family live in other parts of Canada or in the Philippines. In addition to supporting herself, Mary uses her Old Age Security benefit and Guaranteed Income Supplement (GIS) to send money to the Philippines. Providing financial assistance to her family back home is a source of pride, despite the challenges she faces due to her fixed income. Mary was recently diagnosed with Type 2 diabetes, and her doctor prescribed insulin and put her on a strict diet. This was a significant blow, as the unexpected added expenses put a strain on her monthly budget. Mary unfailingly shares her income with her family in the Philippines and has concluded that low-cost housing may be a way to address her problems, but she does not know how to apply for it. She is reluctant to ask for help from the local health and social services centre (in Quebec these centres are known as Centres de santé et de services sociaux, or CSSS) because of a previous unpleasant experience with a social worker: when she had requested financial assistance from her local CSSS, the social worker had recommended instead that she stop sending money to the Philippines. Mary lost faith in the CSSS as a result of that incident; as she explained, the social worker did not understand the challenges she faced every day. She therefore decided not to seek help and still feels stressed as she simultaneously manages her health and takes care of her family responsibilities.

Leni's story: "Medical services saved my life, but I need long-term support."
Leni is a Filipina grandmother who provides care for her husband and three grandchildren. Her daughter works long hours in the secondary labour market and cannot afford child care. Leni and her husband are committed to caring for their grandchildren and to passing on their Filipino heritage. At the time of the interview, Leni had recently suffered a serious accident that severely reduced her physical mobility. Her experience with the health and social services network was particularly good because the care it provided helped Leni to survive that life-threatening incident. However, while Leni was hospitalized, her husband assumed all responsibility for the grandchildren's care, and as she recovered following her discharge, she had to take a backseat and let him continue caring for them. Leni's accident put

emotional and financial stress on the family, and they even went into debt. They later learned from the interviewer that they were eligible for the GIS and entitled to retroactive payments. Thinking about her situation now, Leni says that although the acute care service did a good job of meeting her short-term physical needs, no one was there to help her and her family solve their financial and child-care problems. She also raised the issue of the couple's need for long-term services and follow-up to assist her husband in his caregiving responsibilities and to help her regain her mobility and plan for old age and the future of her grandchildren.

Mrs. S.'s story: "Don't need to worry about her!"
Over the course of a research project, we interviewed several case managers and followed them on home visits. During one such observation, one of the case managers was doing a service assessment of an 83-year-old Sri Lankan woman who had recently fallen after suffering a stroke. As we left the woman's home, the case manager told the researcher, "Oh, I don't worry about Mrs. S. She lives with her family. They're so close, these people. They'll give her any help she needs." However, the case manager had never asked the family about their everyday lives or any caregiving challenges that they might have. In fact, Mrs. S.'s daughter-in-law, who spoke only Tamil, was caring for three young children, and her son had two jobs and was rarely home. They had relied on her to provide child care, and, within eight months of her arrival under family sponsorship, she was in need of daily care herself. Yet government services considered her a low priority to receive support because she was living with her family.

These cases highlight some less common perspectives on aging and the varying degrees of contact that members of ethnocultural-minority immigrant communities in Montreal have with health and social services. They reveal a disconnect between people's awareness about services that are available and accessible to them. Although most older adults in general have difficulty locating and accessing much-needed services, the nature and extent of access and equity problems are unique and complex among ethnocultural-minority and immigrant populations. However, service providers rarely acknowledge that these issues and challenges exist. Instead, prejudicial assumptions – for example, that ethnocultural-minority families, particularly those living in intergenerational households, are always willing and available to provide care – shape the way we think about their care. This assumption may lead us to overlook the issues of emotional and economic distress, isolation, and the "burden of natural caregivers" so often borne by older adults and their families, both in Canada and in other countries. Of greater concern is the fact that this assumption influences the ways in which the needs and experiences of ethnocultural-minority adults are assessed and results in their being assigned low priority in health and social service policies and programs. We now take a closer look at the myth currently underlying the thinking of most healthcare and social service providers.

Identifying the Myth: "Older Adults Prefer Services from Their Loved Ones Because the Family Is There to Care for Them"

If we assume that obtaining care is a matter of personal choice and experience, we don't have to look far to see why some people refrain from seeking help from public services. This lack of demand for help may lead to the mistaken conclusion that there is no need for help. Thus, the perception of personal choice becomes a barrier for families that do not know how to obtain services or have experienced some form of discrimination from those services.[4] This issue goes far beyond health and social services and includes interactions with various programs and professionals, as well as with government services in general. In fact, older adults from ethnocultural immigrant minorities who have faced structural barriers to immigrating to Canada and encountered difficulty finding a job – in addition to intergenerational experiences of poverty during their lives – are reluctant to ask for services out of fear of repercussions or being further exposed to ignorance and discrimination.

Contrary to the idealized view that ethnocultural-minority communities have larger and more-close-knit families, not every member of those communities has a family available to provide care. Since the mid-twentieth century, immigrants who are members of racialized communities have had to face additional restrictions that have impeded family reunification and considerably redrawn the family unit, and in some cases have gone so far as to dismantle it. Immigrants and migrants recently arrived under new labour sector policies, such as the Temporary Foreign Worker Program, the Provincial Nominee Program, and the Live-in Caregiver Program (now the Caregiver Program), must obtain permanent resident status before they may apply for sponsorship for their family members. Sponsorship under the Family Reunification Program is a lengthy process involving a prolonged period of separation. In addition to factors such as relegation to the secondary labour market and, consequently, limited retirement conditions, minority immigrant communities face other challenges imposed by structures that can undermine their everyday lives.[5]

Rarely Considered Structural Barriers That Undermine the Family Experience of Older Ethnocultural-Minority Immigrants

Mary lives far away from her family in the Philippines but manages to stay in contact by providing financial support back home, thus remaining a distant but important caregiver for her family. Now in her eighties, she worries about who will support her if she becomes ill, and she is considering moving to low-cost housing so that she can continue to help her family. Her interaction with the social worker who recommended that she stop sending money back home is an example of how service providers can misunderstand the complex and diverse situations of many older ethnocultural-minority immigrants. We would argue that understanding the everyday lives of these immigrants and the challenges they face means moving beyond the narrow assumption that these families provide care only locally and in the home. For Mary, her identity as a caregiver is important, and the fact that she is willing to risk her long-term health to provide that care beyond international borders is a fact that social service providers must acknowledge and consider in developing care plans. Leni, who is looking for long-term solutions for her later-life needs, had a similar experience. Although she and her husband were able to overcome her life-threatening accident thanks to the extensive follow-up provided by the hospital, they were left to their own devices once Leni was well enough to be discharged and go home. Now she has to adjust to a long-term disability (as a result of her accident), and she and her husband must strike a balance between her retirement and the care of their grandchildren. The fact that they did not know how to apply for the GIS shows that there is a need for long-term interventions to assist some older marginalized adults with securing the benefits they are entitled to.

The myth that ethnocultural-minority immigrant families are always willing and available to provide care is particularly evident in Mrs. S.'s case. The case manager mistakenly concluded that Mrs. S.'s needs would be met simply because her extended family was living under the same roof. The case manager also assumed that ethnocultural-minority families ("these people" – itself a discriminatory remark) could provide the necessary care based on their ethnic origin. In fact, the family's delicate caregiving balance was significantly disrupted by Mrs. S.'s fall. Her son, working two jobs, was no more available to provide physical care than previously, while her daughter-in-law now had to provide care for two generations. Mrs. S.'s lack of French-language proficiency further limited her ability to convey to service providers all of the stress she was facing and her need for support from social services.

Implications and Interventions

In discussions on aging in Canada, we all too often overlook the increasing diversity of our population. Although some multiculturalism initiatives targeting older adults have been introduced in health and social services, certain assumptions about who provides care and, more importantly, *how* that care is provided often undermine efforts to address problems of accessibility and equity within those services. This is particularly true with regard to older members of ethnocultural minority and immigrant families.[6]

Our purpose in this chapter is to dispel the myth that these families are readily available to take on those responsibilities, an idea that is entirely contradicted by their experience. Immigration policies in Canada often deconstruct, reconstitute, and disrupt family relationships in many ways. In fact, not only are adult children largely unable to provide care because they work long hours in the secondary labour market, but, in many cases, older adults must take care of their families in response to the local and transnational realities of poverty and systemic marginalization. As a result, the specific situations of immigrant older adults from ethnocultural minority communities who would benefit from and are entitled to receive formal support are overlooked and their needs are ignored. In general, spouses or adult children are perceived as the designated care providers. Although existing research has corroborated the fact that older adults receive most of their informal support from children and spouses, we seldom consider the factors that might prevent these and other family members from shouldering the responsibility to provide such care.[7] We also rarely consider family circumstances as a whole or the role that older members play as both recipients and providers of care. In the above stories, the older people identified as "the clients" were actually also relied upon by their families to provide care, both at home and transnationally. When illness or disability occurs, the intergenerational reciprocity may be compromised, causing financial and emotional stress for the entire family unit. This kind of situation is rarely viewed as a problem worth considering. The experiences of Mary, Leni, and Mrs. S. illustrate the challenges that some ethnocultural-minority immigrant older adults face in both receiving and providing care.

Taken together, our case studies show that there is widespread misunderstanding about caregiving within ethnocultural-minority immigrant families. By dismantling the myth that ethnocultural-minority immigrant older adults do not seek services because the family is already providing care, we hope to draw attention to their unrecognized precarious situations; to the interconnections among immigration, the labour market, and care; and to how those factors shape the potential financial and emotional insecurity experienced by some families. Understanding these issues may encourage care providers in the public system to acknowledge and accept plural identities and to advocate for greater and more equitable access to services to meet the specific needs of ethnocultural-minority immigrant older adults and their families.

Notes

1 Ilyan Ferrer, Shari Brotman, and Amanda Grenier (2017), "The experiences of reciprocity among Filipino older adults in Canada: Intergenerational, transnational and community considerations," *Journal of Gerontological Social Work*, Vol. 60, No. 4, 313–27.

2 Sharon Koehn and Karen Kobayashi (2011), "Age and ethnicity," in Malcolm Sargeant (ed.), *Age Discrimination and Diversity: Multiple Discrimination from an Age Perspective* (Cambridge: Cambridge University Press), 132–59.

3 These case examples come from our research experience with different ethnocultural-minority communities in Quebec and Canada.

4 Shari Brotman (2003), "The limits of multiculturalism in elder care services," *Journal of Aging Studies*, Vol. 17, No. 2, 209–29.

5 Ilyan Ferrer (2015), "Examining the disjunctures between policy and care in Canada's parent and grandparent supervisa," *International Journal of Migration, Health and Social Care*, Vol. 11, No. 4, 253 67.

6 Shari Brotman and Ilyan Ferrer (2015), "Diversity within family caregiving: Extending definitions of 'who counts' to include marginalized communities," *HealthcarePapers*, Vol. 15, No. 1, 47–53.

7 Martin Turcotte and Grant Schellenberg (2007), *A Portrait of Seniors in Canada: 2006*, Ottawa, Statistics Canada, Catalogue No. 89-519-XIE, <https://www150.statcan.gc.ca/n1/pub/89-519-x/89-519-x2006001-eng.htm>, accessed February 27, 2007.

Conclusion

Public Policy Issues and the Complexities of Aging

Patrik Marier, Anne-Marie Séguin,
and Véronique Billette

As a result of a steep decline in the birth rate following the post–Second World War baby boom and the increase in life expectancy in many industrialized countries, population aging has been a governmental concern since the 1970s. However, it was only in the late 1990s that a tone of urgency began to emerge in public debate, as international agencies and governments published reports on the issue. Among the most influential were publications by the Organisation for Economic Co-operation and Development (OECD), *Maintaining Prosperity in an Ageing Society* and *Reforms for an Ageing Society*, which identified several issues related to demographic changes and provided a variety of possible solutions for preserving economic prosperity.[1] David Foot tackled a similar theme in his book *Boom, Bust & Echo*, in which he argued that demographics explains "two-thirds of everything" – by which he meant phenomena as varied as changes in public policy, economic growth, and even why certain Hollywood films and pop singers become hits.[2]

The pessimistic tone of many of these publications and the identification of demographic change as a threat to various public programs were quickly challenged by other researchers. In Canada, for example, where the average annual increase in the cost of healthcare per person was 3.5 percent between 2000 and 2009, researchers demonstrated that less than one third of this increase was attributable to aging.[3] In fact, the three factors that have been contributing the most to the increased cost of healthcare are the rising number of medical interventions for all population segments, the adoption of expensive technologies, and an overall increase in the use of healthcare services.[4]

With a growing number of baby boomers retiring, these debates have now resurfaced. Our goal here is not to provide an exhaustive evaluation of the studies that fuel these concerns but to demonstrate the extent to which the aging of the population raises complex public policy issues.

The Interdependence of Aging Issues

An increasing number of authors view older adults, all of them erroneously considered to belong to the baby-boom generation, as a homogeneous group with common expectations and interests. This perception is bolstered by the widespread use of statistics that place everyone aged 65 and over in a single category, despite the difference in characteristics and the gaps in age and needs between those in their sixties and those who are older. The growing numbers of seniors and their depiction as a homogeneous group tend to promote an image of older adults as a major political force capable of maintaining their social benefits, sometimes to the detriment of younger citizens, or as an economic burden for younger populations (15 to 64 years of age).[5] These inadequately nuanced depictions accentuate intergenerational tensions. They neglect the fact, as demonstrated in this book, that older adults are a highly diverse population. There are all kinds of distinctions within a given generation of seniors, just as there are among the members of younger groups. Older adults have differing backgrounds and are in an age group that probably has the widest range of socioeconomic and health variations.[6]

A strictly economic view of people's contributions to society also feeds into negative perceptions of aging. Although the number of people over 65 years of age who are still in the workforce is rising, most are no longer working. It would nevertheless be simplistic to define citizens' contribution to society as a purely economic act based on their labour-force participation. Older adults are actively involved in society in various ways, whether by becoming caregivers when their partners are ill, helping out their children, minding their grandchildren, assisting older neighbours, taking the time to listen to people who are afflicted in one way or another, or doing volunteer work. Furthermore, the political preferences of seniors and other age groups are indicative of intergenerational awareness and solidarity. For example, many grandparents oppose any increased pension benefits that would require reduced government spending on their grandchildren's education.[7] Their preferences are thus much subtler than thought in that they demonstrate a concern for the needs of the younger members of their family, their community, and society in general, rather than limiting themselves to supporting programs that would benefit only their own age group.

Another factor likely to aggravate intergenerational tensions is said to be the presence of a public policy bias in favour of older adults – that is, bias that encourages the transfer of resources to older generations at the expense of younger cohorts. Demographic considerations, with the notable exception of pension programs, did not feature prominently in the development of public policies that affect our everyday lives. It is also very difficult to identify and assess the impacts of redistribution between generations.[8] More thorough analyses of whether or not bias exists suggest that Canadian social policies do not generate a bias in favour of older people, unlike in the United States, where access to universal healthcare is provided only to those 65 years of age and older under the Medicare program.[9] These analyses also show that steps taken to facilitate intergenerational benefit transfers do not always achieve the desired outcomes. For example, measures to encourage older workers to withdraw from the labour force in order to combat unemployment do not have a major impact on the unemployment rate among younger people. Several factors, including the decline in some industry sectors and in overall economic conditions, explain why an older worker's withdrawal from the labour force does not lead directly to a job for a younger person, in spite of the high unemployment rate among younger workers. In fact, a recent study showed the opposite: older people remaining active longer in the labour force contributed to a higher rate of employment among younger people.[10]

In short, population aging is a complex and difficult phenomenon for governments to handle because it affects a wide range of public policies. Some of these policies are often in the headlines, such as those dealing with health, retirement, and employment. On the other hand, population aging also has a less well-documented impact on the design and use of public infrastructure and public transit, as well as on policies in areas such as taxation, families, and prisons. To illustrate the scope of the impact of population aging, as part of an ongoing Canadian study on the consequences of an aging population, a social services director mentioned that even foster families were getting older and that this required a change of approach. Given its pervasive impact on public policy, population aging is an issue that requires close coordination among government authorities, including various ministries, departments, and agencies.

Case in Point: Caregivers

Caregivers can be used as a concrete example to illustrate the interdependence of policy actions within the context of an aging population. Caregivers play an essential role for many older adults and contribute on several levels (including transportation, financial management, social and medical interventions, and home support). Many studies report that government services address only 10 to 15 percent of older adults' needs.[11] Caregivers are therefore an invaluable resource for Quebec's Ministère de la Santé et des Services sociaux (MSSS – Quebec Ministry of Health and Social Services), because they provide services and care (free of charge) and facilitate ties between health professionals and those needing assistance. That is why official MSSS policy designates caregivers as partners.

For Quebec's Ministère du Travail, de l'Emploi et de la Solidarité sociale (MTESS – Quebec Ministry of Labour, Employment and Social Solidarity), assigning a larger role to caregivers in the context of an aging population is a problematic issue. One of this ministry's primary goals is to maximize labour-force participation. This means introducing measures specifically for older workers, but also for other populations at risk of reducing their involvement in the labour market, such as caregivers. From the perspective of the MTESS, the best approach would be to provide more services for older adults and develop more respite centres to enable caregivers to remain as fully employed as possible. Labour-force participation is also important for retirement policies. Because of their potential career interruptions and/or diminished working hours in the formal economy, caregivers face the prospect of accumulating lower pension entitlements and are consequently at greater risk of poverty. An employment policy that succeeds in increasing the number of hours of work while reducing career interruptions promotes saving for retirement and the accumulation of pension benefits.

For Quebec's Secrétariat à la condition féminine (Quebec Status of Women Secretariat), the question of caregivers clearly illustrates the socioeconomic issues facing many women. Most caregivers are women, and they perform the vast majority of tasks that require a large amount of time and repeated absences from work.[12] The caregivers who are not paid for this role are often in precarious jobs or are forced to turn down promotions and draw upon their savings; meanwhile, their contributions as caregivers are rarely recognized. This all contributes to the marginalization of their occupational and economic status and accentuates their risk of poverty in the present and later on during retirement, both of which are realities that are more likely to affect women.

How to Address Population Aging Issues

The above section raises another issue: how to deal with population aging issues without giving further credence to some of the myths analyzed in this book, and without replacing them with others. A comparison of steps taken in the ten provinces of Canada to address the challenges and take advantage of the opportunities associated with this demographic change highlights two "new" administrative approaches that have been developed to facilitate policy adaptation: the establishment of seniors' secretariats and the formulation of a national strategy.[13]

Establishment of a Seniors' Secretariat

The aim of creating a seniors' secretariat reporting to its own minister is to facilitate political representation for older adults in government and throughout the civil service in general. The citizens and the many groups that represent seniors thus have a special representative whose role is to make public decision makers more aware of the problems affecting older adults, and to set action priorities. The existence of such a secretariat also helps to make the general public aware of the everyday realities of seniors. However, there are a number of significant disadvantages to this approach. In general, secretariats are not responsible for specific programs or for policy implementation; this means that they have limited human resources. In Quebec, this amounts to 30 full-time staff members; secretariats in smaller provinces typically have a staff of fewer than 10.[14]

Across Canada, governments and their various organizations have tended to refer specific problems concerning seniors to these secretariats and to ask them to come up with solutions. This shows recognition for the secretariats, which are gaining in visibility within government bodies. It is also, however, an acknowledgment of the fact that many public service agencies, faced with staff cuts, no longer have the means to deal with aging-related issues by themselves and must opt to approach secretariats, which, because they are small, simply do not have the resources to carry out this type of work. Moreover, the situation is at odds with the very purpose of creating the secretariats, whose mission is to raise awareness of seniors' issues within departments or ministries so that they can find ways to tackle them within their own organizations (rather than delegate the problems elsewhere). Furthermore, an approach targeted to seniors may send the message that population aging is not a challenge that affects the community as a whole but a specific problem for "old people" that requires its own solutions.

Creation of a National Strategy or Establishing an Executive Council Responsibility

Given the interdependence of many population aging issues, as illustrated by the case of caregivers, the development and introduction of a national strategy is a key OECD recommendation for maintaining economic prosperity. Similarly, the Auditor General of Quebec has pointed out in a number of reports that the government should devote more resources to facilitating the management of demographic changes.[15] Within a Canadian context, the objectives of a provincial (or federal) strategy could include developing greater awareness of the society's characteristics, promoting dialogue with a view to structural reforms, and avoiding the implementation of contradictory measures (such as giving caregivers more responsibilities while at the same time penalizing them for their lower labour-force participation). From this viewpoint, central agencies (such as executive councils and ministries of finance) play a leading role. The main difference between this approach and a seniors' secretariat is that the issue is defined from a societal perspective, which means that the question of demographic change needs to be structured and debated from a comprehensive policy standpoint.

Although some provinces have established seniors' secretariats, none has yet ventured to come up with an integrated strategy or plan to address population aging. However, a number of steps in this direction have been taken. For instance, following the publication of the Auditor General of Quebec's report in 2001, the province struck a working group within the Executive Council to identify issues and actions pertaining to demographic change throughout the public service. The working group made ten recommendations in 2009, including measures to increase the participation rate of workers aged 55 and over and to improve Quebec's net interprovincial migration.[16] Although the government developed a policy on aging called *Vieillir et vivre ensemble. Chez soi, dans sa communauté, au Québec* (Aging and Living Together – At Home, in Your Community, in Quebec), it primarily targeted older adults and did not look comprehensively and holistically at the many policy issues engendered by population aging. In Canada as a whole, few concrete commitments have been implemented to mobilize the various stakeholders and ministries/departments toward a coordinated effort to create a provincial strategy.

How do we explain the absence of such strategies? Two of the many reasons deserve mention. First, strategic planning is much more partisan today. In short, the strategic plans of the various ministries or departments very often coincide with changes in government. Consequently, they tend to be short-lived and have a limited time horizon (to take into account the fact that elections are held every four years). The parliamentary tradition makes it difficult to develop a plan that can survive a change of government. Furthermore, the creation of a provincial plan raises many questions about ministerial prerogative – the powers held by the ministries – because the role of the central agencies would be even more substantial than it is now.

Second, long-term planning, which peaked in the 1970s, was often criticized because of its inability to predict future challenges and find appropriate ways of dealing with them. This is one of the main reasons that many planning administrative units have been replaced by teams whose role is mainly to make financial forecasts with a view to exploring the consequences of various economic and demographic changes, while leaving the task of finding and implementing solutions to other public organizations, such as ministries or departments.

Concluding Remarks

There is an interesting body of political science literature on the definition of public policy problems. These contributions highlight how difficult it is to achieve broad consensus on identifying and resolving societal problems and on implementing solutions. In the case under consideration here, there is no denying that the population is aging. However, the current and future consequences of this demographic change are a major source of disagreement both among people generally and among public decision makers and researchers. These differing opinions are influenced by other historical and partisan debates that widen the gaps between the various positions about the best solutions to adopt. Such divergences can lead to swings between advances and setbacks, abrupt changes in how things are done, or periods when nothing at all happens because it is impossible to reach a broad consensus. The absence of such consensus on demographic change issues may well lead to piecemeal and incoherent policy interventions.

The changes essential to giving greater recognition to older adults and redistributing resources more equitably require the implementation of policies that promote better living conditions for people as they age. Public policies are the outcome of work carried out by elected representatives and by a host of political players (including political parties, interest groups, experts, and citizens), which is why it is important for us all to become aware of the changing situations that older people experience, and the differences in how they age, in order to come up with appropriate solutions.

Among other things, awareness involves better comprehension and acknowledgment of the challenges, needs, differences, and contributions of older adults. Rather than fuelling competition between generations, this awareness must be part of a reflection on intergenerational solidarity that builds a more inclusive society.

The social issues surrounding aging affect society as a whole. As we have seen in the various chapters in this book, issues related to aging are not simply "old people's issues" but matters of general interest embracing a tremendously wide spectrum of areas such as recognition, redistribution, physical and cognitive health, mental health, intellectual disabilities and pervasive developmental disorders, autonomy, sexuality, intimate relationships, violence, work, living conditions, technology, volunteer work, social participation, housing, mobility, prison life, homelessness, mourning, end-of-life concerns, caregivers, and more. These topics are not exclusive to older adults. Intervening in these areas could be beneficial to many groups in society in addition to seniors.

The COVID-19 pandemic, with its multifaceted impacts, is fuelling ongoing debates that have been raging for many years on how to prepare for an aging population and improve the living conditions of seniors. Most notably, across Canada, governments have acknowledged that the status quo is no longer acceptable when it comes to long-term care policies. Researchers have documented these weaknesses and their negative consequences for older adults and their carers for decades. Sadly, it took a crisis of epic proportions to provide the impetus to pledge reforms advocated by many policy actors, including independent public bodies such as Ombuds offices and auditor generals.

Notes

1   OECD (1998), *Maintaining Prosperity in an Ageing Society* (Paris: OECD); OECD (2000), *Reforms for an Ageing Society* (Paris: OECD).

2   David K. Foot (1996), *Boom, Bust & Echo: Profiting from the Demographic Shift in the 21st Century* (Toronto: Stoddart), 8.

3   Neena L. Chappell and Marcus J. Hollander (2011), "An evidence-based policy prescription for an aging population," *HealthcarePapers*, Vol. 11, No. l; OECD (2014), *Health Expenditure and Financing* (Paris: OECD).

4   Neena L. Chappell (2011), *Population Aging and the Evolving Care Needs of Older Canadians* (Montreal: Institut de recherche en politiques publiques/Institute for Research on Public Policy); Chappell and Hollander (2011), op. cit.; Howard A. Palley (2013), "Long-term care service policies in three Canadian provinces: Alberta, Quebec, and Ontario – Examining the national and subnational contexts," *International Journal of Canadian Studies*, Vol. 47, No. 1.

5   Paul Pierson (1994), *Dismantling the Welfare State? Reagan, Thatcher, and the Politics of Retrenchment* (Cambridge: Cambridge University Press, Cambridge Studies in Comparative Politics); Laurence J. Kotlikoff and Scott Burns (2012), *The Clash of Generations: Saving Ourselves, Our Kids, and Our Economy* (Cambridge, MA: MIT Press).

6   Dale Dannefer (2003), "Cumulative advantage/disadvantage and the life course: Cross-fertilizing age and social science theory," *The Journals of Gerontology Series B: Psychological Sciences and Social Sciences*, Vol. 58, No. 6, S327–37.

7   Marius R. Busemeyer, Achim Goerres, and Simon Weschle (2009), "Attitudes towards redistributive spending in an era of demographic ageing: The rival pressures from age and income in 14 OECD countries," *Journal of European Social Policy*, Vol. 19, No. 3, 195–212.

8   Robert Haveman (1994), "Should generational accounts replace public budgets and deficits?," *Journal of Economic Perspectives*, Vol. 8, No. 1, 107.

9   Julia Lynch (2006), *Age in the Welfare State: The Origins of Social Spending on Pensioners, Workers, and Children* (Cambridge: Cambridge University Press).

10 René Böheim (2014), "The effects of early retirement schemes on youth employment," *IZA World of Labor*, No. 70.

11 Jean-Pierre Lavoie (with Nancy Guberman and Patrik Marier) (2014), *La responsabilité des soins aux aînés au Québec. Du secteur public au secteur privé* (Montreal: Institut de recherche en politiques publiques/Institute for Research on Public Policy), No. 48.

12 Maire Sinha (2013), *Portrait of Caregivers, 2012*, Ottawa, Statistics Canada, online catalogue No. 89-652-X.

13 This section is based on a paper currently being written by Patrik Marier on adapting public policies in a context of population aging in Canada's ten provinces.

14 From the 2014–15 management report of Quebec's Ministère de la Famille, which explicitly mentions a 30 full-time equivalent staff increase due to the "repatriation" from the Ministère de la Santé (Ministry of Health) secretariat. Ministère de la Famille (2015), *La famille en valeur: Rapport annuel 2014–2015* (Quebec City: Ministère de la Famille), 14. Secretariat staff account for 7.5 percent of regular-status ministry employees.

15 Auditor General of Quebec (2001), *Rapport à l'Assemblée nationale pour l'année 2000–2001 – Tome II* (Quebec City: Auditor General of Quebec); Auditor General

of Quebec (2010), *Rapport du Vérificateur général du Québec à l'Assemblée nationale pour l'année 2009–2010: Rapport du commissaire au développement durable* (Quebec City: Auditor General of Quebec).

16 Ministère du Conseil exécutif (2009), *Actions gouvernementales portant sur les changements démographiques – état de situation: Rapport au secrétaire général* (Quebec City: Ministère du Conseil exécutif.)

Contributors

Milaine Alarie is an affiliate professor at the Institut national de la recherche scientifique (INRS) in Montreal. She holds a PhD in sociology from McGill University and specializes in gender, sexuality, intimate relationships, family, and aging. She works on issues related to age-discrepant intimate relationships, consensual non-monogamies, and elder mistreatment.

Philippe Apparicio is a full professor at the Urbanisation Culture Société Research Centre of the Institut national de la recherche scientifique (INRS) in Montreal. His research interests include the urban applications of geographic information systems, spatial analysis, and, above all, environmental justice. He holds the Canada Research Chair in Environmental Equity and the City (Tier 2) at INRS.

Ginette Aubin holds a PhD in rehabilitation science from McGill University. After practising as a mental health occupational therapist for 27 years, she has been a professor in the Department of Occupational Therapy at the Université du Québec à Trois-Rivières since 2011. Her research focuses on the inclusion of older adults with a mental disorder and on interventions and environments that are conducive to their inclusion.

Julie Beauchamp holds a PhD in sexology from the Université du Québec à Montréal (UQAM). She is an assistant professor in the Department of

Psychiatry and Neurosciences at Université Laval. Her research interests focus on sexual and gender diversity, aging, and sexuality.

Marie Beaulieu holds a PhD in applied humanities and a master's degree in criminology from the Université de Montréal. She has held the Research Chair on Mistreatment of Older Adults at the Université de Sherbrooke since 2010. She has been a university professor since 1992, and a full professor at the School of Social Work at the Université de Sherbrooke since 2005. She is a fellow of the Royal Society of Canada.

Nathalie Bier is an occupational therapist, an associate professor at the School of Rehabilitation at the Université de Montréal, and a researcher at the Institut universitaire de gériatrie de Montréal research centre in Montreal. She conducts research on cognitive aging, everyday activities, and home support.

Véronique Billette holds a master's degree in psychology from Université Laval and a PhD in sociology from the Université du Québec à Montréal. She has been the coordinator of the VIES research team (Vieillissements, exclusions sociales et solidarités/aging, social exclusion and solidarity) since 2007, and her main areas of interest are citizenship and inequality. She has many years of experience working in the intervention and prevention of violence against women and in mental health.

Rock-André Blondin is a doctoral student in psychology at the Université du Québec à Montréal. His dissertation, under the supervision of Valérie Bourgeois-Guérin, is about older adults who have attempted suicide.

Eleonora Bogdanova is a master's student in sociology at the Université de Montréal. Her thesis addresses identity issues involved in the transition to retirement. She is comparing the identity reconstructions experienced by recent retirees who are single to those of recently retired couples.

Caroline Bouchard holds bachelor's degrees in civil law and international development, and she will soon be completing her master's degree in political science. She has been a senior adviser in intergovernmental relations for the Canadian Medical Association since 2018. From 2013 to 2018, she was a public affairs and governmental relations adviser for the Federation for Ageing in Dignity and Overall Quality in Quebec.

Valérie Bourgeois-Guérin holds a PhD in psychology. She is a clinical psychologist and a professor in the Department of Psychology at the Université du Québec à Montréal. Her research interests include grief, bereavement, end-of-life care, and aging. Her expertise is enhanced by her clinical practice, in which she deals primarily with older adults.

Shari Brotman is a professor at the McGill University School of Social Work. Her interests include caregivers, issues of equitable access to health and social services for seniors in marginalized communities, and access to care in LGBTQ, immigrant, and ethnocultural communities.

Victoria Burns is a professor of social work at the University of Calgary. She holds master's and doctoral degrees in social work from McGill University. Her primary research interests concern the key concept of home support, with a focus on understanding living environments that foster inclusion, particularly for marginalized homeless seniors.

Hélène Carbonneau holds a master's degree and a PhD in gerontology from the Université de Sherbrooke. After more than 20 years of work in recreology in the area of healthcare, she became a professor in the Department of Recreation, Culture, and Tourism Studies at the Université du Québec à Trois-Rivières in 2007. Her research addresses issues of leisure, health, and positive development.

Yves Carrière holds a master's degree and a PhD in demography from the Université de Montréal. He has been an associate professor in the university's Department of Demography since 2013 and is currently the chair of his department. He has conducted research on a regular basis at the Centre for Research and Expertise in Social Gerontology (CREGÉS). His research interests are focused primarily on past and future trends in retirement age.

Julie Castonguay is a social worker who holds a PhD in gerontology. She is a researcher at the Centre collégial d'expertise en gérontologie at the Cégep de Drummondville. She has expertise in various research areas: gerontology, volunteerism, not-for-profit organizations, boomers, home support, and qualitative research methodology (including grounded theory and participatory research).

Line Chamberland is a professor in the Department of Sexology at the Université du Québec à Montréal (UQAM). She has a PhD in sociology and has conducted joint research into various forms of social exclusion experienced by individuals in minority groups owing to their sexual orientation or gender identity, including older adults.

Mélanie Couture is a researcher at the Integrated Health and Social Services University Network for West-Central Montreal and an adjunct professor in the Department of Psychology at the Université de Sherbrooke. In her work, she aims at improving partnerships between older adults, their families, and social and healthcare professionals, as well as alleviating mistreatment.

Bernadette Dallaire (PhD in sociology) is a full professor at the School of Social Work and Criminology of Laval University, Quebec City. She is the co-director of the university's Institute on the ageing and social participation of older adults and a member of the Vieillissements, exclusions sociales et solidarités research team. Her research work has addressed social gerontology, the gerontology-mental health juncture, and mental health rehabilitation.

Chloé Dauphinais holds bachelor's and master's degrees in sociology from the Université de Montréal. Her core research interest is aging experiences at the boundaries of social inequality. Her thesis was on conjugality and aging.

Daniel Dickson is pursuing a PhD in political science at Concordia University. His research investigates how ideas of disability and aging are politically problematized and practically addressed by public policy in Canada.

Michel Dunn holds a bachelor's degree in law from Université Laval. From 1978 to 2012, he was the coordinator of the Life Line team, whose mission is to work with convicted inmates serving life sentences. He is currently working on a successful aging program for older inmates in prison or in the community.

Patrick Durivage, a social worker, holds a master's degree in social work and a bachelor's degree in psychology from the Université de Montréal. As both a practitioner and a researcher, his main interest is gerontological palliative care. For the past 20 years, he has been working in the home care department at the René-Cassin CLSC (local community services centre). In 2016, he was appointed to the Quebec End-of-Life Care Commission.

Ilyan Ferrer is an assistant professor in the University of Calgary's Faculty of Social Work. He received his master's degree and PhD in social work from McGill University. His research focuses on the intersections of aging, immigration, labour, and care experiences in racialized communities in Canada. His work incorporates intersectionality, oral history, and anti-oppressive social work theory and practice.

Julie Fortier holds a PhD in urban studies from the Université du Québec à Montréal. She has been a professor in the Department of Leisure, Culture, and Tourism Studies at the Université du Québec à Trois-Rivières since June 2006. Her research focuses on volunteerism, institutional collaboration, and public participation.

Mireille Fortier is a research professional at the Centre d'excellence sur le vieillissement de Québec and a coordinator at the Institute on the Aging and Social Participation of Seniors at Université Laval. She has a master's degree in anthropology and a certificate in gerontology. Her research interests are social participation and the anthropology of aging.

Zelda Freitas is a social worker with extensive experience in the delivery of psychosocial care to older adults in loss of autonomy. As a research-practitioner and coordinator of the area of expertise in caregiving at the Centre for Research and Expertise in Social Gerontology (CREGÉS), she engages in the research, development, knowledge transfer, and implementation of evidence-based practices related to psychosocial and interdisciplinary intervention in caregiving, palliative care, and bereavement.

Patricia Friesen holds a master's degree in nursing from the Université de Montréal. She worked in oncology and palliative care at the McGill University Health Centre. She is currently working in home palliative care as part of an interdisciplinary team at the Integrated Health and Social Services University Network for West-Central Montreal, which deals with an older multicultural population.

Michel Gagnon holds a master's degree in social services from Université Laval. He has worked with offenders for more than 30 years. As executive director of Maison Cross Roads, he introduced Service Oxygène, which was specifically designed for senior offenders. He is currently working on introducing a gerontological/criminological intervention model for this clientele.

Sophie Gagnon holds a bachelor's degree in French studies and a certificate in journalism from the University of Montreal. She has worked as a journalist for approximately 35 years. For the past 25 years, she has been an assistant editor at *Virage*, a magazine for people 50 years and over, published by Federation for Ageing in Dignity and Overall Quality.

Diane Galarneau has master's degree in economics from the Université de Montréal and has spent most of her career as a researcher at Statistics Canada, working in the areas of labour markets and aging.

Norma Gilbert recently completed her doctoral studies in applied human sciences at the Université de Montréal. Her dissertation was on the topic of aging and measuring loss of autonomy. She has spent the majority of her career in healthcare working with an aging population as a practitioner-researcher.

Line Grenier is an associate professor in the Département de communication at Université de Montréal in Montréal, and a member of ACT. Dr. Grenier teaches predominantly in the areas of research methodologies, media theory, memory and media, and popular culture. She is currently working on a collaborative project on "deaf musics" to better understand how ageing Deaf people access and experience music as a cultural practice today, and how they did so in the past.

Marco Guerrera holds a master's degree in history from the Université de Montréal and a communications certificate from the Université du Québec à Montréal. He is a public affairs adviser for the Federation for Ageing in Dignity and Overall Quality provincial secretariat. He is particularly interested in healthcare access for older adults and the development of a housing market for seniors.

Laurence Hamel-Roy is a doctoral student in humanities at Concordia University. Her dissertation topic is the transformations that have occurred in

Canada's Employment Insurance program since the early 1970s. Her work focuses on the impact of public policy on employment and poverty in the gender and race dimensions of labour.

Sarita Israel holds a bachelor's degree in sociology and social work from McGill University. She is Coordinator of the Area of Expertise to Counter Mistreatment, at the Integrated Health and Social Services University Network for West-Central Montreal. She has also contributed to various research projects, including projects on spousal violence against older women.

Meghan Joy is an assistant professor in the Department of Political Science at Concordia University. She holds a master's degree in planning from the University of Toronto and a PhD in policy studies from Ryerson University. Her research interests include the politics of population aging, theories and practice of progressive politics and policy in cities, and the political economy of the non-profit sector.

Jeanne Lachance is a doctoral student in psychology at the Université du Québec à Montréal. Her dissertation, under the supervision of Valérie Bourgeois-Guérin, is on the topic of issues of transmission in the intergenerational bereavement experience of older adults.

Constance Lafontaine is the associate director of ACT. She develops and leads participatory action research and research creation projects with Montreal-based community partners, including recent projects on escape rooms and their potential for public education on older adult mistreatment. A PhD student in Communication Studies at Concordia University, her thesis explores the intersections of animality and human and non-human aging, including probing multi-species temporalities. Her most recent work probes the production of social robots as pets for older adult care.

Sophie Laforest is a professor in the Kinesiology Department at the Université de Montréal. She holds a bachelor's degree in physical education, a gerontology certificate, a master's degree in rehabilitation, and a PhD in epidemiology. She has received grants for much of her research and has published articles in scientific journals, over 20 of which have high international standing.

Annette Leibing holds a PhD in medical anthropology from the University of Hamburg in Germany and is a professor in the Faculty of Nursing at the Université de Montréal. Her research interests include illnesses of aging, new medical technology pertaining to aging practices and approaches, seniors' accommodation (institutions/home), and prevention.

Marie-Michèle Lord holds a PhD in biomedical science from the Université de Montréal. She is a professor in the Department of Occupational Therapy at the Université du Québec à Trois-Rivières and a regular researcher at the Centre for Research and Expertise in Social Gerontology (CREGÉS). Her research focuses on the well-being and social participation of seniors, and she is interested in the health of aging workers.

Maxime Lussier is a postdoctoral researcher in rehabilitation science at the Université du Montréal. He holds a PhD in neuropsychology from the Université du Québec à Montréal. His main research interests are related to cognitive plasticity, gerontechnologies, cognitive training, and factors that can modulate normal cognitive aging.

Patrik Marier is a professor in the Department of Political Science at Concordia University and the scientific director of the Centre for Research and Expertise in Social Gerontology (CREGÉS) at Centre intégré universitaire de santé et de services sociaux du Centre-Ouest-de-l'Île-de Montréal. He is also a researcher in charge of the Vieillissements, exclusions sociales et solidarités research team. His forthcoming book analyzes how Canadian provinces are planning for an aging society.

Antonin Marquis is a doctoral student in psychology at the Université du Québec à Montréal. Under the supervision of Valérie Bourgeois-Guérin, his research is on the experience of suffering of people who request medical aid in dying in Quebec.

Paula Negron-Poblete is a professor in the School of Urban Planning and Landscape Architecture at the Université de Montréal. Her work addresses the impact of urban structures on the mobility of vulnerable populations. Her current research is on the mobility of seniors who live in peripheral areas and medium-sized cities, with an emphasis on walkability.

Ignace Olazabal holds a PhD in anthropology. He is the director of the gerontology program in the Faculty of Continuing Education and an adjunct professor in the Anthropology Department at the Université de Montréal. His main research interest involves social aspects of aging baby boomers in Quebec. Among other things, he was the co-editor of a book comparing baby boomers in Quebec and France (*Les baby-boomers, une affaire de familles*), published by Presses de l'Université du Québec.

Pam Orzeck is an assistant professor and the director of field education at the McGill University School of Social Work. She has extensive experience in clinical and community practice in social gerontology and healthcare.

Manon Parisien is a planning, programming, and research officer. Trained as an occupational therapist, she has a master's degree in community health from the Université de Montréal, a certificate in health services management, and a teaching certificate. Her primary field of interest is the co-construction of state-of-the-art practices in the promotion of health and rehabilitation.

Marie-Pier Petit holds a PhD in psychology from the Université du Québec à Montréal, where she is a postdoctoral researcher. Her research interests include sexual and gender diversity as well as violence and abuse across the lifespan. She completed a research internship on elder abuse at the Centre for Research and Expertise in Social Gerontology.

Danis Prud'homme holds a degree in business administration from the Royal Military College in Saint-Jean and a certificate in fundraising management from the University of Indiana. He has been the executive director of Federation for Ageing in Dignity and Overall Quality since 2008. He is frequently called upon to comment publicly on seniors' issues.

Jonathan Purenne holds a master's degree in demography from the Université de Montréal, with a specialization in retirement issues. He has been working at Employment and Social Development Canada since June 2018, conducting research into retirement, retirement timing, and the labour market for older adults.

Emilie Raymond is an associate professor in the School of Social Work and Criminology at Université Laval and a researcher at the university's Centre interdisciplinaire de recherche en réadaptation et integration sociale, at which she leads the Participation sociale et villes inclusives research team. She is interested in the social and citizen participation of seniors with disabilities and makes extensive use of participatory research approaches.

Kim Sawchuk, the principal investigator of the ACT team, is a professor in the Department of Communication Studies at Concordia University and Concordia University Research Chair in Mobile Media Studies. She has written on aging and community-based research practices, age-friendly city policies, how older adults engage with digital media, algorithms and representations of age, and aging and activism. Her most recent projects in this area explore the connections between crisis communications, social isolation, and digital disconnection.

Anne-Marie Séguin has a PhD in geography from Université Laval. She is a full professor at the Urbanisation Culture Société Research Centre of the Institut national de la recherche scientifique and a member of the Vieillissements, exclusions sociales et solidarités research team. Her work focuses on the social and territorial aspects of aging, exclusion, and environmental equity.

Andrée Sévigny holds a PhD in social services from Université Laval. She is a retired researcher at the Centre d'excellence sur le vieillissement de Québec. She is a member of the Institut sur le vieillissement et la participation sociale des aînés (IVPSA) at Université Laval and of the Centre collégial d'expertise en gérontologie at the Cégep de Drummondville. She is interested in the social participation of older adults, especially volunteer efforts by – and for – older adults.

Julien Simard holds a master's degree in anthropology from the Université de Montréal and a PhD in urban studies from the Institut national de la recherche scientifique (INRS-UCS). He is currently doing a postdoctoral fellowship at the McGill School of Social Work. His research is centred on the urban and spatial dimensions of aging.

Pierre-Yves Therriault holds a PhD in biomedical science from the Université de Montréal. He is a professor in the Department of Occupational Therapy at the Université du Québec à Trois-Rivières and a regular researcher at the Centre for Research and Expertise in Social Gerontology (CREGÉS).

His research focuses on the design of structured activities to promote enhanced human thought in dealing with treatable problems and promoting skills development.

Isabelle Van Pevenage is an in-house researcher at Centre for Research and Expertise in Social Gerontology (CREGÉS) and an adjunct professor in the Sociology Department at the Université de Montréal. She has a PhD in sociology from the Université de Montréal. Her research program is structured around life trajectories and identity transitions, including end-of-life circumstances and family solidarity.

Isabelle Wallach is a professor in the Department of Sexology at the Université du Québec à Montréal. After obtaining a PhD in ethnology from Paris Diderot University (Paris 7) and a postdoctoral fellowship in social gerontology (Centre for Research and Expertise in Social Gerontology – CREGÉS), she specialized in aging and sexuality. She is a member of CREGÉS, the Vieillissements, exclusions sociales et solidarités research team, and the UQAM Research Chair on Homophobia.

Isabel Wiebe holds a bachelor's degree in geography from the University of Bonn, Germany, and a master's degree and a PhD in urban studies (Institut national de la recherche scientifique). Her research area is seniors' mobility needs in the context of an aging population. Her dissertation is on the mobility practices and experiences of seniors in everyday life in the Montreal neighbourhood of Rosemont–La Petite-Patrie.

Index

Note: "(f)" after a page number indicates a figure; "(t)" after a page number indicates a table; CHSLD stands for centre d'hébergement et de soins de longue durée (long-term care facility); IDD stands for intellectual and developmental disabilities.